FORWARD TO INDEPENDENCE

Fitz de Souza

My Memoirs

Copyright © 2019 Fitzval R.S. de Souza

The views and opinions expressed in this book are the author's own and the facts as remembered by him.

All rights reserved.

ISBN 978-10-93146-88-2

Contents

	Acknowledgements	iv
	Foreword, The Rt Hon. the Lord Steel	vi
	Preface, Hilary Ng'weno	vii
	Introduction, Victoria Brittain	xi
1.	The Story of Our Family in India and Goa - From the 1800s to 1929	1 +16 ↓
2.	Zanzibar in the 1930s	14
3.	Dreams and Ambitions - 1938 to 1945	34
4.	Arriving in England - 1947 to 1948	54
5.	How I Got Into Politics - The 1950 General Election	76
6.	Return to Kenya - 1952	99
7.	A Little Background about Asian Migration to Kenya and the Goan Identity	125
8.	The Fight for Justice and a Dramatic Turn of Events in Kenya in - Late 1952	139
9.	The Trial of the Kapenguria Six and Operation Anvil December 1952 to April 1954	161
10.	Behind the Iron Curtain and Other Excursions - 1953 to 1957	183
11.	Kenya: The Promise of a New Dawn - 1958 to 1962	197
12.	Majimbo v. Harambee: The War of Ideas, Plots and Manoeuvres; Events from 1963	223
13.	Assassination of an Idealist - 1965 to 1966	249
14.	Dangerous Times - 1967 to1969	269
15.	The Asian Exodus From East Africa Accelerates - The Early 1970s	280
16.	Milestones	292
17.	After Mzee	301

Acknowledgements

It has been suggested several times by my family and friends, that I set down a memoir and that it be not only my personal story, but something of the history and journey of our family, their origins in Goa and India, and their subsequent settlement and life in Zanzibar and Kenya.

I thought this a good idea and indeed found it difficult to write of my own journey without weaving in a broader narrative, particularly that of East Africa. After reading several books on the subject however, I became more confused than at the outset. The reason for this is the partial nature of history writing, each author, however neutral their intentions, bringing a particular slant to the facts and events described.

However, my children in particular have been pressing me hard to put words onto paper and I have had little choice but to accede to their request. And when my son Mark presented me with a dictating machine, my other children, Veena, Roy and Maya, and my wife Romola lent their equal support, and my dear friend Carmen Couto, now Carmen Moniz, offered to type everything out for me, I realised I had no further excuses. I am extremely grateful to all of them for their assistance, which has been a tremendous encouragement.

I would also like to thank the seasoned author and journalist Hilary Ng'weno, who gave a good deal of his time and knowledge in discussing Kenyan political history, Jane Stewart for typing the transcripts of Hilary's interviews with me, Amrik Heyer for her invaluable practical support and encouragement, John Parker for the many hours he spent with me to make my book a reality, and our dear friend Judith Heyer for her expert help and contributions, especially concerning the time in Kenya we shared with her and her family. I am grateful also to Hilary Ng'weno, Victoria Brittain and David Steel for their helpful comments and the kind words they have written.

'History,' someone once said, 'is written by the winners,' but this was decidedly not the kind of book I wanted to write. I hope that in what follows you will find a story that justly records and pays tribute to all those who are deserving of mention.

Fitz de Souza

This is a remarkable book, beautifully written and describing in graphic detail the author's experience of the transition of Kenya from violence-torn colony to independence. Fitz de Souza speaks with authority as one active at the centre from lawyer to Jomo Kenyatta to Deputy Speaker in the Nairobi Parliament. His sketches of the participants are quite breathtaking and moving.

His is a life lived to the full – I could not put it down and read it all in just two sittings.

David Steel

The Rt Hon. the Lord Steel of Aikwood

Preface

by Hilary Ng'weno

When I was doing a documentary on the life and times of Fitz de Souza for the series of documentaries that I called *Makers of a Nation* I came to learn a lot more about Fitz than I had known as a senior journalist in Kenya. I first met Fitz when I was a trainee reporter on the *Nation* newspaper in Nairobi before I became editor in chief of the paper in 1964. In neither role did I make friends with politicians. In fact there are only two politicians that I can call friends – one of them was Fitz and the other was the late Joseph Murumbi.

While doing the documentary on his life I learnt that Fitz had been at Lincoln's Inn in England studying law with the Jamaican Dudley Thomson, one of the lawyers who with Fitz defended Jomo Kenyatta and his five colleagues at Kapenguria after they had been arrested in 1952 and accused of being leaders of the Mau Mau rebellion against the British colonial rule. It was Fitz that the Kenya African Union (KAU) approached for advice on whom to hire to defend Kenyatta and his colleagues. Fitz and his Goan friend, Pio Gama Pinto, were two of a very few non-African KAU members at the time. Fitz introduced KAU officials to Achhroo Ram Kapila, a young Kenyan Asian lawyer who had already made a name for himself for defending Africans in a number of politically sensitive cases. It was later decided to invite Dennis Pritt, a famous British lawyer, to lead a team of lawyers, including Fitz and Kapila, to undertake the defence of Kenyatta and his colleagues.

And I learnt that Fitz was one of the people Jomo Kenyatta sought to meet after he was released from detention in August 1961 and took over the leadership of the Kenya African National Union (KANU) of which Fitz was now a member. Kenyatta made sure Fitz was at his side in February 1962 when he led the KANU delegation to the second constitutional conference held at Lancaster House in London to chart out Kenya's path towards independence. Fitz was KANU's chief legal adviser at the conference.

In the May 1963 general election before Kenya's independence, KANU nominated Fitz as the party's candidate for the Asian area of Parklands in Nairobi. As an intern journalist for the *Nation* newspaper I covered one of his campaigns and was impressed at his penchant for socialist rhetoric that seemed to make Parklands Asian businessmen and voters uneasy. Nevertheless, he was elected MP for Parklands, thereby becoming the only Kenyan of pure Asian descent to get elected to independent Kenya's first Parliament. When in 1964, Parliament met for the first time Fitz was elected Deputy Speaker and as Deputy Speaker he would try to be as neutral as he could in the great ideological struggle that was going on in the ruling party KANU between the left-leaning radical wing led by the party's vice-president Oginga Odinga and the conservative wing led by Tom Mboya, the party's secretary general. Within the radical wing was Fitz's friend and Odinga's ideological strategist, Pinto, who had been nominated to Parliament. But on the 24th of February 1965, barely two months after Kenya became a republic with Kenyatta as its first President and Odinga as Vice-President of the country, Pinto was assassinated.

Pinto's murder would take away from Fitz and many of Pinto's friends all political interest. For several days after Pinto's murder Fitz pestered the Police Criminal Investigations Department (CID) to come up with the killer or killers of his friend but the Police never arrested the real killer. A hapless driver called Kisilu Mutua was later arraigned in court, convicted and sentenced to life imprisonment for being an accomplice in Pinto's murder. More than 50 years later Mutua was still protesting his innocence and Pinto's friends were convinced he was killed by a high-ranking officer of the Kenya Police intelligence branch called the Special Branch.

A year after Pinto's murder, Odinga was forced out of the ruling party KANU and subsequently resigned as Vice-President to go and head a new opposition party, the Kenya People's Union (KPU). Kenyatta appointed Murumbi as the country's second Vice-President, but like Fitz, Murumbi had been devastated by Pinto's death and did not stay long as Vice-President. By the end of 1966, he had resigned and quit politics altogether, devoting the rest of his life to business and collecting African art and books about Africa.

In the end, Fitz too, like Murumbi, decided to quit politics following the second major assassination in Kenya – that of Tom Mboya on the 5th of July 1969. Though the country's politics between the right-wing and left-wing politicians had soured by the time Mboya met his death, it was Fitz to whom Mboya's family turned to for sorting out some of Mboya's estate issues. Fitz did not vie for a parliamentary seat in the general election held in December 1969. Instead he went on to practice criminal law for a while, but he found criminal law rough on his nerves. As he said later, he would be very adversely affected when a client he was defending on a capital offence would be convicted and hanged, especially if he was convinced that his client was innocent. Fitz would later spend the following years practising civil law until he finally retired from law practice.

I used to meet Fitz at his home in Muthaiga in Nairobi with his wife Romola or at Murumbi's home also at Muthaiga. Joe Murumbi's home was a great art museum and it was so wonderful seeing the great works of art and books he had collected. Joe died on the 22nd of June 1990 and was buried just outside the Goan cemetery at the Nairobi City Park where Pinto had been buried 25 years earlier. His wife Sheila died nearly ten years later on the 7th of October 2000. Fitz and I were members of Sheila's funeral committee and we sent a formal request to President Daniel arap Moi for the City Council to allow Sheila to be buried near her husband and Pinto at the City Park cemetery. Sheila's funeral service was conducted by Anglican Reverend Mutava Musyimi and Catholic Church Father Angelo D'Agostino – simple, but very moving.

More recently, I got involved with Fitz while he was beginning to write his memoirs, something I had pressed him to do back when Sheila died in 2000. I interviewed him many times, mainly on Kenyan political issues so that the interviews, which were recorded, could help him in writing his memoirs. That exercise was an eye-opener for me. I had never met an elderly person who could remember so many details about his past. I would ask Fitz the same question after a few weeks and he would reply almost in the same words and phrases he had used before. He was remembering personalities and events of the years before and soon after Kenya's independence in 1963 and Fitz wasn't just remembering events touching on his life. He was remembering Kenya's history of which he was one of the great makers. The story you read in this book is not just about Fitz. It is a story about the foundations of the Kenya nation. And it is for that reason that I feel very strongly that Fitz Remedios Santana de Souza will forever remain a legend for many Kenyans.

Hilary Ng'weno

Journalist and former editor of The Daily Nation and The Weekly Review, founder of The Nairobi Times, television producer, author and historian

Introduction

by Victoria Brittain

Fitz

Fitz de Souza is a man of memories from his unique insider/outsider status in Kenya's struggle for independence from Britain and the early days of its uncharted path under Jomo Kenyatta. A vanished world of optimism and idealism rooted in Goa, Zanzibar, Kenya's Rift Valley, London's Inns of Court, and the dying days of British colonial rule in Kenya is unveiled in his subtle understated book. De Souza was Deputy Speaker of the first Parliament of independent Kenya, a trusted friend to Kenyatta and of all the aspiring politicians of the moment, many of whom he knew well from the prisons and courtrooms of violent pre-independence days. He was a man who in those heady days of independent Kenya could have had any ministry he wanted, and was offered any stretches of farmland he wanted by Kenyatta. Unlike so many others he wanted none. The life he chose was a very different one of idealism, matter-of-fact self-sacrifice and extraordinary hard work.

His story is of a time of serial dislocations – his doctor father like many Goans took the long sea route from India to East Africa. He went alone, ahead of his family, on a chance offer of a practice, first in Zanzibar's Stone Town where people were so poor that many paid the doctor with fish instead of money, then to more financial stability on the mainland in remote Magadi, 70 miles west of Nairobi. Young Fitz, still in his early teens, then chose to stay alone in Zanzibar in the school he loved and with the friends made in his 14 years living there. That teenage self-sufficiency would be just what he needed to carry him through years of studying for the Bar in London thousands of miles from his family or anyone he knew. He passed the law exams when he was only 19, after years spent with like-minded friends from other colonised countries; kind landladies; little money; studying in bed to keep warm. He was still 18 months too young to be Called to the Bar.

The idealism runs through all his anecdotes of his early years in Britain, the shock and deep sadness he felt at the death of Gandhi; the excitement at the discovery of London's Speakers' Corner; of the Methodist minister Donald Soper; of the principled anti-colonial MP Fenner Brockway; his surprise nomination as a Labour candidate for Municipal Councillor in Southend (again under age); endless exhilarating talking at meetings of Indian and East African students' groups; a brush with Conservative MP Patrick Wall where he managed to hold his tongue when faced with a blatant defence of colonialism and racialism in East Africa.

Back in British Kenya in 1952 it was inevitable that de Souza's closest friend would become the legendary, magnetic Goan journalist/freedom fighter Pio Pinto. As a 17 year old working in India, Pinto led agitation for Goa's independence from Portugal; then returned to his Kenyan birthplace rather than risk deportation to a prison camp in another Portuguese colony, Cape Verde. Through Pinto, de Souza widened his anti-colonial ideas. Here he tells a unique and inside story of the growth of the warm alliance between the Indian political activists led by Pinto, and key African trade unionists.

In the urgency of the times the two young Asians shared every thought, every analysis, and even took turns initially to sleep in the one bed Pinto had.

The Kenyan nationalist movement faced British intransigence in maintaining the apartheid system and land occupation by white settlers, which was Kenya in those days. Anger was at boiling point.

The violence of those days when the British declared a state of emergency was extreme, with 150,000 Kenyans detained in brutal camps after 32 white settlers were murdered by Mau Mau rebels. At least 12,000 Mau Mau were killed in the conflict. Many Kenyan political and trade union leaders were imprisoned, including in 1954 his friend Pinto. De Souza was part of a group that had gone to Kenyatta, President of the Kenya African Union, telling him his own arrest was imminent and that there was an offer from the Indian Government of sanctuary and from the Emperor Haile Selassie of Ethiopia to send troops to get him out. Kenyatta's refusal to leave his people chimed with de Souza's attitudes. And as a lawyer he was for a time able to be active in visiting hundreds of prisoners, including Kenyatta, to whom he smuggled letters in defiance of British regulations. Then his own father was arrested at work in Magadi and told that his son was a terrorist. De Souza was tipped off by a phone call in Portuguese (a signal the police were listening) from his mother saying that the police were looking for him. Telling her not to worry and that he was on his way to Mombasa, he drove in the opposite direction to Uganda thinking that way he could be in safety and more useful than in prison.

He was useful, in particular as liaison with the Indian Government who were ready to push their former colonial power into concessions, such as the release of Pinto. The British soon knew the colonial game was up all over Africa. For Kenya, three long, testy conferences followed in Lancaster House in London. Kenyatta insisted that de Souza (as a PhD and a barrister) be seated next to him, and he proved himself to be a leading and passionate speaker whose words marked the conferences. But at the final conference, in early 1963, Kenyatta called his close group to a private meeting and told them that the country had had enough of negotiating and he was ready to make compromises on the proposed constitution despite none of them agreeing with it. De Souza argued fruitlessly against his leader's willingness to agree to terms he did not intend to stick to once in power. The idealist had collided with other people's reality. At that time he did not understand it, but the coming years at the heart of Kenyatta's administration would reveal acute tensions of tribal loyalties inside the political class and critical external pressures as the UK, the USA and Israel consolidated their influence inside this key Western ally in the Cold War period.

Three political assassinations marked de Souza's days in Kenyatta's administration – Pio Pinto in 1965, the Luo politician Tom Mboya from Western Kenya in 1969, and the socialist politician J.M. Kariuki in 1975. They were the ominous signs of how the character of the country had already evolved into something very different from what young men like de Souza had dreamed of creating for its people.

A fourth assassination, of Bruce Mackenzie, the Minister of Agriculture, a South African-born former RAF pilot in the Second World War came from outside and well illustrates the ruthless geopolitical high stakes world that did not suit de Souza. Mackenzie was killed when his airplane blew up over the Ngong Hills with a bomb placed in a present from Idi Amin of Uganda as payback for Mackenzie's role in Kenya's assistance to the Israelis' ending of the 1976 Entebbe hostage crisis. An Air France plane was hijacked to Entebbe by a Palestinian splinter group of the PFLP and two German revolutionaries demanding the release of 40 Palestinian prisoners in Israel and 13 in four other countries. Forty-five Ugandan soldiers and three hostages were killed and 30 planes of the Ugandan air force destroyed by the Israeli rescue raid. The leader of the Israeli commandos was also killed – he was the older brother of Israeli Prime Minister Benjamin Netanyahu. Mossad's chief had a forest planted in Israel in Mackenzie's name. De Souza recounts a telling, earlier Mackenzie moment when they were together in London with Kenyatta after his release from prison. Kenyatta, who had no money, would enthusiastically eat three or four steaks at dinner, and they were staying at the Cumberland Hotel in central London, all well beyond their means. Mackenzie paid for everything and when de Souza protested and insisted on sharing the cost, told him that in fact he was not paying anything as the consul at the Israeli Embassy had arranged with the hotel owner, Joe Lyons, to cover all the group's expenses.

By the time I knew Fitz de Souza and his family in Nairobi in the late 1970s he had bowed out of politics, 'increasingly aware of the entrenched nature of tribalism and the virtually one-party system.' He still knew everyone in power from years before, but his discretion never slipped and he said little about all he knew and what he was thinking of current Kenyan developments. His generosity and welcome into his family circle was a privilege. Years later, I would think of de Souza when I had spent years with other rare, modest politicians in other post-colonial African countries. They, like him, had spent their lives in the service of the ideal of building a society based on social justice and rule of law, and had similarly been personally defeated by the harsh realities of power based on corruption and tribalism allied with ruthless external actors. But always there is a younger generation with the same idealism for a national project for the people, and for whom these individuals are role models not to be forgotten, and Kenya's younger lawyers have been de Souza's heirs for decades.

Other strands of Kenyan society across this period have been caught for future generations in books as different as Ngugi wa Thiong'o's *Petals of Blood* and James Fox's *White Mischief*. Fitz de Souza's unique memories and reflections on the Goan and Indian world of East Africa evoke the work of the great East African/Canadian writer M.G. Vassanji's novels like *The In-Between World of Vikram Lall*, *The Book of Secrets* and others. Vassanji is an Ismaili Muslim of Gujarati heritage, born in Nairobi and brought up in Tanzania before going to live in Canada. He too is a man of dislocations and a rich cultural and societal heritage from a lost world that de Souza has brought back.

De Souza and the idealists of his early world could never have imagined the Africa of today – newly colonised by China, and with nine foreign countries having military facilities on the continent. They range from the old colonial powers of France and Britain to Turkey, Japan, Germany, Saudi Arabia, the United Arab Emirates, and China, whose base is under construction. The USA has a military presence in 11 countries, even after withdrawing from three others when the Americans gave up on the hunt for the old Ugandan warlord Joseph Kony. Meanwhile, across the continent ageing kleptocrat leaders are long out of tune with the people. Wars, famine, repression, corruption and economic desperation have taken a toll most graphically illustrated by the growing phenomenon of the hundreds of thousands of African refugees who daily flee their countries, and when possible their continent.

Victoria Brittain

Former foreign correspondent for The Guardian in East Africa, author and playwright.

Chapter One

The Story of Our Family in India and Goa

From the 1800s to 1929

'Swaying palms, white sands and sparkling waters – a tiny, glorious slice of India hugging the country's western coastline, bounded by the Arabian Sea.'

This seductive description from a modern-day travel guide alludes as perhaps you have recognised to Goa. The tourists and backpackers who now flock there each year in search of paradise were not the first foreigners to arrive on Goa's shores. Several centuries before the advent of package holidays, a certain contingent of explorers, setting sail in search of spices, arrived in Goa with more serious intent than a fortnight in the sun. In 1510, an invasion fleet led by Portugal's Admiral Afonso de Albuquerque, whose countrymen, ravenous for this tiny glorious slice of India and seeking a base for their profitable trade with the East, left some 6,000 of its Muslim defenders dead, the Hindu population largely suborned and Goa swallowed up into the Portuguese Empire.

Prior to the arrival of the Portuguese, it was in Goa that my Hindu ancestor Narain Purob along with his Maharashtrian family regularly offered water at the roadside for weary travellers. Without painting them as ardent philanthropists in any way it pleases me to think of them having this charitable role in their community, a simple duty and tradition performed alongside earning their day-today living from farming. A sense of collective social responsibility was reflected similarly in the rural life in Goa, where the villages had grown up around agriculture over the generations, with groups of friends and families pooling their resources to manage some land, constructing often quite complex irrigation systems connected to rivers on higher ground. With sufficient water the resultant paddy fields could produce two crops of rice a year, enough to feed everyone and make the village relatively affluent. These areas of land are still known as the Communidade or Community Fields, with the tenancies auctioned every two or three years, a proportion of the proceeds and rents then donated to the local school and church, the balance divided among the male heirs to the Communidade over the age of 14. These heirs are known as Zonecars, and though I left India several decades ago I believe I would still be entitled if I chose to collect it, to the Zone payment from my village.

With the Portuguese had come Christianity. Some historians claim that the religion was not forcibly imposed and that the villages were left largely undisturbed. Yet, there is evidence of horrifying attempts at subjugation, including the discovery of 600 severed heads, thought to be those who refused to convert. The Hindu rite of sati, the burning of a widow on her husband's funeral pyre, was made illegal, but not stamped out. Gradually, churches were built and at some point my forebears became followers of the Catholic faith, though as will be seen, exchanging the Bhagavad Gita for the Bible would not easily uproot other aspects of their deeper cultural heritage, in particular their beliefs and practices in relation to caste and the dowry system.

My paternal grandfather, Jose Francisco Remedios Santana de Souza, was born the youngest child of a farmer in the village of Ucassaim in the district of Bardez, Goa. The system of communal farming did not prohibit simultaneous private ownership, and the family was relatively well to do, owning several rice fields and maintaining elegant horse-drawn Victoria carriages. It might therefore be assumed my grandfather had been born with a large silver spoon in his mouth, but circumstances proved otherwise when his father died, leaving a now elderly widow, an eldest son, my grandfather, and in between the two boys, five sisters, all as yet unwed. The practice of marriage was a serious business; before all the delights of colourful silks and coconut cakes, feasting and dancing could commence, behind the scenes a great deal of hard, often protracted bargaining had to be done over the dowry. Paid by the bride's family to the groom, a dowry for each of these girls was an absolute prerequisite for marriage; the alternative for many women was a life of abandonment, poverty and often shame through no fault of their own. My cousin May, just before she died, told how as a young woman her wealthy father had refused to pay 2,000 rupees on top of the 80,000 he had already offered her prospective husband's family, and as a result she had remained a spinster all her life. May was bright and highly educated, but the system was harsh for those who lost out; all the beauty, accomplishments and sweet-naturedness in the world could rarely compensate for a girl who could not, or in May's father's case would not, provide the required dowry.

    The more admirable corollary to dowry wrangling in Indian and Goan communities was, and to a large extent still is, the custom for the relatives of those who are left for whatever reason in need, to do their best to support those less fortunate members of their family. In this instance, it was my grandfather who took on the familial responsibility, selling the fields that would have been his inheritance in order to furnish his sisters with sufficient dowry to find them husbands. To earn a living himself he took a job with the Bombay branch of the extensive Eastern Telegraph Company, thence posting to Cochin where, according to my mother, he became the first Indian Telegraph Master; to be the first in any profession or walk of life previously the preserve of Europeans has traditionally been a matter of great pride among Goans and Indians.

Once he had established himself in a career my grandfather had his 'happy day' and got married to a Goan girl whose family was in the timber export business. The couple had seven children, four boys and three girls. The sixth child, the youngest of the boys, born in 1888, was my father. He attended Guirim School in Goa and experienced by all accounts a happy upbringing. My grandfather saved and invested wisely, buying a large tract of land on which he planned to grow cashews, mangoes and teak. My father and his brothers held fond memories of accompanying him on excursions along the river in a small Garawa, a type of canoe using only oars, and alighting at the British agricultural station to buy Mancurada, a finely grafted mango to take back and propagate. Cultivating the land took considerable labour, but when the project was complete, along with the mangoes and teak the family had planted 450,000 cashew trees. From the cashews they would distil and sell the strong Goan liquor feni. Shrewdly spreading his investments, my grandfather was also buying property in Bombay, including the nearby Malabar Hill.

On leaving school my father had done well enough to set his sights on becoming a doctor. One of my grandfather's houses in Bombay was near Dhobitalou, conveniently placed for the medical school, and he and my father shared these living quarters for a while, along with a cook brought from Goa and half a dozen or so fellow students. While in college he became friendly with a girl, the daughter of a Doctor Sequeira, and by and by as they were seen regularly in each other's company it became assumed among their peers that the two of them would get married. My father was certainly of the same mind, and being a dutiful son he sought his family's blessing on the intended union. When his mother learned more, however, she ruled against it, telling him that the girl was 'not of our caste' and warning that if he had daughters they would be 'half-caste' and no one would marry them; he would, she prophesied darkly, be cursed by his own children for inflicting such a fate upon them. The fact that the girl and my father were both Goan Christians made no difference; caste remained the overriding factor in deciding who could marry whom. I remember hearing my aunt Tia Urbina Monteiro attempting to explain this anomaly between Christian belief and the rigid stigma of caste with the decree that: 'everything in the Bible was correct except for caste'. But caste she maintained 'was made by God'. I would challenge the notion by saying it merely suited her because she was a Brahmin, the higher caste.

As a young man my father must have felt unhappily torn. Reluctant or unable to act against his parents' wishes, he continued I believe to yearn for the girl, nurturing the hope that somehow or other they might yet marry. For the immediate future however, the unfolding drama of world events was about to alter the course of his life in other ways, for just as he qualified as a doctor, Britain was plunged into the bloody conflict of the First World War. To the East, her troops would be engaged once more in the age-old struggle for control of India's border with Afghanistan, while in the meantime deploying across the region to launch attacks on the Turkish railway lines in Arabia. Being a good horseman, boxer and generally fit and sporting, my father along with nine of his fellow medical school graduates, all Goan Christians, accepted an invitation to join the British Army. In the Cavalry he was immediately given the rank of Lieutenant, followed swiftly by promotion to Captain and a salary of 900 rupees a month, a princely sum at that time. Sent first to Peshawar he travelled there by train, and thence rode on horseback to the Afghanistan capital Kabul for what would be a four-year posting as part of the Indian Medical Service treating war casualties and those suffering from disease. Relating these exploits to me he would talk of negotiating hazardous routes along mountainsides with death-defying sheer drops below, while around him lay the corpses and skeletons of shot horses and men. It indeed sounded adventurous to my youthful imagination, but it was only later on when I saw for myself pictures of Afghanistan's harsh boulder-strewn landscape, devoid of either roads or proper footpaths that I realised just how arduous the work of a field doctor there must have been.

Among the troops and the local populace there was apparently much talk of T.E. Lawrence and his leadership of the Arab revolt against the Ottoman Empire, and the name of Lawrence of Arabia was one to instil awe and reverence in some. Lawrence's role was a curious one, for although ostensibly a figurehead of the British, his apparent immersion in Arab culture and championing of their cause could well serve as inspiration for those seeking to throw off the chains of imperial domination elsewhere, including Britain's 'Jewel in the Crown', India. Already becoming a tenacious spokesman for radical reform and later 'swaraj' or home rule in India was the young Mahatma Gandhi, recently returned from South Africa. Opinions on Gandhi were sharply divided, and there being few doctors in the area my father was to have the opportunity to meet those of differing allegiances. Among the prominent leaders he knew in the North-West Frontier were Dr Khan Sahib and Abdul Ghaffar Khan. The latter, a towering 6 foot 6 Pashtun was dubbed the 'Frontier Gandhi' for his friendship with and utter devotion to the man Winston Churchill was to call 'this thin naked fakir'. Abdul Ghaffar Khan's political opponent, who supported M.A. Jinnah and the Muslim League, was Abdul Khayim Khan, whom my father also knew and got on with quite well. Maintaining friendly relations with those across the political spectrum was no doubt pragmatic and unavoidable, and does not in any way imply that my father was lacking in beliefs of his own. His first duty I have no doubt, he saw as striving to be a good doctor, treating all of his patients without fear or favour, being honest and compassionate and living by the principles of the Hippocratic Oath. He saw his work as trying to cure people, and if his patients appeared to be poor he would not charge them, even providing them with medicines out of his own pocket.

Following the armistice of 1918 my father stayed on in Kabul for a few more months and then returned to

Peshawar. With the war over, the calls for independence were growing louder and anti-imperialist sentiment spreading. Such feelings were set to escalate far higher when in 1919, at Jallianwalla Bagh in Amritsar, British Brigadier General Reginald Dyer ordered his troops to open fire on a crowd assembled peaceably in the gardens there. When the bodies were recovered the British reported 379 civilians killed, while the Indian National Congress put the figure at 1,000. The incident was even more shocking for the fact that the troops had fired on those attempting to flee through the narrow walled entrance to the gardens. The outrage would fuel support for the Indian Non-Cooperation Movement. Those defending the action claimed that the crowd had ignored a public order banning large gatherings, alleging many of them were armed with makeshift weapons and that their mood was hostile. This attempted justification would not help the innocent victims or their grieving families. Churchill described the incident as 'monstrous', while the legendary Indian writer Rabindranath Tagore renounced his knighthood from the British in protest. The memories of those who witnessed the slaughter would never ever be erased. One story tells how the young Nehru, overhearing British soldiers in a railway sleeping compartment heartily rejoicing about how many Indians had been killed, committed himself from that moment to the fight for independence. Twenty-one years later, activist Udham Singh who had been wounded in the massacre, made his way to Caxton Hall in London and shot dead Sir Michael O'Dwyer, who when Lieutenant Governor of the Punjab in 1919 had commended Dyer's actions.

After discharge from the Indian Medical Service my father found a small shop premises in a bustling bazaar called the Qissa Khawani from which to set up a practice, with living accommodation above. His patients were largely the indigenous Pashtun people, whom he found friendly and hospitable. Yet he learned also to be wary. If daring to look them in the eye there was unmistakable steel, a glimmer of ferocity and danger that made the onlooker recoil. Allied to this sense of menace, and the most alien aspect of the culture for an outsider, was an adherence to repressive, cruel and atavistic customs. The prevailing culture was one of extreme patriarchy in which women, having few if any rights, were kept hidden away. The first time my father was called to treat a female he was warned by her father that he must on no account set eyes upon her. At this point the man drew his hand across his own throat in a slicing motion and pointed to my father, and then to the room in which the daughter was hidden. The message was clear: if this rule was not observed both my father and his patient would be killed without hesitation. When my father tactfully pointed out the difficulty of offering treatment under these conditions, the reply was to the effect that his being a doctor was surely sufficient to provide a cure. It therefore has to be said that my father was not always truthful in his diagnoses, as when summoned, again by an important elder, to a household whose daughter was about to be married. He was informed that before accepting her, the girl's prospective husband wanted a guarantee that she was a virgin. Again the hand was drawn chillingly across the throat, and my father was made aware that if the girl were discovered not to be virgo intacta, she would lose not only the chance of a husband, but also her life. He then enquired tentatively if it was the husband-to-be that would kill her, to which the girl's father replied no, he would do it himself. Realising the danger he too was in, and not knowing what else to do, my father looked thoughtful for a moment. Then assuming a bold and confident smile he declared that all was as it should be with the girl and the marriage could go ahead. From that day on he said, every female in Peshawar he was called on to examine for this purpose was a virgin.

    While my father strove to make his living and do some small amount of good in this often unnerving environment, his father had reached a position where he could afford to take life a little easier, and in his mid-fifties retired from the Eastern Telegraph Company, returning to Bombay and the large estate in which he had invested.

There was a problem however, as my grandmother was unwilling to live in Bombay, desiring instead to reside among her own people back in Goa. I believe there was advice at the time against such a move presumably on the grounds that it would be financially imprudent to sell the Bombay estate, which was considered an extremely good investment, today worth hundreds of millions of pounds. The question of where they should live became the subject of some dispute, but in the end, with his wife adamant he acceded to her wishes, enlarged his ancestral house in Ucassaim and there they settled. There was of course still the estate in Goa, called Cujira, where the rice fields, cashew trees, teak and prime mangoes he had assiduously planted with the help of his sons continued to bear valuable fruit and give some peace of mind about providing for the future of his offspring.

    My father would visit his now ageing parents when time allowed, though with responsibilities also to his patients and the journey by road and rail from Peshawar to Goa taking several days this was not perhaps as often as he would have wished. There was also the unresolved issue about when and whom he might marry. Unwavering in their opposition to the girl he had known as a student, each time he saw them it is likely his parents would have aired their thoughts on propitious matches, either cajoling or hoping to stir his interest. With this bone of contention left hanging, he would perhaps have felt a stab of remorse, as so many of us do along with our natural grief, after receiving the sad news that his father had died. When subsequently his mother became unwell, his visits to Goa became more frequent. Travelling by motorcycle he would embark on the long trek, passing through hot deserts, taking the 'bike on the train where possible to speed up the journey. Her condition looked to be serious, and with no known cure he decided to stay on in Goa to look after her. This must have been a testing time, my grandmother enduring chronic pain, and having what would now be termed cancer of the uterus, the indignity of profuse bleeding; my father told me frankly that the necessities of cleaning and attending to her was embarrassing for both of them. He also recalled the awkwardness whenever the thorny subject of marriage arose. But these aside their relationship was amicable, and being a doctor and her son he was no doubt the best carer my grandmother could have had, a duty he fulfilled until after two long years of illness she passed away.

With both his parents deceased, was my father now free to marry the person he had long ago set his heart upon? One might assume so. There would remain disapproval among some, and the concern of having children labelled as untouchables, but these would arguably have been easier for him to transcend than the love and respect he held for his parents. Like time and tide, however, marriage waits for no one and the girl he had cherished was already committed to another. My father's extended family had not sat idle either, and had made alternative arrangements for his wedding. While welcoming the prospect of becoming a husband now, he did have one particular qualm about the intended person. This was not over her caste, for like him she was a Brahmin, an educated teacher and her father a doctor. The problem was her age, which he had been told was just 16. My father was now 35, and marrying a girl young enough to be his daughter seemed to him somehow not right. When his objection was reported back to her family, however, they promptly replied that no, no, there had been a misunderstanding and their daughter was in fact 24. It was a woman's prerogative to adjust her age but when marriage was at stake it could as easily be readjusted it seemed. My father remarked that never had he seen a girl grow up so fast.

My parents' wedding took place in Bombay in the early spring of 1923, and very soon it was confirmed that my mother was expecting. In those days one did not know the gender of a child while in the womb, intensifying the suspense for patriarchal Indian and Goan families, for whom a son carried the greater kudos. Parents were very aware of the practical implications too; male heirs could be expected to earn money, to have a dowry bestowed upon them on marrying, rather than the parents having to fork out, and thereby be better placed in every way to look after their elders financially in old age. An Indian couple that produced only daughters would be considered unfortunate in this respect. As my mother's time grew close, my father arranged for her to go to Rajkot, to a hospital and doctors he knew personally. On the 29th of December 1923 she gave birth to a healthy baby boy. Both parents were delighted and they gave him the name of Rix.

Though my father had strong reservations about returning to Peshawar, he was at least familiar with its challenges as a doctor and, perhaps thinking that things might improve, he decided to go back there for the time being at least. Being married now gave him an advantage professionally; previously he could only treat females with the aid of a local woman carrying out proxy examinations and reporting back the symptoms through a closed door, a haphazard method compromised by barriers of language and culture. Now, however, my mother was able to come on board as his willing assistant in this capacity. She was fluent in the local language as well as English and although medically a layperson was a quick learner and brought a calm and reassuring 'bedside manner' for the women. Despite this my father was not, contrary to what some of the locals seemed to believe, a miracle worker. Suppose they took umbrage if through no fault of his, a patient one day died? Each time a gunshot rent the Peshawar air his uneasiness increased.

His family meanwhile was expanding, my two-year-old brother Rix having been joined by a sister when on the 6th of March 1926 in Peshawar, our mother gave birth to Iva. Having two young children did not unduly confine them, and indeed my father continued to visit friends and relatives in Goa, having now bought a motorcycle with a sidecar in which he would convey my mother with Rix and little Iva hundreds of miles from Peshawar and back. It was during one particular stay in Goa that he got talking to a very personable older physician by the name of Manuel Albuquerque, who was to make him a proposition. Dr Albuquerque had for a number of years been domiciled in the British protectorate of Zanzibar, situated just off the east African coast, during which time he had established a thriving medical practice, and it seemed built up other business interests. Dapper and clearly well to do, he was now looking to retire and asked my father if he would be interested in buying a half share in his practice. By now approaching his late thirties, my father might well have considered the time ripe for a change of scene. His concerns about continuing to work in Peshawar, with its atmosphere of brooding unrest and the ever-present danger of unwittingly offending the volatile tribesmen, had not abated. Here was the chance to escape the harsh and unsettling life of the North-West Frontier and a possibility for his children to grow up in more congenial surroundings. Zanzibar was a polyglot of Arabs, Indians, Africans, Europeans and a small community of Goans, living side by side in what was by all accounts a contented community overseen by the steady hand of the British administration and its local officers. It sounded ideal. On the other hand, having never been to Zanzibar he felt slightly unwilling to take his young family so far across the sea without further knowledge, or some stronger motivation.

Unforeseen by either of my parents, certain events, unrelated in themselves, were about to create what would potentially be the catalyst. The first event was deeply personal, being the birth in 1928 of my parents' third child. My father's commanding officer in the army, a man called Fitzpatrick, had told him that Fitz meant 'son of' and choosing now to adopt this custom my father named the boy Fitz Valentine after himself. How proud he must have been to have a second son. At just a few months old, however, the infant contracted meningitis and shortly after died. Might this blow have jolted my father to think more seriously about upping sticks and leaving India altogether? To seek out fresh surroundings at such a time would not be surprising. However, neither in those days was infant mortality; the loss would have been upsetting undeniably and my parents would have grieved, but life had to go on.

It did not put an end to their relations, for soon there was another baby on the way. Very worried that meningitis might also take this child, my father had my mother admitted to the Sequeira Hospital in Bombay, which had better conditions and a friend of his among the medical staff. Exactly a year and one week after her previous child had died my mother gave birth to another boy. I was given my late brother's first name and christened Fitzval Remedios Neville Santana de Souza.

Chapter Two

Zanzibar in the 1930s

In certain aspects the world I entered was one of stability. British India, the Raj, was, ten years after the Jallianwallah Bagh massacre and contrary to some predictions still intact. In Britain itself the Conservative Party under Stanley Baldwin had survived the upheaval of the 1926 General Strike and remained for now in power. The agents of change, however, were waiting in the wings. In January 1929, the Indian National Congress proclaimed its official goal as that of total independence for India. June saw the fall of the British Conservatives and the Labour Party in office. In the USSR Stalin took no chances with opposition and expelled Leon Trotsky who, like millions of the dictator's enemies, real or imagined was already living on borrowed time as the Soviet Union withdrew further behind the Iron Curtain. It was said by Krushchev at the Warsaw Convention that if Stalin ever sent for you, you had better say goodbye to your family for the last time. Ideological chasms deepened even as the physical distances between nations were narrowing at least for the rich, signalled on the 1st of April 1930 by the first non-stop passenger flight between Britain and India.

    If the world at the beginning of 1929 was a place of relative calm, it was the calm that comes before a storm. Though few realised it the economy was walking a perilous tightrope in the industrial powerhouse of America, stretched over the few hundred yards of New York's financial district Wall Street. The decade following the devastation of the First World War, which saw the USA and much of Western Europe riding a wave of prosperity and excess, was dubbed the Roaring Twenties not only for the exuberance of its high society events. Growing wealth in the cities had fuelled ever-growing optimism and a stock market that seemed to defy the laws of gravity. In this brave new world it appeared that not only the rich could get richer, and to secure their slice of the American Dream alongside the Rockefellers, Vanderbilts and Carnegies, huge numbers of ordinary citizens begged, borrowed and mortgaged their homes to buy shares in anything and everything, while brokers obligingly extended credit to eager investors. The stock market rose and rose, and kept on rising. It was like a marvellous party at which the music never stopped.

At the end of October 1929, triggered by a financial scandal and falls the previous month in London, to people's horror and disbelief the US market started to follow suit. With spirited attempts to bolster confidence by block buying of shares there followed a roller coaster ride as the indices spiked and dropped dramatically. Calling the market's bluff proved a forlorn hope. Greed succumbed to fear, panic selling set in and some $30 billion was wiped off the value of the stock market. Many Americans had lost everything they owned, some in despair throwing themselves from the Manhattan skyscrapers, a compelling image exaggerated perhaps in legend of fools destroyed by the temple of Mammon that had so enchanted them with dreams of riches.

What did all this mean on the distant shores of India where the livelihood of so many ordinary people derived from that most solid of assets the land? In that age of late imperialism and vastly unequal trading relationships the reverberations were soon being felt. The British seeking to protect their own economy banned imports and Indian farmers who had ceased growing grain in favour of cotton and other 'cash crops' to supply Britain's textile mills found they no longer had a market for their commodities. Harsher still, under 'triangular trade' colonial policy prevented India exporting her produce to other countries. The Imperial government banned jute exports other than to Britain, which paid low prices and impoverished the producers. Such punitive economic restrictions would force many Indians to sell the family silver and gold instead to pay their land rents and taxes.

For my father, still very reluctant to return to Peshawar with his family, what were the choices? He could stay on in Goa perhaps and take a stake in the family's cashew feni refinery set up by my grandfather. This trade would presumably be as hard-pressed as any as the depression took hold and considering himself first and foremost a medical man such an enterprise was unlikely to appeal. (The family refinery was in fact successful and was awarded a gold medal in Belgium for its products. As a young man I was sometimes asked to taste the drinks for quality which having seen the raw ingredients being 'treaded' by numerous bare feet was not pleasant!) Practising medicine in Goa might have been possible though there were already established doctors there. Manuel Albuquerque's offer of a partnership and a new life in Zanzibar was still open. Should he now accept it?

It was in April 1930 while secluded with his family amid the lush mango groves of Goa that fate took a hand in his decision. Reports came from Peshawar that his friend Abdul Ghaffur Khan had been leading a non-violent pro-independence protest through the Qissa Khawani bazaar when British troops had opened fire on the crowd, killing some four hundred people. As more details emerged it was confirmed that riots had subsequently broken out, the bazaar set alight and most of the buildings in it including my father's house and surgery burnt down. Sadness on hearing this tragic news must have been accompanied by immense relief that the de Souza family had been out of the province at the time. The Jallianwallah Bagh massacre 11 years previously had taken place some 200 miles from Peshawar; that this latest violence had occurred literally on my father's doorstep was an alarming reminder of how volatile the 'tinder box' of the North-West Frontier was, and the danger that could flare up from any quarter. With his premises destroyed, there in any case appeared no question of going back.

Goa meanwhile was experiencing its own degree of discontent. Dr Antonio De Oliveira Salazar had come to power in Portugal, passing the Colonial Act, conferring preferential incomes on Portuguese employees in Goa, in contrast to their Goan counterparts. The free visits to Portugal that had been extended to Indian Goans under the previous liberal administration were also withdrawn, along with other curtailments, which seemed only right if it came with greater independence. A revitalised independence movement led courageously by Dr Tistao Braganza Cunha established the Goa Congress Committee, affiliated to India's National Congress, whose fight for independence from the British Empire was, with the galvanizing support of Gandhi's non-violent civil disobedience campaign, stepping up. Goan nationalists meanwhile were advocating that given the intransigence of the Portuguese administration, it would be better to wage their campaign for freedom from outside the country. The world both at home and abroad seemed to be entering a febrile state, and a mood for radical change was in the air.

Though favouring both Goan and Indian independence, my father was not actively political. Any dilemma about how or where to uphold the cause would for him, I believe, have been secondary to supporting his family and furthering his vocation in medicine especially for the poor. In 1932, two years after the destruction of his surgery in Peshawar and at the age of 44, he packed a suitcase and prepared to leave Goa, setting out alone on a voyage of some 16 days across the Indian Ocean, his destination the island of Unguja (the African name) or Zanzibar, the largest of the archipelago also known collectively as Zanzibar. He had obviously not rushed his decision, indeed was not yet decided. But assuming the recommendations of Albuquerque and others proved accurate, this remote, old-established British protectorate might indeed provide him with a solid future and be a happy environment in which to raise his children. If such impressions were borne out on arrival, he would then send for the family.

Zanzibar comprises several small and two large coral islands, Unguja and Pemba. The principal island Unguja lies at its shortest distance some 12 miles from what was in the 1930s, the German territory of Tanganyika (now Tanzania), on the African mainland. Zanzibar's topography is fairly low-lying, with few steep gradients, its shores fringed by beautiful beaches of soft sand, while outlying coral reefs teem with varied marine life. The island's history is dramatic and chequered, its population by the mid-20th century reflecting a long evolution of incursions and settlements. Early inhabitants were of Bantu and Swahili origin, until the arrival of Arabs from Persia and elsewhere. In ancient times when a polygamous Arab king died his successor would be chosen from his various families through trial by combat, the losers expelled and put to sea, to perish or seek their fortune. These dispossessed half brothers of Arab rulers sailed as far as Africa, and if finding fresh water would establish a base. Some were believed to have come simply to escape the periodic droughts in their homelands, and Arab settlements stretched down the east African coast to Port Elizabeth.

Portugal claimed Zanzibar in the early 16th century, although a British ship arriving in Unguja in 1591 found no military presence. After an alleged mass slaughter of Europeans by the Sultan of Mombasa in 1631, however, the Portuguese established a fort on Pemba, as they endeavoured to do in all their colonies, along with ships, to quell any uprising.

The Sultanate of Oman took over in 1698, the new ruling Arab elite establishing spice plantations in 1818. Local women valued cloves as decorative earrings and to enhance their recipes. But such was the huge industrial demand for cloves from overseas – notably in cigarette manufacture – that many of Zanzibar's indigenous farmers had their coconut trees, a useful source of rope and string as well as nourishing food, cut down to make way for the more valuable spice. Ivory, sold en-route from the African mainland, where the Arabs had exercised control was also highly profitable, but more lucrative still was human cargo and slaving would make fortunes for some, the most notorious of them Tippu Tip. By the mid-1800s an estimated 50,000 slaves were passing through Zanzibar's markets each year until the trade was eventually curtailed through British intervention.

In 1890, Germany and Britain, competing for dominion over the territories of East Africa signed the Heligoland–Zanzibar Treaty, an agreement giving control of mainland Tanganyika to the Germans, and Zanzibar to Britain, which declared the islands a protectorate, installing the loyal Sultan Hamad Bin Thuwaini as their vizier. Three years of peace followed, ended by the sudden death of Sultan Thuwaini, allegedly poisoned by his cousin who promptly appointed himself ruler, replaced the Union Jack with his own flag and surrounded the palace with armed supporters. Nearby British gunboats were mobilised, an ultimatum issued, and after a brief stand-off a bombardment commenced. The wooden structure of the palace quickly collapsed and thirty-eight minutes later so did the defending army, after fighting what became known as 'the shortest war in history' and suffering some 500 fatalities. The cousin who had led them fled to the safety of the German Consulate. A new tame vizier was soon found and Zanzibar was peaceful again.

The Sultans of Oman had long encouraged Indian traders and merchants to the islands, and Goans too had established a small but significant presence. In the mid-19th century, Burton and Speke hired two young men from Goa to assist on an exploration into the African interior; their quest the source of the Nile. Travelling via Zanzibar, Valentine Rodrigues and Gaetano Andrades, together with hundreds of African porters spent two years on the trek, finally reaching a huge expanse of inland fresh water, which Speke promptly named Lake Victoria after his British Queen. Remarking afterwards on the tenacity of his two

Goan assistants, Speke also observed that 'Rodrigues picked up Swahili and was handy at cooking and sewing, while Andrade was a kindly nurse, and though physically weak, courageous.'

Such practical skills combined with endurance and adaptability were evident in the Goans who, hearing about Zanzibar perhaps from Rodrigues and Andrade or by word of mouth, began slowly to follow in their footsteps. It was no mass migration; a local doctor recorded the number of residents of Goan descent in Unguja in 1870 as 30, and by 1948 a census counted 598, together with 83 on the neighbouring island of Pemba. But though small in number, the Goans who settled in Zanzibar would make their own distinctive mark, as merchants, clerks, butlers and chefs, and in tailoring, photography, education, music and the arts.

This then was the place on which my father first set eyes in 1932. Waiting for him was Dr Albuquerque, affable and welcoming in his handsome silk suit, with a rickshaw driver in attendance. He showed my father around, and in Stone Town took him to an impressive property with a prominent name board that read 'Surgical Hall'. This was the building he owned and he reaffirmed his offer that my father could begin by leasing or buying a section of it on instalment terms, and have an ample share of the patients. Here was a ready-made living that could be taken up at once, and not only was there a reassuring absence of gunshots and fearsome Pashtuns to contend with, but the palm-fringed beaches and fragrant air of Zanzibar were pleasingly reminiscent of Goa.

It seems my father's mind was soon made up, for my mother swiftly received an encouraging missive from him followed by arrangements for her to bring my brother and myself out to join him in Zanzibar in a few months time. It was agreed that for the time being my sister Iva would stay behind in Goa with relatives. Although we would be making this fairly long trip over the sea without him, my father having been with my mother in Peshawar during some arduous and testing times was confident of her resourcefulness and her willingness and ability to cope with such a journey. He also arranged that our family servant, a young Goan boy called Thomas would travel with us to assist, and thereafter remain with us in Zanzibar. My father's time there prior to our arrival would allow him to find suitable accommodation and familiarise himself with the place.

Although I was just under four years old I have vivid memories of this my first voyage; the sharp tangy aroma of the salt water, the yawning ocean as we left Goa, and the long sunlit days afloat, stopping off at the beautiful islands of the Seychelles en-route, then the thrilling moment when the glinting outline of Zanzibar came into view. Dominating the seafront stood a square building of impressive size and symmetry, faced with imposing pillars and tiered verandas set around a tall clock tower. I was to learn this was the Beit al Ajaib, or House of Wonders, so named by locals when it was completed in 1883 as a palace for the then Sultan, the first building in Zanzibar with electric light. Close by the House of Wonders arose the older castellated ramparts of the Arab Fort, a seat of power whose solid brownstone walls had witnessed battles and bloodshed over the centuries. Such sights and the stories they told were quite a source of romance to a little boy.

And there on the harbour was my father! As he greeted us with smiles and kisses, even to my young eyes and ears there were things around us that felt familiar. Some of the people seemed so too, which with 100 or so other Goan families already on the island was unsurprising. These families were clustered mostly in Stone Town, within the vicinity of the imposing St Joseph's Catholic Cathedral, whose twin spires, visible from almost every part of the island seemed to a young child gazing up at them to stretch as far as heaven itself. All around was a bustling scene in which Africans, Comorians, Indians, Ismailis, Omanis, Persians, British, Europeans and Goans ate and worked and slept, and worshipped any number of gods in half a dozen or more tongues, their daily soundtrack the buzz of motorbikes and traders' cries, the Muezzins' calls to prayer and St Joseph's bells ringing out for morning Mass and the evening Angelus. Throughout the streets and alleyways the natural incense of nutmeg and mace, and the precious cloves from the picturesque rows of laurel-like bushes that flourished on the red hills beyond the town perfumed the air. It was within this lively, sensual and cosmopolitan setting, which would form the backdrop to the next few years of my childhood, that my father had found a dwelling for us.

Stone Town was something of a misnomer, for much of it was built not of regular stone but the coral from which Zanzibar itself was formed, lending the walls a rough-surfaced, warm reddish appearance. Leading off the wider precincts ran narrow streets of tall, closely built houses, accessible only on foot or by bicycle. Down just such a street lay our house, rented from an Arab landlord named Bwana Udi for 25 rupees a month. Heavy, ornately carved brass-studded front doors opened into the ground floor room above which were two further storeys, and at the very top a cement terrace for potted plants part roofed with corrugated iron. On this small roof garden we grew many pretty flowers, including the fragrant scented jasmine whose petals the ladies liked to wear. My parents slept on the second floor, my brother and myself on the one below, while our faithful Dachshund dog had the ground floor to himself.

The house was well placed; my father could walk in two minutes to his practice at the Surgical Hall, or cycle to collect medicine from the dispensary at nearby Kiponda. My mother, who had a job teaching at the Aga Khan School would take a rickshaw there each morning, her salary a modest 90 rupees a month, less than many a local cook might earn. My brother was immediately enrolled in the nearby St Joseph's Convent School in the Shangani area by the seashore, which would also be my first seat of learning, beginning at four years old in the kindergarten. St Joseph's, housed on the site of a former hospital and run by a group of German Catholic nuns, had expanded steadily since its inception in the late 1800s, and at the time of my enrolment there were around 25 pupils in the kindergarten and I believe almost 200 in the whole school, about three-quarters of them Goans, alongside Hindus and Muslims. This interfaith mix, even within a Catholic-run school was part of the legacy fostered by the Sultans of Zanzibar as an 'oasis of tolerance'. The schoolchildren all played happily together. One day when I was at home, a boy I knew from school appeared before me as if by magic in one of the rooms. 'How did you get in here?' I asked him. He smiled and said he lived next door and had climbed over the roof and jumped down into our house. His name was Sajjad Ali Gullam Ali, a Muslim boy, and he and I would become best friends for life.

Sajjad and I were soon exploring the neighbourhood, getting to know our way around the maze of narrow streets and alleys that made up Stone Town. Only a few yards from our homes sat the imposing former residence of Tippu Tip, the Omani descended trader who had made his fortune from what were once called the three pillars of the Indian Ocean economy; cloves, ivory and slaves. The slave trade was abolished in 1876, but slavery remained legal in Zanzibar until almost the end of the 19th century, 30 years before my young friends and I were born. The evidence of this gross practice could still be seen though in the low-ceilinged chambers in which the slaves had been routinely manacled. Tippu Tip had died in Stone Town in 1910 from malaria so it was said. However, his exploits were so cruel that the stories could fill our youthful imaginations, and sometimes passing by his house or the old slave market, we thought we could hear people crying out in pain and despair. If only we could have been there to help the poor souls we would say to one another. But then what could we have done, we were just boys. It might also have been that slavery in some form or another still went on in secret in Zanzibar and therefore just possible that the voices we heard were not imaginary.

The nuns who taught us, the Sisters of the Precious Blood, were not of the fearsome variety but kind and caring, their lives devoted to our welfare and development. Some of their rituals and refinements, grand-looking candelabra on the dinner table and so forth were quite surprising and different to anything we had at home. Years later when taking up invitations to visit the families of some of them in Europe, I saw their well-to-do origins and realised the sacrifices they must have made in going all the way to far-flung Zanzibar in the service of God and the education of children.

There were some very nice English people too, including Dr Taylor who lived by the Cathedral. He would become a close and trusted friend of my father, and whenever we had cuts or minor ailments we would be sent straight to Dr Taylor. Many of the Goans it should be pointed out, regarded themselves not as Indians but as Portuguese, in other words European rather than Asian. The question of any putative Portuguese ancestry was glossed over in the proud assertion of having 'Portuguese blood in our veins'. Like the supposed blue bloodedness of royalty, the stuff could it seemed also have a nationality. The British encouraged or colluded in this notional European-ness of Goans, selecting them not only for the Civil Service, but also as loyal and efficient cooks and domestic staff in their homes and exclusive social institutions, the British Club and the Yacht and Golf Clubs. But no Goan, however good a golfer, sailor or whatever was allowed membership or use of the facilities of any of these clubs. Some Goans worked for the Arabs in the Sultan's Palace and elsewhere, but something like 80 percent then in Zanzibar were British Government clerks. Their salaries were based on the rather ridiculous principle that those who had passed the Cambridge Senior Exam were paid a starting salary of 90 rupees per month, while those that failed received just half this amount. At the same time what might now be termed a glass ceiling was also firmly in place, with the most senior vacancies in the service reserved strictly for the British, often a fresh-faced young upper-class fellow who had arrived straight from the 'mother country'. What were termed 'Head Clerk' posts, however, from the customs office to communications, transport and prisons, were filled almost exclusively by Goans.

Goans enjoyed their own social establishments with several clubs catering for different trades and professions such as the tailors. The most prominent club was the Goan Institute, one rung down the hierarchical ladder as it were from the British, which did not admit Africans or Arabs as far as I know. Within the Goan Institute, caste divisions also played their part, and at one point 13 dissatisfied Kshatriyas, seeking more say in how things were run set up their own group known as the 'Number Thirteen Club'. The Goan Institute was by and large though a happy place for socialising, recreation and dancing with its own bar and accomplished musical band, where my young friends and I would while away many hours playing carom, an absorbing table top skittle game, and each Christmas Santa Claus would arrive with gifts for the excited children. The convivial atmosphere also encouraged many a teenage courtship and marriage. The chosen segregation of the Institute – elective at least on the part of its members – was rarely reflected in any overt intolerance of others outside its confines. As described, in day-to-day affairs the assorted ethnic and religious groups of Zanzibar carried on their patchwork lives in close proximity, with two well-attended mosques situated near to St Joseph's Cathedral. My father's Muslim patients were also far more friendly and open than in Peshawar, which must have been a relief for him. There was some quiet resentment of Indians, and mutterings of alleged hard-nosed business practices, but our mixed community, provided no boats were rocked, was one in which everyone got on. And at the head, as visible guarantor of harmony and contentment, the Sultan of Zanzibar, Sayed Khalifa, would be seen regularly out and about, walking or driving up and down and smiling and to all intents and purposes the leader of the Arabs and ruler of the islands. In reality he was a puppet, an acceptable face for the populace, as any British administrator put in his place would more likely be shot than waved at.

    The harmony within our home on the other hand was genuine, though as with all families there could be areas of conflict. My father was generally the more indulgent parent, buying me small gifts of balls and books he thought I might like. My mother was the voice of authority and the discipline she applied in her work at the Aga Khan School was extended to the domestic sphere. Duty and honesty were held in high regard, as was thrift. I recall the day she gave me a brand new pencil sharpener. A sharpened pencil at all times was a prerequisite to good handwriting, the basis of all learning, and it was impressed upon me how precious a tool this little object was, the keenness of its blade seemingly a constant reminder of what was expected of me in school and in life. My parents both being professional people set great store by education as the most vital and valuable key to success and in this vision the pencil sharpener seemed a resonant symbol. My mother was especially concerned that I should take great care of it, I must never lose it she told me, for if I did she would be very angry. Next day at school I sharpened my pencil dutifully and, at the end of the first lesson placing the sharpener squarely on my desk lest I lose it in the rough and tumble of the playground, joined my friends there for the mid-morning break. On returning I was horrified to see the sharpener had vanished. My heart was pounding in distress yet I felt too shy to tell my teacher.

    Dragging myself home with leaden feet, I confessed to my mother. Her warning had been no exaggeration, she was furious with me and as a punishment forbade me to sit down. I kept thinking she should have advised me to keep the sharpener in my pocket at all times, but she had not, also that our classroom had no cupboards, drawers or the type of desks that opened for storing possessions. In putting it on the desk I had done what I thought was best but been the victim of a thief. I was very upset with my mother. I was made to stand up for over an hour until my father came home and spoke quietly on my behalf, pointing out that I had learned my lesson now that some people are untrustworthy. I was very grateful for his support, and so relieved that he saw the innocent intentions behind my naïve action. It was an early object lesson in the realities of the world, though not the last, and more serious demonstrations of human mendacity were destined to befall me in the years to come. And who knows, although my dear mother's seemingly excessive iron discipline over a cheap pencil sharpener was intended to inculcate in me the importance of taking due care and attention, something of my disbelief and outrage that day, the painful and isolating experience of being accused of a crime which, albeit trifling another person had committed, and the arbitrariness of supposed justice, might have planted a potent seed in me.

A similar influence could have been a growing awareness of the social divisions around me, and how inexplicably harsh they seemed. For while Zanzibar was indeed a kind of happy melting pot, it only melted so far, beneath which lay a rigid echelon system. At the lower end were the Africans, who worked mainly as porters and dockhands and had their own residential area outside the town. Jockeying somewhat for position above them were the Goans, Arabs and Indians. The Africans, having little choice, appeared on the surface at least sanguine about their place in the scheme of things, while those with ambition or 'ideas above their station' might claim Arab blood. One day walking in what we called the shambas, an area of shrubs and small trees, I chanced upon our servant Thomas in intimacy with a local girl who looked African but called herself an Arab, perhaps to make herself more desirable. Fearing my parents' censure Thomas swore me to secrecy. A little later he disappeared and we never saw him again. His covert relationship was understandable, for within the Goan community caste prejudice in general remained strong.

I discovered these attitudes could also impinge on me when I made friends in the neighbourhood with some children whose surname was Coutinho, the eldest of whom was Max. When my mother found out she told me quite forcibly to stay away from the family. I pleaded that these were nice, friendly, children, why should I not play with them? My brother Rix then became sweet on one of the sisters, Zita, and they began to meet away from the house. One day, while sorting through our laundry, my mother found a letter in Rix's pocket. It was from Zita, and read, *'Darling, I love you, let's get married...'* Mother confronted Rix and beat him furiously, refusing to give him food. I found him crying. My father took no part in the punishment, but neither did he feel able to intercede. The Coutinhos' only crime it seemed was that they were regarded as untouchables. When in defiant mood I would announce to my mother that she could shout at me all she liked, but when I grew up I was going to marry one of the Coutinho girls. I felt no malice in this, nor as I recall any actual desire to do as I said, but just to speak out against this inhuman notion. My mother worked very hard and I was very appreciative of her, but she did believe strongly in the caste system. I didn't agree with it, and it sent me a little further away from her, as far as my brain was concerned. She had grown up in Karachi and Goa, and her father, a surgeon, used to say, 'I am a secular Brahmin.' There was a deep mythology, and Hindus whose forefathers supposedly came from some province containing a mystical river, believed they were the kingpins of society and got away with a lot, quite literally.

In Zanzibar, the church preached the equality of all people in God's eyes, while on the ground it too discriminated. This fact, and the known tendencies of some priests for affairs with married Goan women, gave the more zealous elements a job of work in keeping their flock within the fold. Unlike some families that recited the rosary several times a day, we had no ritual of prayer at home, and while my mother made a show of observance, my father was not religious. We attended Sunday services and confession and I knew the whole Latin Mass parrot-fashion without understanding a word of it. As a pupil of St Joseph's I was expected also to go to church first thing every day on the way to school, or risk being sent home. Each morning the nuns would ask each of us: 'Did you go to church this morning? And remember, no lies now!'

Our local priest Father White would pursue backsliders and one day he called at our house demanding to know from my father why I had not been attending. I was very surprised, as I didn't think I was that important. I told him: 'I don't go because you are all a bunch of racists.' 'What do you mean?' he said. 'We are not racists we are people of God.' I said, 'Yes, that is where I think the shame lies, you are supposed to be people of God but you are racists.' He repeated: 'What do you mean?' I said, 'Look, you have hospitals where you don't allow black people to come in. You have schools, reading rooms, nurseries, all run by the Catholic Church for Catholics, but only white Catholics.' Father White shook his head: 'No, no, my son.' 'Don't bother with the "son",' I replied. He then tried to explain to me that it was not a question of a colour bar, but that African and European cultures were different; the church believed in equality, but not in mixing the two cultures. I was reminded of this line of argument some years later, on hearing an Englishman remark, 'I don't mind a black man being my brother, but I don't want him to be my brother-in-law.' Father White then tried the tactic of appointing me head server in church, which being a responsible position that I found difficult to refuse was successful at least in getting me into the building even if my heart and mind remained somewhat elsewhere.

If the fact that the priesthood had its share of hypocritical or dubious characters came as no surprise to someone of my father's experience, more unsettling for him were certain discoveries regarding a member of his own profession, especially that the individual concerned was none other than his business partner Dr Manuel

Albuquerque. Well-spoken and smartly dressed, the doctor had always seemed a pillar of the community. Whenever his rickshaw stopped by our football pitch or on the street and he deigned to say hello to us children, we would feel very special, as if we had been addressed by royalty. The first warning bell sounded when my father happened one day to enter the storeroom where Albuquerque kept some of his medicines. He found the place full of cobwebs, the bottles and jars covered in thick layers of dust. On inspecting some of the contents he strongly suspected they were bogus and more likely to harm than cure anyone. When my father broached the matter, Dr Albuquerque seemed to deny any notion that his medicines were either ineffective or unsafe. Still not entirely certain himself my father allowed my mother to volunteer in what has to be said was a brave experiment, imbibing a tiny amount of one of the potions. That night she became violently ill. As she sat on a commode crying and distressed, it was clear that all the so-called medicines in the cobweb-infested storeroom should be destroyed.

  Whether Dr Albuquerque agreed to this or not I do not know. What did come to my father's attention were other questionable aspects to his partner's affairs, most glaringly Albuquerque's tendency to overcharge his patients, particularly the Arabs. This might have seemed unworkable given that the depression had hit Zanzibar as hard as anywhere. Albuquerque, however, was playing the long game. When an Arab patient said he had no money he would obligingly offer him a loan and even draw up paperwork so that everything was in black and white. Few of the Arabs signing these documents realised that not only was the rate of interest excessively high, but that the loan was secured against their property. When they were unable to meet the repayments, Albuquerque would apply to the courts for foreclosure.

  It was legal but unscrupulous, exploiting the Arabs' language barrier, and no doubt their trust in Albuquerque as a man of medicine. By this modus operandi he had acquired a considerable number of properties in Zanzibar. Those Arabs he had taken advantage of were unlikely to feel well disposed towards him, explaining perhaps his keenness for my father to take over his practice, while he discreetly withdrew from the scene. As all this dawned on my father he finally had it out with Albuquerque. The two men had a huge row, and when my father made it plain he wanted to quit the partnership there were angry threats and talk of litigation. Our dream of a new life in Zanzibar had suddenly begun to turn sour.

Despite all of this, Albuquerque was widely respected. It is said that in 1903 he contributed to the detection of bubonic plague in Zanzibar and worked hard to combat the disease. Quite the opposite of a revolutionary, he became Portugal's consul general to the Sultan of Zanzibar, and his palatial mansion in Anjuna in Goa was built as a replica of the Sultan's Palace. Dr Albuquerque died in 1956, and a life-size marble statue of him has now been erected on a pedestal in the garden. My abiding boyhood memory of the man is of a rather grandiose figure, smiling and waving to everyone as his servant pedalled him in a rickshaw along the seafront.

Playing marbles in front of our house in Zanzibar

Myself (top row, second from left) as a boy scout

On the beach in Zanzibar with my friends (top row, left)

Chapter Three

Dreams and Ambitions

1938 to 1945

We had been in Zanzibar some six years when the dispute with my father's medical and business partner Manuel Albuquerque came to an acrimonious head. As often happens in life, as one door was slamming shut another fell open, albeit in this case through sad circumstances. In the small area of Stone Town called Kiponda, quite nearby to us, a member of the Ismaili community, an elderly Muslim doctor by the name of Merchant had recently died. Having known and respected Dr Merchant, now that his busy practice was available to purchase my father was willing and ready to take his place.

Kiponda being so close there was no need to relocate, though my father did in due course move us to a different house in Stone Town. My mother kept her teaching job at the Aga Khan School, while my brother Rix and I continued our studies at St Joseph's. I use the term study advisedly, for though at first gaining top marks, somewhere between the age of eight and nine I had started to fall behind. I was beginning to take after my brother, who as a keen sportsman devoted most of his energy to games, in and out of school. Rix, tall and handsome, was also distracted by girls. He was always very good to me though and often took me to the big sports grounds in Mnazi Mmoja, meaning 'one coconut', where football, hockey and 'pitch and staff' were played. Putting our shoes and shirts on the grass to mark the goalposts, the football and hockey players would sometimes fight over the space. My brother would always come and help me. He was very generous and everyone liked him. As far as ideas went, over caste for example, he was very like our mum, but he would always defend people physically, especially from the larger boys. I liked him very much.

The great outdoors was an ever-present diversion and our idyllic family camping trips lasted three or four weeks in the school holidays. In term time, in the playground or at the Mnazi Mmoja, there was football. After a match we would go and listen to the police band, led by Captain Bustard, and in the Victoria Gardens, away from the flowerbeds and ornamental fishponds some Goan clerks had set up an unofficial badminton court. One afternoon at the Gardens, hearing a splash, the next second we saw a father rescuing a child who had tumbled into the pond. As I recall, this was the first time I set eyes on a little girl called Romola. Our forbears had been distant cousins, and her uncle had first come to Zanzibar in 1890. More recently, her father and mine had been fellow students at medical college in Bombay. Romola's family had a wonderful house right beside the sea, so close that at high tide the windows had to be shut, and a wild almond tree with huge leaves. Romola's brothers, one of whom won the Goan Institute Silver Cup for table tennis, were keen on all kinds of sports, and I would often call at the house to play cricket with Ehrlich, Orlando and Armando. Another great game was building intricate battleships of sand for our war games. While we boys gleefully bombarded each other's funnels with fistfuls of sand, Romola would sit in the window reading, as if we boys did not exist for her, occasionally lifting her head from her book to smile.

I would idle away many hours like this on the seafront, playing, fishing and swimming with Sajjad and my other friends. These were blissful carefree times such as every child should experience, but there could be risks for the unwary, as I would discover through an unnerving experience. It was a gloriously hot day, and leaving my companions to their games I had taken to the sea to cool off. I swam out strongly, full of energy and revelling in the refreshment of the water. It was such a beautiful day, the sunlight reflected on the surface dazzling to the eye, and I became oblivious to all but the physical pleasure I was enjoying. It was only when I noticed the shoreline looking distinctly smaller, that I realised with alarm how far I had swum out. I now risked being swept either so far out to sea that I could not get back, or along towards the docks where the floating rubbish lured hungry sharks.

A scarcely less horrific threat was the Arab ships, whose crews watched for boys who had swum too far out, waiting to snatch them from the water and take them away as slaves. This was no myth and happened almost every day, and although it was said to have befallen only African youths I kept a keen lookout for any dhows as I tried to swim with all my might now back towards land. The current, however, proved too strong, so I resorted to floating on my back, keeping as still as possible and praying I would drift back in at some point. Half an hour must have passed before I had floated several hundred yards down the shore and found myself by the Sultan's Palace. Hauling myself thankfully onto terra firma I ran back to retrieve my clothes, where I found my friends laughing and playing merrily amongst themselves and quite unaware of me. 'You b*******!' I exclaimed vehemently, the stress of the ordeal finally hitting me, 'I could have been drowned or eaten by sharks or kidnapped as a slave!'

Keen to nurture a sense of responsibility in me and hone my skills in arithmetic, my mother asked me to oversee my father's bookkeeping. The tasks were straightforward enough; he would show me how to make up the patients' bills on a Saturday then send me out to deliver them and collect payment. Another duty was to empty his pockets on his return from surgery at the end of each day, tot up the contents, deduct any 'float' and record the net amount, before then handing my mother whatever she required for the household. Once a week I would carry the remainder to the Zanzibar Post Office and deposit it in our family savings account, which earned 2 percent annual interest. In this way I got a little bit of experience of accounts and the value of money and felt very grown up handing over the coins and notes at the window, having virtuously resisted any temptation to swipe so much as a cent for myself. I was in any case given a small amount of pocket money, 50 cents each week, but really I was so proud of the trust my father placed in me that I could not think of abusing it.

Despite encouragement I was still not applying myself with similar discipline at St Joseph's. A staff shortage had meant that my first teacher, Sister Robertina, had to take two classes. Though kind and methodical, the only subject she was really strict on was religion, and it was the same throughout the school, and nobody could question what was said. Sometimes the priests came in and gave us catechism. They were regarded as very important people and the nuns warned us never to ask them certain things, especially to do with the human body. We also wondered why the pages of some of our textbooks had been torn out. Nothing was taught about sex or reproduction. When my father did try to tell me about the 'birds and the bees' I thought it was all very strange. A girl called Zita Cordoza once asked me, did I know where babies came from. Well I knew that people got married. What else? They kiss I suppose I said. I had seen dogs on the street getting stuck together, but thought they were just biting one another. The facts of life remained a mystery to me, and would for some time. I remember the first time I saw a woman's breasts; she must have been about 75 years old, cycling down a lane. When she asked me what I was looking at, I pointed and said, 'What are those for?' She replied, 'That's where you get milk from.' I said, 'Why don't you cover it, it might get cold.' Another girl then told me how a man's seed gets put in the woman's pot, and described the parts of the body involved. I felt it was very dirty, and that my father being a doctor would know that this was all made up nonsense.

When I went to look through his medical books, however, and saw the diagrams, I realised with a shock that what I had been told appeared more or less true.

My favourite teacher was Sister Zeglinda, the youngest member of staff, whom the Headmistress would shout at in German, making her cry. We had no idea what was being said, but our hearts went out to her and we would willingly have beaten the Headmistress for her unkindness. We also felt sorry for our teachers when the school inspectors came in. These were very tough Irish people, and when one of them sat at the back, even the German nuns would get nervous and begin to stutter. Adding to their embarrassment and ours, the inspector would then shout at them in front of all their pupils and tell them they were stupid.

Speaking and studying English, I was learning French as a second language, and picking up some Swahili. Our German teachers had trouble pronouncing some English words, saying 'drought' like 'rough' for example, and in French lessons, one of our Seychelles pupils (three brothers, Phillipe, Emile and Jules, had arrived from the islands) would correct the master's grammar and pronunciation, which some days made him angry, sometimes grateful. I loved British history, from the story of King Alfred burning his cakes to the Black Hole of Calcutta. Geometry came in useful on the one afternoon each week when we practised carpentry, sawing and screwing plain pieces of wood to make chairs for the church. What I liked about all of mathematics was the intellectual trial of strength, to be asked to prove a theorem, knowing there could only be one right answer, and the challenge of finding it. At one point I was finishing maths tests with time to spare and would go over the paper again to check my answers.

When studying for the Junior Cambridge, lessons ran from 1pm until 7pm at night, and as the afternoon wore on and it grew dark outside we boys longed to escape. Then one day a friend showed me how, by inserting a 5-cent piece into a light socket then replacing the bulb, it not only made a pleasing bang, but all the electricity went off. When no one was looking I tried it out in our classroom. Sure enough the whole school was plunged into darkness and the teachers were forced to send us all home. I performed the trick several times for the class though the girls weren't very appreciative of my efforts. Nor were the teachers, who lived in the attached buildings and had to sit with candles all evening until the power was restored. After a prolonged investigation I was caught and caned.

My standard of work at St Joseph's continued to slip. Zita Cardozo, who had asked me where babies came from – already knowing I think – was, unlike Zita Coutinho a Brahmin, so my mother had no objection to our friendship. She was a pleasant girl, and though a little too religious for my taste, we were both mad on carom, and at the Goan Institute played the skittle game avidly together night after night. It was a wonderful timewaster, and along with the tennis and table tennis, badminton and other pastimes, my powers of concentration were wanting when I got in the classroom or had homework to complete. My brother Rix, whose single-minded pursuit of sports had left his academic achievements wanting, seemed happy and carefree enough, so why I thought, worry one's head about tests and exams? Rix was such a fine sportsman, excelling at cricket, hockey, football and badminton. I shared his enthusiasm particularly for table tennis, practising night after night, dreaming I would one day be a champion.

One problem not of my own making, especially when Rix was not around to look after me, was bullies. I had been advised early on that the best way of deterring them was to befriend the largest boy you could find, do his bidding and he would then be your protector. I therefore approached a likely looking fellow and asked: 'Will you be my best friend?' He looked at me and replied: 'Your best friend? You are useless, a tiny little thing. What can you do for me? Nothing doing.' I felt very humiliated. The bullies' favourite sport was to stamp on the feet of any smaller pupil they saw wearing conspicuously good shoes. My parents made a point of my having smart, polished footwear at all times, the shoemaker coming to our house each year to measure me up for handmade shoes, these being the days before branded footwear such as Bata arrived in Zanzibar. Other pupils were jealous I suppose and I was a prime target, my shoes at the end of the day scuffed and marked and my feet bruised and sore. The chief culprit, a boy named J. de Cruz, made me so angry and upset on one occasion that I went round to the official British residence where his father worked as a cook. He was a kind man, who during the evening dances would pass us titbits from the buffet. Two armed policemen on the door just stared at me as I ran right past them crying and into the kitchen. 'Look what your son has done!' I shouted at the cook, showing him my shoes. 'Don't worry,' the cook reassured me. I knew he had punished his son when next day at school Wenceslau gave me a furious beating.

My father listened sympathetically but said that I must find my own solution. I think he wanted me to stand up for myself, and also feared that any intervention would make matters worse for me, saying that if parents got involved in their children's fights, their opponents would only take it out on them later. Necessity being the mother of invention, I was forced to draw on my own resources. My father advised me to gather together all the boys who had been bullied. This I did, and told them we must band together. We would call ourselves the 'High Gang' and I would be the leader, which they accepted. From now on when any of us was troubled by a bully we would wait until after school and leap on him, beating him until he begged us to stop. When the first such strike was carried out it proved very effective, and the 'High Gang', as I would discover several years later, became an institution at St Joseph's.

The idea of helping one another was also instilled in us by the Wolf Cubs. A photo of me in my uniform, taken on my Box Brownie camera would become a cherished possession. Goans were keen photographers, often having their own portrait studios or taking pictures for weddings and dances at the Goan Institute. It was there that I learned the foxtrot, rumba and waltz, another hobby to detract me from my studies. Eventually my father received a letter from the school. Calling for me, I saw tears in his eyes as he said, 'Et Tu Brute?' Being unfamiliar with 'Julius Caesar' I asked what he meant. He read out the letter, in which the teachers regretfully informed him of my declining performance over the past year and all my missing homework. They also noted that the work in my exercise books looked very similar to that of other pupils and suspected me of copying. Looking at me sternly, my father told me how Rix, despite extra tutoring had still not passed his exams and would now be sent to a government school in India, very much a last option. 'Do you want to be the same?' he asked. He then told me the story of Caesar, whose brutal murder as depicted by Shakespeare was compounded by the shock and horror of finding his most trusted general and closest friend Brutus among his executioners.

I too was shocked. What could I say? Metaphorically stabbing my beloved father in the back could not have been a more extreme opposite of my feelings towards him. I was very fond of him, and he of me. Looking back I saw that his cherished dream must have been for his sons to qualify as doctors and to earn sufficient to look after him and my mother in their old age. Concerns about Rix, and now this sudden discovery that I might be heading for the academic scrap heap, must have caused him great pain. I felt very guilty and made a promise to myself that I would henceforward study hard. Seeing the remorse on my face, my father also made a promise, expressing it in terms of a deal: that if I improved and did well enough in class, he would buy me a brand new Raleigh bicycle. The desire to make him happy was inspiration enough, but the prospect of a gleaming Raleigh bike gave added zest to the turning over of a new leaf.

It was around this time though that I became aware that my parents had another source of worry. Now old enough to understand the relative cost of things, I realised the source of my mother's anger over seemingly insignificant items like the lost pencil sharpener; namely that we were short of money. Why should this be? We didn't have a lavish lifestyle, like most people my father used a bicycle to get around or for speed his motorbike, which he was very keen on, but we did not then own a car. Our only entertainment was the radio and newspapers and though frequenting the Goan Institute my father was not a drinker. The fact was his income was less than might be expected of a successful doctor. He had paid in small regular instalments for Dr Merchant's practice, and it was indeed a busy one, but this was not the same as profitable. With no government health service of any kind, obtaining fees from the patient was the only way a medical man could earn a living, but some days looking in my father's pockets there was little to be found for our housekeeping, let alone to take to the Post Office.

It was not that he was inefficient or idle, far from it. The reasons were twofold, firstly the economic depression in which, like much of the world in the 1930s Zanzibar was mired. Competition for resources was intense, and the Clove Growers Association under the chairmanship of Mr Bartlett, known for his charismatic limp, was committed to ensuring optimum returns for its members; when Britain proposed the Clove Bill, legislation regarded as commercially punitive, the ensuing protests brought British troops onto the streets of Zanzibar, and a friend of our family, a promising law student in his early twenties, was sadly killed. Second was my father's lax attitude to money, or more precisely his generous nature; when my football club's expensive leather ball was stolen, he had no hesitation in buying us another. The same applied in his work, those patients who could afford to would pay him, but many genuinely could not. The narrow open sewers that ran down the centre of the Zanzibar streets gave rise to dysentery, viral fever and other serious conditions, and people who contracted these diseases he could not turn away, money or no money. Most of his patients were Africans, what we called the Swahilis, and a few Indians, and with many settling their bills in kind, often were the days he returned home with crabs or fish or coconuts in lieu of cash. Many were shopkeepers, small traders; one man, a watch seller used to give him a watch every so often. These I would invariably take to pieces, fascinated by the precise intricate mechanisms, though with no proper screwdrivers had trouble putting them back together and ended up with quite a collection of old timepieces, none of which worked. Abdul Kareem Munghi, a hardworking Indian man who made washing soap for clothes and utensils and sold it door-to-door, and one or more of his nine children were always falling sick, which kept us well supplied with soap at least. When patients had no money and needed medicine my father would go and buy it for them, out of his own pocket, from the chemist's shop.

My mother was increasingly disapproving of her husband working for free. I could see why she had asked me to keep scrupulous accounts. She also made her views clear: 'Look at him, we don't have money to eat, and he is giving free medicine to these people.' My father's justification was that it was, 'the duty of a doctor to treat people, to make them all right. You don't send a person to die because he has no money. If you have money you must spend it on them first.' His sense of vocation could not be faulted, but mother also had a point; he had a family of his own to support. From time to time he was obliged to raise some cash by selling parcels of his land in Goa, prompting my mother, fearing the complete dwindling away of our family assets to remark with some force: 'You cannot be Santa Claus forever.'

For my part I felt determined to fulfil my promise of renewed commitment to studying. At the end of that year I waited nervously as the results were read out in school. To my utter joy I heard that I had come top. Instead of waiting to collect my prize, however, I ran out from the back to find my father. 'So where's my bicycle?' I panted eagerly. As he took my hand I felt despondent for a moment but he just meant we had to go to the shop to choose it. There was no Raleigh to fit my size, but on payment of 107 shillings we left with an eminently suitable Phillips model, another British brand. The world was opened up for me; though used to walking great lengths, having a good bike now, it wasn't long before I was cycling 15 miles or more in an hour to already favourite haunts, or discovering even more distant regions of Unguja. In my excitement though, I forgot again about the power of the elements. Hearing about a festival being held at Fumba, on the far side of the island, Rix and I decided to pay a visit. After a long hot cycle ride, we reached Fumba. The place was alive with music, singing and dancing, everyone having fun. When Rix announced it was time to go, I said I would stay a little longer. The cycling was also catching up with me. Sitting down on the beach, my head started to throb and soon I was feeling very unwell. I had barely the energy to wheel my bike, let alone ride it all the way home. Dizzy and almost unable to stand, I had no idea what to do.

Then I heard a voice calling: 'Fitz, what are you doing here?' Looking up I saw a family who were friends with my father. They soon realised I had a bad case of heatstroke. 'Come on let's get you in the boat.' The family had a small motorboat moored on the seafront. It was the quickest way home. Skirting the coast, we bumped swiftly across the waves and halfway around the island until the familiar outline of Stone Town came into view. The family brought me to our house, where my father thanked them profusely. As he took in my weak and feverish state, I had never seen him look so worried. Having read Mahatma Gandhi on the deficiencies in Western medicine, he quickly prepared an 'Onion Bath', an ancient Indian remedy, which required mashing several pounds of raw onions to cover my whole body. After sitting up with me for three nights, he saw with relief that I was gradually recovering. If it had not been for the swift action of our friends with the boat, and my father's subsequent care, I believe I would have died.

My horizons were also expanding intellectually. I formed a club with friends for exchanging books we obtained from weekend auctions of property left by departing British families. Putting 10 cents each in the kitty we could often pick up 20 books for a shilling. My father approvingly added to my growing library and one volume he gave me would have a profound effect. It was Mahatma Gandhi's autobiography 'The Story of My Experiments With Truth', charting the author's upbringing and early years, his political awakening as a young lawyer in South Africa, abstinence from alcohol, simplicity, non-violence and a philosophy of education for all, principles that he both preached and endeavoured to live by. I began to follow Gandhi's work and ideas with great interest.

In 1939, we learned that Britain was at war with Germany. 'Pray for victory,' the German nuns would tell us. Victory for whom, I wondered. At first, day-to-day life in our small, multicultural community under the British flag continued much as before. A few miles across the sea next to Kenya though lay the German controlled territory of Tanganyika. We began to see British troops drilling along the coast, practising probably for what we would later learn were the D-Day landings in Europe.

All evening we sat by our neighbour's radio listening for news. One night we heard an ominous tolling of bells come over the airwaves, followed by an electrifying, upper-class English voice: 'German calling, Germany calling, today our glorious navy destroyed 32 battleships of the arch imperialist powers...!' William Joyce, better known as Lord Haw-Haw, was a former member of the British Union of Fascists, who had defected to Berlin and was now broadcasting official Nazi propaganda. Later on I would be fascinated with the legal ramifications. Caught by chance at the end of the war and tried in England for treason, an appeal argued that the charge was invalid; as an Irishman born in America and subsequently a naturalized German, he was not a British subject and could not therefore be guilty of treason. The prosecution countered, that having lied about his nationality in gaining a British passport, and voted in Britain, he owed allegiance to the Crown. The case was upheld, and on the 3rd of January 1946, Joyce was hanged.

As the war escalated we felt the effects of rationing, with no butter and, considering the number of chickens in Zanzibar, surprisingly few eggs. In India meanwhile a war of words had broken out, with the British presuming on the colony's support, while Congress, though condemning Germany's actions, would not involve India in the conflict without consultation. The British then offered some minor concessions to the Indians, prompting Gandhi's reaction that 'the old divide and rule is to continue – Congress has asked for bread and it has got stone.'

By March 1942 Britain, fearing a Japanese invasion of India through Burma, sent Sir Stafford Cripps to speak to India's leaders, promising future independence in return for their allegiance now. Gandhi, while opposed to Nazism, which he dubbed 'naked ruthless force reduced to an exact science' was also suspicious of the British offer, calling it 'a post-dated cheque, issued on a fast-failing bank.' Amid a mood of mistrust discussions broke down, and under the slogan of 'Quit India' immediate British withdrawal was called for. Hopes now ran high among supporters of independence. Watching from afar, my family and I, though Goan, identified strongly with India in the struggle. The hopes were swiftly dashed however when on the 9th of August 1942, the British without warning arrested the entire Congress leadership. It was my 13th birthday. There was a great sense of shock, and I must confess we all felt sympathy for the Germans, not because we really liked them, but thought that if the British suffered a loss of face, got a bloody nose as it were, they might be a little more amenable to justice for their colonies. It was a case of 'my enemy's enemy is my friend'. It was only later when I learned more about Hitler and the full horror of the Nazi regime that I realised Gandhi had been right, and felt a little ashamed.

Another kind of shame hit me at about this time. The appearance of hair in places other than my head coincided with some strange sensations. My body seemed out of control, and at night I would sometimes awake to a sticky sensation around my lower half. I would get up quietly and wash my pants, hoping they would dry before the morning with no questions asked. When I got the chance to speak to my brother about it he assured me it was quite normal and happened to all men. As to how and why though, I was still not entirely sure.

While my father's fears about my schooling had been allayed, his worries over money continued. In that same year of 1942, however, a communication from an old army friend, Colonel Nawaz Khan, brought with it the possibility of improving his circumstances. Colonel Khan was now looking to return to a military post, and it had occurred to him that my father might like to take over his current job of Medical Officer in Charge at the large soda ash works at Lake Magadi in Kenya. It would mean moving a long way, Magadi being situated in the Rift Valley, some 75 miles southwest of Kenya's capital Nairobi. Financial concerns aside, we had been very happy during our ten years in Zanzibar, but here surely lay the probability of a more regular income in place of ad hoc payments and watches, soap and fish. My father may equally have been drawn by the simple desire for change, refreshment and a spirit of adventure. Whatever his motives, Magadi must have seemed attractive for he duly replied to his old friend and gave his grateful assent to the offer.

I felt uncertain. The move would mean leaving my friends and familiar surroundings, but also interrupting my education which I took rather seriously now. I was worried about what school I would go to in Kenya. I could not quite envisage the glow of achievement and security I felt at St Joseph's in some other unknown environment, and my all-important Cambridge Senior Certificate exams were not far off now. As with our move to Zanzibar, my father arranged to go on ahead to Magadi, see what it was like, and if all was well he would send for my mother and me. Rix would shortly be sailing in the other direction back to India to finish his schooling. To reach Magadi meant crossing the sea to the port of Tanga in German Tanganyika, thence travelling by rail into Kenya, changing trains for the final leg. Ships being scarce at that time, my father had to wait several weeks for a passage, the only type of vessel available an Arab dhow. With little wind to fill the sails and no ancillary motors or tugboats, the 25-mile crossing took him five whole days, one and a half of them the last mile into Tanga harbour. Despite this he described it as an enjoyable trip, recalling with amusement his fear of being eaten by sharks, as, to use the toilet, he had to grip two ropes and hang out over the side.

His impression of Magadi positive, and the managers of the Magadi Soda Company being pleased to engage him, he began making arrangements for our relocation. Having done a lot more thinking, I had decided that I would definitely prefer to stay on in Zanzibar and continue at St Joseph's where I felt sure of a better chance to succeed in my exams. Though I was a boy still, and one who had never lived away from his family before, there were many people around who knew us and would surely look out for me, and I felt quite confident in being able to survive on my own. My father, however, saw it differently and did not like the idea of my being so distant. When I got to Nairobi though, finding a school place and accommodation, where the going rate of 10,000 shillings for one room was prohibitive, proved difficult. When asked if I would prefer to go with Rix back to Bombay or Goa, I pleaded that I would much rather return to Zanzibar. My father still seemed very reluctant, but after some consideration eventually gave his consent.

And so as a 14-year-old schoolboy, with my parents far away on the African mainland, I became independent, a young man about Stone Town, Zanzibar, a private tenant renting a small house at 15 shillings a month, and employing one of my father's former patients as my part-time servant for five shillings, paid from my 150 shillings allowance sent each month from Kenya. The servant would make me lunch then return to his duties as a messenger in the law courts next to the school. I soon settled into my new life, always healthy and full of energy, until one morning I awoke to feel a fever coming over me. Drained suddenly of strength I languished at home for two days. On the third day some nuns from St Joseph's, concerned about my absence from school, came looking for me. It turned out to be a touch of malaria.

With attentive care, particularly from my best friend Sajjad Ali Gulam Ali, I was soon well and we were all hanging out again after school, sharing biryani at one of the little Indian shops, or eating at one another's houses and enjoying long convivial strolls until late in the evening. We had such pride in our close-knit group, looking after each other and fearing nothing and no one, that in those balmy days of friendship the future seemed to stretch before us, an unending road of exciting possibilities and ever-happier times ahead. Down which particular path though would my own future lie? Who or what were my influences? My father would always be my first role model, while on the world stage Gandhi was certainly becoming a source of inspiration. An elderly Sikh, the only taxi driver in Zanzibar, eking out a living with his small Austin Seven from his house near the market square in Stone Town, provided, in the person of his son Basant Singh Gill, who was away in England, another. Spoken of proudly by his father, the young man's return home one day caused huge excitement, people rushing up to shake his hand and talk to him, and every mother in town hoping fervently that their daughter might marry him. Basant was indeed a very impressive and charming fellow with equally charming friends and spoke English very fluently. When I asked him what he had been studying in England, he told me he was training to be a barrister. He was also a keen billiards player, which I later found was almost a prerequisite in the profession. My best friend Sajjad's father was a lawyer and Sajjad was intending to follow in his footsteps.

It was at about this time while Britain and its empire were still at war that the calls for Indian independence would surely be heightened by a terrible turn of events in Bengal. Gandhi had been warning of rice shortages since 1941 and by 1943 the situation had become so severe that it would, over a period of just a few months, lead to the death from starvation of three and a half million people. Historian Madhusree Mukherjee has presented the British Prime Minister of the time, Winston Churchill, as bearing much of the responsibility. In her book *Churchill's Secret War*, published in 2010, Mukherjee wrote that between January and July 1943, India exported huge quantities of rice, estimated as sufficient to keep almost 400,000 families alive for a year; it went instead to maintain Britain and the European theatre of war. Churchill refused urgent pleas to export food to the colony, claiming there was a shortage of ships, this while cargoes of wheat from Australia passed by India, bound for storage in Europe.

In India, hoarders took advantage of the crisis, exacerbating the dire shortages for their financial gain. Fearing a Japanese invasion of the colony by sea, the British also employed a scorched earth strategy – what they called 'denial policy' – seizing boats along the Bengal coast and destroying rice stocks. In researching her book, Mukherjee had traced survivors of the famine, who recalled people drinking the leftover water in which rice had been boiled, children eating leaves and grass and the bereaved having no strength left to cremate their loved ones, whose bodies were fed on by dogs and jackals. Some men left for Calcutta to seek work, while desperate women prostituted themselves to provide food for their families. In this very sad time for Bengal, as Mukherjee describes it: 'Mothers had turned into murderers, village belles into whores, fathers into traffickers of daughters'.

The famine lasted until almost the end of 1943. Those that survived brought in their crop of rice, but by the time shipments of barley and wheat reached the people in need in November, tens of thousands had died. Bengal's population was estimated at 61 million, and while many of them had starved that autumn, Britain's food and raw materials reserves had grown to 18.5 million tonnes for a country of 47 million. Not all of the British were indifferent to the plight of the Bengalis; Lord Wavell, who had been made Viceroy of India that year, described the Churchill government's attitude to the country as 'negligent, hostile and contemptuous'. Remarks made by Churchill on the other hand, suggest a very contrasting attitude, as when speaking to the Secretary of State for India, Lord Amery: 'I hate Indians... they are a beastly people with a beastly religion,' while to a meeting of the British War Cabinet, he declared that the famine was their own fault, 'for breeding like rabbits'. Apparently, when the government in Delhi sent a telegram to London about the famine, Churchill's only response was to ask why Gandhi had not died yet.

In Madhusree Mukherjee's view, it was 'not so much racism as the imbalance of power inherent in the social Darwinian pyramid that explains why famine could be tolerated in India while bread rationing was regarded as an intolerable deprivation in wartime Britain'. Soutik Biswas, who reviewed *Churchill's Secret War* for the BBC, was of the opinion that: 'For colonial apologists, the book is essential reading. It is a terrifying account of how colonial rule is direly exploitative and, in this case, made worse by a man who made no bones of his contempt for India and its people.' (Source: 'How Churchill Starved India' by Soutik Biswas, online correspondent for BBC News in India. 28th of October 2010.)

In Zanzibar we were relatively fortunate. The average standard of living, always very basic, had deteriorated under the economic depression of the 1930s and Britain's entry into the Second World War had brought trade restrictions and shortages. Compared to Bengal and many other parts of India, however, people on the islands of Zanzibar could either grow or obtain food of some kind, sufficient in most cases at least to avoid starvation. Poorer peasants in the south and east of Unguja and on Pemba, unable to sustain a living in the rocky terrain, sold their labour to the Arab or Shirazi clove plantation owners or migrated to Zanzibar town to find work. A lucky few had access to education, which could bring opportunities, and a happy day dawned for me in December 1943 with the news that I had passed my Senior Cambridge Certificate. This success brought with it the realisation that I would soon be leaving St Joseph's, and saying goodbye to my friends. The sadness was mingled with a growing excitement. A new adventure was about to begin. It was agreed that I would now leave Zanzibar and make my own way across the sea to Kenya to join my parents in Magadi. There were some belongings of ours that my father wanted brought to Magadi now, and I was asked to make the arrangements. The furniture was not worth much, but along with his motorcycle that he had left behind, it all had to be shipped. Wartime restrictions made movement of goods extremely difficult, but after some effort Julius Fernandes, Chairman of the Goan Institute and Chief Customs Clerk, kindly provided the necessary permits, and everything was packed up and taken to the harbour.

As I set sail from Zanzibar the war in Europe was coming to an end, yet India's future lay still unresolved. By now a keen and devoted disciple of Mahatma Gandhi, I had decided to spend my life fighting not only for the freedom of India, but of Goa too, and carried within me a burning sense of justice on behalf of all those to whom it was denied. I had read an article that said if you want to fight the British you've got to learn their rules and use those rules against them. This was the most effective means of bringing about change, by reason and argument and using the laws and procedures that had evolved over hundreds of years. At the same time I noted that the article's author had agreed with Karl Marx: that laws are the rules of those in power, designed to keep them in power; one therefore had to show that some laws could be wrong. I thought these were very perceptive ideas, and from them I had found my life's goal and knew that I wanted more than anything to become a lawyer.

I had little idea of the specifics of achieving this aim, other than that it would require a lot of hard work – studying endless cases no doubt, learning the intricacies of the legal system and all sorts of rigorous examinations. But like the much-feted taxi driver's son, I would go to England and there receive the finest legal training in the world. Arriving in Magadi, overjoyed to see my father after such a long absence, I told him proudly of my ambition. To my shock and disappointment, however, it seemed he did not wish me to become a lawyer.

My father instead suggested that since I had done well in Maths and English at school why did I not study for a degree in Engineering or Literature? But what, I protested, did he have against me doing law? He replied that unfortunately he had never met a lawyer who wasn't a crook. 'Okay,' I said, 'I will make you a promise: if I am a lawyer I will be an honest one, if I think a client has done something wrong I will tell him to plead guilty, I will never do anything to make you ashamed.' He could see I was sincere and serious, but there was another problem; sending me to London and supporting me there would cost more than for my brother and sister in India, and with tears of sorrow in his eyes he told me that, because he had very often treated his patients for free, he had not saved enough cash for me to pursue my ambition.

Chapter Four

Arriving in England

1947 to 1948

It seemed that my father's salary from the Magadi Soda Company was only just enough for us to live on. Being the only doctor in a large district, he regularly treated other Africans, but as in Zanzibar, most of these unofficial patients could at best pay only in kind, or offer to trade in their sheep or cattle, often at a poor rate of exchange. Some walked 50 miles or more, or if they were unable, a fellow tribesman would bring him word, and he would go to them. The company having given him use of a car, I began to go along on these visits, and on the long, pockmarked road from Magadi to Nairobi, practice my driving. Other vehicles being scarce, there was little chance of a collision, but this also meant that in the event of a breakdown one could be stranded for several hours, or even days. Once when another car got stuck at the same time as ourselves, the driver, a German, asked us to push him out first. Having done so, he was about to drive off and leave us, forcing us to run after him and, after some rudeness on his part, persuade him to assist us in return.

Such an attitude, typical of the way many Europeans treated Asians and Africans, was also irresponsible, for though there was astonishing beauty in the Kenyan wilds, and wonderful creatures to behold, such as the flock of magnificent pink flamingos I once came upon, there was also danger. Once, I saw some men working on the road, seemingly unaware that just a few yards away, watching them from a low tin roof, sat a leopard. Another time, my father and I found a whole pride of lions eating a zebra in the middle of the road. Unable to skirt around, we had to wait in the car at a distance until the males, cubs and females had all had their fill, which though fascinating, took three or four hours.

Out in the bush after dark, the temperature could also plummet. One day on the way to Nairobi we came across a car stopped in the road, the driver alone. My father said that we must help him, for if left there all night he might die of cold. He was surprised to find it was an old school friend whom he had not seen for many years, Dr Dias. After getting his car started we followed on to Dr Dias's residence in Nairobi, a typical iron-framed and timber house with a corrugated iron roof, built on stilts to keep out the damp, on River Road. We learned that he had married a French Seychelles woman, though they were now separated and he had a mistress. His acquaintance with my father renewed, I was invited to stay at the house, which had several guest rooms. In the mornings he was very pleasant and kind to everyone, a perfect gentleman, but come the afternoon his mistress would arrive, and then he would start drinking, usually a whole bottle of whisky, and get very angry, shouting and swearing at people. After a long sleep he would get up very shamefaced, apologising for his behaviour, until midday when the pattern would repeat itself. I thought if this is what alcohol does to a person, I don't ever want to touch it, whisky was poison. My father said not to tell anyone. Dr Dias's work was confined mainly to the cutting of African patients' uvulae, which was believed to eradicate illness.

It was while staying at River Road that I began attending the Nairobi law courts, often spending three or four hours listening to the cases and seeing what went on. I made some good friends at the courts, who were generous enough to help me, among them Mr Nariman and Mr Nowrojee. I was also directed to Mr A.H. Malik, a bearded gentleman in his fifties, whose private office was in

Whiteaway Laidlaw, the famous department store in Nairobi, where he was, I think, chief accountant. Just come from England, he was also Chairman of the Barristers and Bar Students Association, which I applied to join, and once admitted I was invited to the regular dinners held at Mr Malik's home on 6th Avenue, Parklands. While everyone else wore 'black tie' though, I would turn up in my khaki shirt and shorts. When my father heard, he immediately looked out a dinner suit that more or less fitted me and insisted I wear it. I think he was just in time, as I found out later that an item had been put on the agenda to ban me for improper attire.

Mr Malik also kindly provided the addresses of the Inns of Court in London and advised me how to apply. In the court library I met a young man called Raj Khanna, who had also just returned from England and whose father our family already knew quite well. Raj talked to me about his own experiences and was likewise encouraging and helpful. With a lot of useful information now, I sat down, and in careful longhand wrote to each of the four Inns of Court in London, explaining that I wanted to become a lawyer, had passed my Senior Cambridge and had an exemption from Matriculation. A further letter was dispatched to Gibson and Weldon, an educational firm in London, to begin their correspondence course that covered all aspects of English Law except Criminal.

A promising reply came a few weeks later from Lincoln's Inn. I tore it open eagerly, only to find that not only would I have to wait until I was 16 but must pay £200 towards the admission fee. My 16th birthday was not far off, but £200 was a lot. My father, now behind me in my endeavour, and still upset with himself about the money, announced he would sell all his land in Goa. This would raise a huge sum, millions in today's money, but once gone, the land could never be recovered for the family and I thought he should not do it. After further remorseful head-scratching, at my suggestion he agreed to surrender an insurance policy held with South African Mutual as it was then called (later Old Mutual), while I wrote to Lincoln's Inn to ask about paying in instalments. They replied that this was not normal, but since I seemed a boy who was very interested they would allow it. They did insist, however, that before being admitted I must pass an examination in Latin, which they would arrange for me to take at the courts in Nairobi in a few months time. I only knew a bit of Latin, and with no one to teach me, went to the Church Mission Society bookshop, bought all the Latin books I could find and returned to Magadi to begin learning the conjugations, grammar and all.

On the day set for the exam I travelled to Nairobi and reported at the court as instructed. I was told however that the officer in charge of such matters was absent and they knew nothing about any exam. Feeling let down, I wrote to Lincoln's Inn telling them of my preparations and the long train journey to get there and how unfair it was that they had failed to make the arrangements. I think they were impressed with this, as a profuse apology arrived, assuring me they had written to their officer in Nairobi, but would assume I had adequate knowledge of Latin now, waive the requirement for me and admit me as a student.

This was joyful news, but there was a further obstacle before I could set sail for England, for although the substantial £50 sea fare could be paid from my father's insurance policy, tickets were scarce. As luck would have it, a space was found on a Union Castle ship out of Mombasa leaving quite soon. If I did not take it, however, it would mean waiting another six months, and I knew I had to go. Preparations now began in earnest for my departure; my father had already spent weeks buying up tins of corned beef, a rare commodity and only available from soldiers, NAAFI canteens and the like which together with other staples, including almost a whole salted pig, filled one large trunk. He also thought I would freeze in England, and packed ten blankets, plus woollen sweaters and scarves. His chief concern was that, unlike India, we knew no one in England who could look after me. Then there was the worry that I might, as with the sons of others he had known, meet an English girl and marry her, and he would never see me again. I tried to reassure him on all these points, yet he remained anxious.

One piece of news that pleased him that year of 1947 was the announcement in February, by British Prime Minister Clement Attlee, that India would be granted full self-governance by at the latest June 1948. My father believed in democracy and that no nation should rule another, especially one several thousand miles away. Having grown up and studied in India and lived through some of the worst excesses of colonialism such as the Jallianwalla Bagh massacre, the prospect of imminent independence must have been a significant event for him and his generation. The diplomatic machine moved swiftly after Attlee's announcement, and by June the so-called 'Mountbatten Plan' was in place, which included the principle of Partition. The Indian Independence Act then received royal assent on the 18th of July 1947. A few days later I was getting ready to sail for England.

My mother and father and a few family friends came with me to the station at Magadi, and in the early light we said our farewells. I had to stay overnight at Konza, and then pick up the six-thirty onward train. Arriving at Mombasa with my seven trunks of various sizes, I boarded the Llanstephen Castle, an old troop carrier built in 1913 and now on her first voyage after a hasty conversion to accommodate 231 first-class and 198 tourist-class passengers. Two Indians and myself were put into what must have been the worst cabin of all, situated amidships with no windows or portholes and always very stuffy and hot.

We thus spent most of the time on deck, where I was quite excited to see the dances, music and games taking place, and got talking to other young passengers. There were many in their teens and twenties, boys and girls, from South Africa, who went out of their way to be friendly and look after us. Some of the girls were quite forward and made me feel rather shy with their advances. After stopping at Port Sudan and then Aden, on my way up to the deck one morning I glanced through a window and was surprised to see that the entire ship seemed to be on dry land and the engines were emitting a low growl, and I thought we had run aground. Looking more closely I realised we were in the narrow channel of the Suez Canal heading towards Port Suez. None of the South Africans were about and the ship seemed almost empty. Later I learned that they were all Jewish, secretly en-route to fight for Israel, and the ship had made an undisclosed stop during the night for them to disembark.

At Port Suez and Port Sudan, though none of us had money to buy, it was thrilling to see hordes of little sailing boats draw up, the Arab vendors clinging to the tops of slender 20-foot masts, selling everything from silks and handbags to rude postcards. From here we continued north, across the Mediterranean to the Italian port of Genoa where we would dock for seven days. The ship now became our hotel, and, free to go and explore, the officers suggested we might make some spending money by buying a few cigarettes from the ship's bar to sell at a profit ashore. Amazingly we found we could make ten times what we paid, and trading one packet of cigarettes a day gave us more than enough lira for meals and taking buses to see the sights, such as Campo Santo. With cash to spare, I even bought myself a beautiful woollen overcoat for the winter. We had been warned not to stray off the beaten track, but one day when someone asked me to follow him and he would give me a better price, I got greedy. Rounding a corner I saw a group of rough-looking fellows, and realising my mistake, as one of them grabbed me, I kicked him in the groin and took to my heels.

Our next port of call was Marseilles, then Gibraltar. The voyage had so far been smooth, but in the Bay of Biscay the ship began to pitch and roll and many of us were seasick. The calm of the English Channel restored us and brought the long-awaited British coast in sight. Drawing nearer, I looked forward to seeing before me a land of beautiful historic buildings, but as we entered the mouth of the Thames and steamed slowly up towards Tilbury Docks, all was fog and rain. When the view cleared it was disheartening to look out on nothing but the backs of hundreds if not thousands of grimy terraced houses. Not long ago the East End had been battered by the Blitz and things looked pretty bad still.

Although I had no one to meet me, during the voyage I had met some amiable people also bound for England, including one of my fellow cabin passengers Mr Prithamlal Vishwanath Rawal, a middle-aged Brahmin from Lorenzo Marques who prayed morning, noon and evening, and an Irish boy born in Cairo called Ambrose Fanning, who had been in the army. Ambrose told me that his brother John was currently a medical student at King's College London and renting a room near a big shop called Whiteleys, and that if ever I needed any help, I should go and see him. Another was Peter Carey-Harper, a charming ex-RAF pilot aged about 35, now settled in South Africa and coming to London for a holiday. Hearing that I knew no one in London, he offered to assist me in finding accommodation and getting to know my way around, which I most gratefully accepted.

Peter helped me get my seven trunks on the train and up to St Pancras Station, where, as I couldn't afford porters, we manhandled them to the left luggage room. From here I followed him down the escalator to the Underground, an exciting first experience for someone like myself who had never before left East Africa. I was very impressed at the speed and frequency of the trains, hurtling in and out every few minutes, and I remember thinking how small the world would seem if a similar system stretched around the globe.

We alighted at Queensway Station, bought the Kensington Post and found a telephone box from which to enquire about rooms to rent. Peter had some pennies for the calls, but although the phone was working, the coin box was full, so a bucket had been placed beneath. I must say I was very impressed with the British sense of honesty, for the bucket must have contained several pounds worth of pennies, which no one seemed tempted to steal, and Peter and I dutifully added two pennies for each call we made. Finding a room still available, we made our way to number 55 Inverness Terrace, a row of high white-painted period houses, where Mrs Harrison, a tall, thin lady, very kind and friendly, greeted us. Although in the basement, the room was not too cramped, and the rent of £3 per week, excluding breakfast but with all other services, seemed reasonable. Peter and I agreed to share for the time being, and pay half each.

After settling our things in and snatching a sandwich in a nearby café, Peter went off on some business and I decided to have a look around. It was about 2 o'clock in the afternoon, and the only places I knew of were Piccadilly Circus and Soho. Uncertain of the Underground route I set off on foot. It was almost three miles but somehow I found the way, the sights and sounds of London carrying me along. Along the Bayswater Road, women called out, 'Want a bit of fun dear?' At Marble Arch I crossed the wide road into Hyde Park and came upon Speakers' Corner, where all sorts of orators, anarchists, preachers, philosophers, people attacking the British Government and those who just talked about nothing, were in full flow, some drawing quite a crowd. I thought they were very courageous and interesting, and stayed for a couple of hours listening to the various debates. Later I would return here and speak myself, to make the case against colonialism.

Continuing on through endless crowds, young and old, English and other nationalities and lots of American servicemen, I eventually reached Soho and wandered through the narrow alleys with their small cafes and tobacconists, delicatessens and drapers. At Piccadilly Circus buses and taxis circled the winged statue of Eros god of love, while tourists took photos and idled away the time.

In the evening the neon signs lit the streets, and it wasn't until 10pm, after some tea and sandwiches in Soho, that I thought of making my way back. Not sure about the way, I remembered seeing the Midland Bank near my accommodation, so asked a policeman if he would direct me there. 'Which branch?' he replied. I said, 'Is there more than one?' 'Yes, about 400 in London!' Fortunately, I remembered my new address and the officer took out a pocket book and looked it up. It was about midnight when I finally arrived back at 55 Inverness Terrace. I was cold and tired, and must have seen hundreds of thousands of people, more probably than in my whole life, and exchanged barely a word, yet it had been a great and exciting day, and I felt London was one of the most wonderful places in the world.

The next morning I set out early for Lincoln's Inn, arriving at about 8.30am. To me it was extremely imposing, like a cathedral, with a large stone gatehouse and high arching roofs. There were very few people about, but then I hadn't realised that lectures didn't begin until 10am. 'You're new here aren't you?' said another early arrival, introducing himself as Dhole Singh, from Trinidad. 'Would you like some help?' Dhole showed me the Great Hall, the Library, and at my request, the Under Treasurer's office, where I assumed I would have to report and sign some papers to begin my course. I was very surprised that they weren't really interested, just mentioned the notice board for the lectures, that I could use the library, do whatever you want, etc., and that was that. After the grand upper parts of the building, I was very disappointed in the Common Room, a tiny basement where we took our lunch of sandwiches or fish and chips – a great contrast to the formal dinners held upstairs, in great pomp and style.

A couple of days later, while Peter Carey-Harper was still away, I received a visitor at Inverness Terrace. It was Prithamlal Vishwanath Rawal, my fellow passenger from the ship. I wasn't sure how he had found me, but he seemed very pleased to see me, as well as anxious, confiding that he had some serious problems and needed my help. Although a multimillionaire, his London agents were away and he had to attend a very urgent conference. Could I possibly give him a short-term loan of £200? I said I only had £25, and he replied that would be fine. I said, 'I can manage £20,' but he insisted he would need the whole amount, promising that he would pay me back without fail the very next day. He then wrote down the addresses of his agent and the hotel he was staying at. I handed him the £25. Then seeing the woollen overcoat I had bought in Genoa, Rawal asked if he might borrow it to wear to the conference, as it was so cold now. Again I agreed, thinking, as with the money, that 24 hours was nothing. Besides he was such an honest respectable man, why should I refuse?

A day went by, then two, and there was no sign of Rawal. I thought perhaps he had got held up somewhere. I had no money for meals, or to travel to my lectures. I eyed the trunk containing all the tinned food my father had collected, but was reluctant to open any of it, feeling it would be the last straw. Eventually I telephoned his hotel, only to be told he had run away and given their name to lots of people. They understood he was a shopkeeper from Quelimane and was last believed to have fled to France leaving a trail of debts behind him. I would be lucky, they said if I ever got my money back.

I felt very depressed and angry with myself. What could I do? I knew no one in England, had no bank account or income. My father had arranged to send me a monthly allowance via his employers, which I was to collect from the ICI offices in Victoria, but the first payment was some weeks away. I walked the streets, almost at the point of holding out my hand to beg, until, standing on the pavement in Queensway staring in the windows of a department store, I saw the name Whiteleys and remembered it was where Ambrose Fanning had said his brother John lived, and that I might look him up. After ringing a few bells and making enquiries, someone directed me further along towards Paddington Station, where I was let in to a flat and found John Fanning at a table over some books. I think he was studying medicine some of the time at St Mary's Hospital nearby. Explaining how I had met his brother Ambrose, I told him my story, to which he was immediately sympathetic. Giving me two pounds out of his own pocket, he said I might return it if I could, but not to worry if not. He warned me never to lend money in future; it was a hard world, and we had all been taken for a ride at some point, but I had got off cheap, so be careful next time.

After enjoying a proper meal, the first I had eaten in three days, I sent a telegram to my father, saying briefly what had happened, and could he please send me some more money. The reply came promptly, followed by another £25. He did not scold or question me, probably judging the experience itself harsh enough. I did write to the British Consul General in Quelimane, who confirmed that Rawal was a big-time conman with 42 convictions for fraud. The Portuguese Police had traced him to a shop in Ballards Pier, Bombay, and many years later I went there with an idea in my head of beating him up, but never found him. Even though I guess he would have been quite elderly by then, I had found it very hard to forgive the man. But as Christmas 1947, my first in England, approached, I had to try to put such mistakes behind me, concentrate on the future and work hard to fulfil my dream of becoming a barrister.

The New Year brought a terrible shock. It was the 30th of January, and I had been strolling in Hyde Park opposite the Dorchester Hotel when on a newspaper billboard I read the headline: 'Gandhi Shot Dead'. People were crying, not just Indians, and I too soon had tears of sorrow and disbelief in my eyes. For many of us, Gandhi had seemed a kind of father we had never met. Distressed by partition and the violence that had followed, he had been on a prayer vigil when the assassin struck. Everyone though had been shocked by the slaughter after partition; some English people reacted by telling me, 'we should come and rule you again,' suggesting that they thought India incapable of governing itself without descending into bloodshed.

After about a month of sharing the basement at Inverness Terrace, Peter Carey-Harper announced that he had to move on. Unable to afford the full rent on my own, I spoke to the Accommodation Officer at Lincoln's Inn and she very kindly found me a place in a working class area at 46–48 Highbury Grove, a row of houses converted to a student hostel. Behind was the large Corsa Radio Factory, whose siren blared out at seven each morning as the workers all trooped in, and again at five in the afternoon when they could go home. We all had very small single rooms with no central heating, and mine being in the basement, with a single light bulb fixed on the high ceiling, was like an icebox. I did most of my reading lying in bed, huddled from head to toe under six or seven blankets. When the beautiful glowing fire was lit upstairs in the lounge, there would be 40 or 50 people sat around it. Many of them were lawyers or law students – from the West Indies, East Africa, India, Britain and America – and there were a lot of interesting discussions on politics and law.

The hostel charged £2 10s a week for bed, breakfast and dinner, and lunch on Saturday and Sunday. With rationing in force, our food was of course very simple; cornflakes, mashed potatoes and cabbage and occasionally a bit of fish, and tea or coffee for breakfast, lunch at Lincoln's Inn usually a sandwich and a cup of tea, then soup and potatoes followed by stewed apples back at the hostel in the evening. But we were quite happy. I hadn't come to England to have a good time or eat sumptuous dinners, but to become a lawyer as soon as possible. I spent as much time as I could studying, which meant seven days a week, and only allowed myself one evening off each week, when I would go out exploring different parts of London, walking to save money on the Tube or buses, and because I believed one saw much more of a country this way. My weakness was bridge, which I could already play a little, but several of the students here were very keen; my game was soon improving, but like carom, it took up one's time. Two months after moving to Highbury, snow started falling over London. Though only a light powdering, being the first time I had ever seen it, I was thrilled, and ran outside to take photos with my Box Brownie camera.

One evening, about three months after moving to Highbury Grove, I was sitting at dinner in the basement, when the landlady entered and said to one of the students, 'I want you out, you left the tap on in your bedroom and flooded the place, and it's ruined the carpets and ceilings – pack up your things and get out now.' Another of the diners from our table got up to protest, 'If you send him away, I shall go too.' The landlady replied, 'Go then,' whereupon another student made a similar pledge, and received a similar retort. At this point I added my voice in solidarity, saying that if anyone were evicted, I also would leave. She would not back down, however, and neither would we. Leaving our meals unfinished, the three of us in the protest packed and departed, while the one who had allegedly left the tap on, made other arrangements.

Standing outside on the pavement with our suitcases, it was cold and dark, and we realised we had no idea what to do next. A helpful policeman suggested we head for Finsbury Park, where there were several boarding houses. We jumped on the Number 19 bus, alighted when the conductor announced our destination and, carrying our two suitcases apiece, walked from boarding house to boarding house, hotel to hotel, for street after street in search of vacancies. There were several, but most at rates we could not afford. Other places were more reasonable, but had just one or two single rooms, and by now feeling a strong bond with one another, we agreed we would rather stay together. I must say, we didn't find a single trace of racialism; at one hotel, an Air Force man told us how he had bought the entire place for £700 and that he would love to put us up. His only available room though was a triple, which we regretfully declined. After trying over 30 places without success, we had walked a mile to Manor House and it was now past 11pm. Asking another policeman, we were directed to number 323 Green Lanes, where, he told us, two lovely old ladies ran a beautiful boarding house, why didn't we try there? Though nervous about calling so late, we found the establishment and rang the bell. The ladies were so kind and almost dragged us in, offering one single and one double room, which, after such a welcome, and our long walk, we gladly accepted.

It was only now I learned the names of my fellow self-elected exiles: Alex Sequeira and Meryl Seriwardena. We got on very well together and soon became like brothers. Alex, in his mid-forties, held a parliamentary position in Aden and had been sent to learn the job of Clerk to the Council, attending the House of Commons each day to study procedure. He felt very lonely in London, missed his wife and children and suffered from sleepless nights. Meryl, 29, was a former deputy mayor in Ceylon, now studying for his Bar Finals and though also married had no children yet. He and I both took our law very seriously, sitting down with our books every evening, taking turns to make tea or coffee at 10pm and 11pm, and pushing on again until 2 or 3 in the morning. Sometimes, to cool our heads and get some air we put on our overcoats and went out for long walks. If feeling rich, we would stop for refreshment at one of the little roadside kiosks or horse-drawn carts, selling tea and cheese rolls to truck drivers and other night roamers. From what we could understand through their rich cockney accents, we found it interesting to hear these men's conversations, and although sprinkled with crude jokes, their laughter was always good-natured. Meryl and I must have looked a funny sight, two Indian boys who just nodded and smiled occasionally, hanging out in the middle of the night. And yet without ever knowing them beyond the lamp-lit pavements, the men's camaraderie seemed somehow to embrace us and we felt a sense of belonging.

In our law studies formal teaching was only a part of the process. The professors were very good and gave you an insight but if you did sufficient homework time spent in the classroom could be superfluous. One day a professor said to me, 'You are obviously not interested in my lecture.' I replied that I was. He said, 'Then why are you not taking notes?' I said, 'Because I know what you are going to say.' I had read the chapter of his book, to which he was now referring, the previous evening. I proceeded to recite from memory the gist of what came next. Looking quite astounded he said, 'I'm surprised you remember it so well.' I said, 'Yes, your book is very good.' We delved more deeply into the subject through our own discussions, in the YMCA, at our boarding house, in tearooms and cafes. Former students came to debate the finer points with us. Some of them were retired colonels and majors, who could have very conservative ideas, especially in matters of religion and race. Being no respecter of older people in that sense, if I thought someone was talking rubbish I would say so. The most important thing to remember was that although laws might be fixed, their interpretation was what mattered, and crucial to the outcome of a case.

In that first year at Lincoln's Inn I was studying Criminal Law, and eager to see the judiciary at work in real life, I began going almost every day to the London Law Courts. This was not a requirement of the course but for my own interest. I wanted to gain an insight and see how the big lawyers conducted the cases. Some were quite exciting, occasionally shocking. In one divorce case the wife pleaded that her husband had given her gonorrhoea. When the judge asked her how she knew this, she said did he want her to go into it, to which he replied yes. So she described her symptoms in lurid detail to the whole court. In another divorce the husband alleged his wife had had sex with their dog, and if the judge wanted evidence he should see the scratch marks on her back. I left the court at that point but I believe the story got into the Sunday papers.

Other forms of entertainment could be had at the picture houses, which in those days showed documentaries and newsreels as well as fictional films. I had gone to the cinema as a boy in Nairobi, the Capitol and the Empire. I remember being depressed sometimes, because all my friends had been in Zanzibar still and I had no one to talk to. The people in the films I watched were rich and lived in fantastic palaces of marble and gold, but these illusions felt like a fool's paradise, and emerging back into the real world I would feel even more down and eventually I stopped going. Many Indian films are like this. I had read the novel 'Gone With The Wind' and heard that the film, then being screened in London and showing among other things a baby being born, had caused dozens of men to faint and be carried out on stretchers. At least it was about real life though, and a war fought to end the injustice of slavery in America.

Illusion and reality could catch anyone out, especially somebody new to a place, as I still was. Always wanting to explore and learn, whenever I had time I would go out for walks, wandering the London streets at random, fascinated by the architecture and history around me. One day I came upon an impressive looking building with high walls like a castle. I thought this must be a grand old English house, with great halls and servants' rooms, etc. Stood by the large wooden front door was a policeman, so I went and asked him if I might go in and look around. He smiled and said I should first go and read the sign on the wall. It was Holloway Women's Prison. The policeman told his colleague and they had a good laugh.

By October 1948, Meryl and I, having both worked hard on our Criminal Law, opted to take our Bar Finals that December. After months of gruelling study we also felt exhausted and that we were no longer taking anything in. Friends recommended we relax and take a break from routine: 'Close your books, and just go somewhere.' Someone else mentioned you could go to Paris for £5, and a few days later we boarded a ferry at Newhaven bound for Dieppe, and from there took the train to Paris. In Gare de l'Est, recommended for its cheap hotels, we found a single room for half a crown (2 shillings and sixpence), with running water only on the ground floor and a single hole in the floor toilet on the seventh. Walking half a mile with a towel, we could pay the equivalent of threepence to use the public baths. These minor privations aside, Meryl and I had a lovely time, saw all the famous historic sights of Notre Dame, Sacré-Cœur and of course the Eiffel Tower, spent less than £4 each over the whole week and came back refreshed and ready to work at our studies again.

I am glad to say we did quite well, both gaining an Upper Second, and we were very happy with ourselves. It was now time for Meryl to return to Ceylon. We were both sorry to say farewell, having become close friends over the past few months, learning and supporting each other, sharing what seemed a great adventure as well as a common goal. The parting was tinged with a particular sadness, since the night I had seen Meryl injecting himself. He had told me he had to do this every day having been a diabetic since the age of five. It seemed such a shame that he had never been able to enjoy sweet things. My sorrow was infinitely greater when he confided to me one day that he did not think he would live for very long.

Alex Sequeira meanwhile was still very unsettled. He would disturb the household by getting up in the night and pacing up and down, and looked generally ill at ease. He had been to see a doctor and from what I could gather, had been told he was going through what they now call the male menopause. Another friend then suggested that, as his wife was far away in Aden, to calm himself down he should seek some sexual relief, and took him to visit a prostitute. Apparently this was not a success; he said he could do nothing, as he kept thinking of his wife.

Meryl, a brilliant speaker, while not ardently religious, followed the Methodist faith, which he maintained was better than Catholicism. Although very disappointed in the Catholic Church for its racism in Zanzibar and Kenya, I was still a strong believer and had never considered alternative sects. Finally Meryl said, 'Look Fitz let's go to my church then I'll come to yours and we'll each see what the other is like.' We took the bus up to a Methodist church in Palmers Green. The people there were so warm and friendly, coming up after the service and asking who we were and where we were from, introducing us to their children and saying, come to our house, come to tea, come to dinner, even the single girls. They really looked after us and by the time we left we must have had 15 or more invitations. The next week we went to a Catholic church. There were no invitations. No one even spoke to us they were so full of themselves.

I hadn't realised there were two types of English worshippers, the high church like the Anglicans and Roman Catholics who were very insular, and 'low' church nonconformists like the Methodists and Congregationalists, who were very friendly to foreigners. The other differences between them were not in matters of principle, but things like the altar, which in Anglican and Catholic churches was higher and faced away from the congregation, while the Methodist and Congregationalist ministers tended to face more towards people. I began to visit other Methodist churches and saw that their focus was on sermons. At Kingsway Hall Holborn the minister was the Reverend Donald Soper, later Lord Soper, a socialist and teetotaller and a fantastic speaker who was very passionate about tackling poverty.

Donald Soper was a regular at Speakers' Corner in Hyde Park, where I was fascinated by all the different characters; politicians and religious fanatics, some serious, others amusing and a few who seemed just crazy. Anyone who had something to say could get up and say it. One Sunday morning when I was there someone asked if anyone would like to come up and take a turn. I said yes, and stepping up onto a soapbox I began to speak about the evils that the British were perpetrating in foreign lands, the colour bar and how the church supported racism. The audience was quite receptive if to some extent self-selecting, tending to gather around speakers that they agreed with. A few older-style British people shouted out: 'You are talking rubbish, there is no colour bar in Africa.' I replied that they should come to Africa and then they would see it for themselves. One black American girl told me that if a white person wanted to understand the colour bar in the USA all they need do was paint themselves black for a day. I returned and spoke most weekends from then on. Each time the police would come over and take my name and address. But this was the world-famous Speakers' Corner, and apart from the hecklers I saw no one prevented from voicing their opinion. Elsewhere, later on, things would be different.

With fellow passengers on the ship to London

Arriving in London, with fellow passengers on the ship including Peter Carey-Harper on the left

Outside Lincoln's Inn

Soon after I first arrived in London

Meryl Seriwardena and myself

Chapter Five

How I Got Into Politics

The 1950 General Election

It felt quite momentous the day I went to purchase my gown and wig, measured and fitted by London's oldest tailors, Ede and Ravenscroft in Chancery Lane. Although not yet qualified, I needed them for the 'dinners', which all students were required to attend before being Called to the Bar. These occasions had originally been intended to teach etiquette, table manners and the art of civilised conversation to newcomers from the English Yeoman class. Once they had learned the basics of the English legal system and been taught to behave like good middle-class people, they would be Called to the Bar. They would assist the poorer and less articulate peasants and serfs to present their cases to the Commissioners for Excise or Commissioners of Assizes, who in large part were commissions-earning tax collectors for the monarch. The legal representation was deemed a public service and the Yeoman barristers were expected to work gratis. In practice however, their gowns had a side pocket into which it became customary for the client to discreetly slip a small sum of money. If this did not happen, they were powerless to file a suit and for a long time remained reliant on their client's whims or ability to pay, and hence tended to seek some kind of fee in advance.

At the dinners wine was also served, and as a teetotaller I was to find myself very popular, my fellow students all hoping to be given my unwanted ration of alcohol. I understood that some of the dinners I had attended in Nairobi could count towards the requisite 12, though by the time I had passed my Bar Finals, I still had a few to attend. There was though, no rush, since according to the rules I could not be Called to the Bar until the age of 21, and I was still only 19 and a few months. What should I do for the next year and a half? One idea that had lain at the back of my mind, a sort of secondary plan for my career, was to try for the Indian Civil Service (ICS) as it was then called. The ICS had always been considered an elite government institution, important in the running of the country, and paid good starting salaries. On contacting the High Commission for India in London, I was told the ICS exams were currently being reconstituted – presumably to take account of India's recently acquired Independence – and that the age range for new entrants was restricted to 22 to 24. They said though, that I might take a temporary job with them until the exams were restarted. This sounded ideal as it gave me a chance to earn some money while keeping my options open. Mr P.N. Haksar, who was No 2 I think at the High Commission, was very charming and went out of his way to help, and the Educational Attache, Professor Sunderam, said he was writing to the Government of India to allow students to take their ICS exams in England.

I duly reported to the Indian Civil Service offices in a building once belonging to Lord Nelson, in Clifford Street, just off Regent Street near Piccadilly Circus. My temporary job was titled Chief Filing Clerk in the Councillor's section, at a salary of 2 pounds 19 shillings and 1 penny per week, after tax. I liked working there, although there was very little to do. The most enjoyable part was greeting all the different people coming to apply for visas to go to India. I would sit each of them down and talk for about 20 minutes or more, learning about their occupations and interests and their views of India and world affairs. It felt a privilege at my young age to meet so many intelligent people who wanted to see India and to hear their thoughts and expectations of the country.

My only other duties were to go through a dozen or so letters every day, find the relevant file for each and take them to the Consul, or officer in charge, Mr Sharma, who would draft replies and pass them to his secretary to type. Then at the end of the afternoon it was my job to gather up all the files and return them to their correct places in the metal cabinets. The problem, when there were no visa applicants to brighten up my day and no letters or files to deal with, was acute boredom. Colleagues and I passed the time at the window, watching the comings and goings of the street corner prostitutes and their clients and inventing silly names for each of them. I also took to reading novels which, being in an open-plan office, soon drew the attention of Mr Sharma who told me off, saying that if an officer walked in it would look as if I had nothing to do. I replied that in fact this was so and if he was worried about my being idle why not give me more work? An unofficial role did come my way, for though Mr Sharma was very proud of being a double MSc, I noticed his letters were riddled with grammatical and spelling mistakes which I was pleased to correct, and he, careful not to let anyone else know, was pleased to accept.

One day a letter of Mr Sharma's caught my particular attention. Addressed to the Government of India, in it he claimed that his office in London was terribly under-staffed, that there was a growing backlog of visa applications, and with complaints about the situation running high, he urgently needed a further ten members of staff. I stared at the letter in amazement knowing full well that visa applications were simply forwarded to the Ministry of Home Affairs in India and issued only if and when an OK was received. When I had previously asked Mr Sharma why he did not issue any visas himself he had replied that it was better the Indian Government decide, then, if a mistake were made, it was their responsibility. He was in effect, simply acting as a postman. I told him I thought the request in his letter was quite ridiculous; here we all are, I said, sitting doing almost nothing and you are writing to India saying we are all overworked and exhausted. He then explained to me that to be a successful civil servant you had to tell your superiors you were overworked and need a lot of staff; that way you become boss of a big department and can apply for an increase. The alternative is that they will always assume you are under-worked, sack some of your staff, and you might never get promotion.

Thinking this was a very strange way to run such an institution, after three months, getting fed up with so little to do, I wrote a long letter to the Indian High Commissioner, Krishna Menon, explaining what I thought about the Civil Service, telling him how under-employed we all were, and how everybody tried to appear busy while doing nothing at all. Referring to the entire Indian High Commission in London, with its 1,200 or so employees occupying numerous huge buildings including our own, plus a seven-storey premises on the Edgware Road near Marble Arch and another in Jermyn Street, I said I thought something should be done to reduce the overall number of staff and outgoings. To my great surprise I got a telephone call from Mr P.N. Haksar, saying he was very shocked to see my letter, which had been passed to him, and would very much like me not to send it to the High Commissioner. I said, 'I am sorry, but this is exactly what I feel, and if I have to leave my job in order to say so, then so be it.' He then put the phone down and the next minute had come into the office. 'You know,' he said looking at me with a concerned expression, 'you will want to be an ICS officer sooner or later, and it would be bad for you if you resigned in these circumstances.' I replied that I had changed my mind about that, I did not any longer want to be a civil servant, in any part of the world, and was quite happy to leave. After trying for almost an hour to persuade me to reconsider, he then tried a different approach: did I realise that if my letter was actually read by the High Commissioner, dozens of people might be sacked? And, did I realise what would happen to their wives and children if that happened? With their parents unemployed, those children's welfare and education and their whole future would suffer. Would I like to see that happen as a result of my actions?

Mr Haksar had pierced my Achilles heel. I began to see things in a different light, and that perhaps in standing up for what I thought right, I was being more like a traitor or a spy. I certainly didn't want others to suffer on a point of principle. Asking Mr Haksar for my letter back, I said, 'thank you very much' and tore it up in front of him. I also confirmed that I was resigning. He replied that if at any time I wanted to come back he would make me an Executive Officer straight away, would even do so now if I liked, on a starting salary of £5 10s a week. I said that was very nice of him, but repeated that I had no further intention of being employed by the Indian Government as a civil servant. From now on I would work for myself, independent and responsible for my own affairs. This was where I left it.

And so it was, that after three months of shuffling papers for the ICS in Piccadilly I returned to what I now realised was my true ambition, and took up my law books again, resumed attendance at Lincoln's Inn each day, picking up the thread and thinking how best to fill the time remaining until my 21st birthday when I could be Called to the Bar. I would have liked to take an LLB (Bachelor of Laws) but since I could not afford the fees, I had taken the Bar exam first, which would (at that time) allow me to practise law after being called. In the meantime, I enrolled as an external LLB student at London University, attending two or three times a month.

One day I met a very charming young man called Manu Devani. Discussing education, he said to me, 'Fitz, have you heard of Economics and Politics?' I admitted I knew little of the subjects as academic disciplines. 'Come on then,' he smiled, 'I'll teach you a bit.' Manu took me along to the Indian YMCA (Young Men's Christian Association), housed temporarily in a terrace of properties in Woburn Square, the original premises in Fitzroy Square having been destroyed by the Blitz. Inside were 30 or so small rooms, for accommodation, private reading and study and communal gatherings and discussions. No formal membership was required, you could just turn up and get to know people, and the atmosphere was welcoming and relaxed. Manu was retaking his Intermediate BSc Economics that year, and conversing with fellow students in a subject he clearly relished was helping his revision. Listening to the discussions I soon became fascinated and signed up myself as an external student with the London School of Economics and Political Science, commonly known as the LSE, to do the Intermediate BSc Economics. As my interest grew, I asked about the possibility of becoming an internal student, which they said would require a three-year commitment. Mindful that in less than two years I could qualify at the Bar, I asked if I might do the BSc within that time. The Registrar was very kind, and said that the LSE liked to encourage people who were keen, as I obviously was, and that one more student would not make much difference; she would therefore authorise me to attend all the lectures and seminars as an external student, take the Intermediate exam in June and see how I got on. She didn't even charge me the £4 a term. All this was down to Manu, a fantastic person, who, when he discovered I had no money to celebrate on my birthday, arranged and paid for a party for me.

  I was soon busier than when employed full-time, with lectures during the day, and part-time jobs as a waiter and postman. Delivering Christmas cards and parcels, I would see more of the English people's kindness as they offered me a seasonal tipple, and would make them laugh by preferring tea. Then would come fruit picking in East Anglia, arranged by brothers John, Martin and David Ennals, three students who had set up a holiday employment service for fellow undergraduates. Hard work by day, and, allowed to eat freely, putting me off strawberries for life, the balmy evenings by an open fire, guitars playing softly, bore romantic fruit for some of the boys and girls. Friends and I had also been invited by the British Council to visit Switzerland, which I was looking forward to after sitting the Intermediate. June came around very quickly, but having read a great deal about economic theory, I entered the examination room confidently. Halfway through however, disaster struck when my fountain pen suddenly disgorged a sea of ink over my work. Fearing that the stained paper would ruin my chances, I hastily adjusted the pen and set about copying all my answers onto a clean page. The next moment the invigilator strode over, accusing me of using a crib sheet. I explained about the ink spill, but his suspicions were aroused, and even when I needed the toilet he insisted on following me right in.

Afterwards, convinced I had failed, I told Manu I didn't want to wait around for the results, and went off to Switzerland. It was the first time I had seen the famous Alps, and the change of scene and of fresh air took my mind off the unhappy memory of the exam. On returning to London a fortnight later, however, against all my expectations I was thrilled to discover that I had passed the Intermediate and could continue studying for the BSc Economics. The Registrar also recommended I try the LSE's new campus in Southend-on-Sea where I would, she said, benefit from a more intensive teaching programme. When I learned that Southend-on-Sea was only a short train journey out of London on the Essex coast, I took her advice and made the necessary arrangements. My landlady at Manor House was sorry to see me go. Now her longest-residing tenant, I had got to feel quite at home over the last few months, helping her out with the business and putting the 'room to rent' cards in the tobacconist's window.

Accommodation seemed plentiful in Southend-on-Sea, where quite by chance I found a boarding house owned by a Mrs Harrison, the same name as my first landlady in Inverness Terrace. It seemed a good omen, and this Mrs Harrison was similarly kind and welcoming. The campus here being much smaller, student life felt more intimate and we were all soon friends. In no time at all I was enjoying a great social life in the cricket and hockey teams, playing my favourite sport of tennis and joining picnics and excursions. I had also discovered the sublime, uplifting pleasure of classical music when, after many hours working in a shop I was able to afford my first-ever electric record player. My first record was Bizet's *Carmen*. A staging at the Albert Hall brought the whole story to life for me, and listening to the beautiful *Flower Song*, the *Habanera* and the rousing *March of the Toreadors*, I have to say, my spirit woke up.

It was in Southend-on-Sea that I first got involved in organised politics. My landlady Mrs Harrison happened to be Chair of the local Conservatives, and a frequent visitor to her house, whom she would treat as an honoured guest, was Henry Channon, the MP for Southend and Chairman of the British Conservative Party. Channon had I believe married into the Guinness family, and although now separated from his wife, they had continued to support him in his political career. Having a strong supporter of socialism, myself, under the roof of a staunch Tory, naturally gave rise to some lively debates. Mrs Harrison and I argued almost all the time, as I did with her other residents, who were all older people, including a former police commissioner from Hong Kong, a retired butchery owner, and others from the diplomatic service, who all shared her political views. Ridiculing what I saw as their biased and sentimental support for the Empire, I would point out the iniquities of Britain's former rule over India and those still existing in the colonies. Mrs Harrison was a caring person and sincere in her views, but knew nothing about life in the colonies for the colonised. In that sense, through no fault of her own perhaps, she was uneducated, while those of her tenants who had direct experience as colonial rulers were what has, sometimes, been called "dis-educated". Our disagreements were never personal or too heated, but when things got intense and I criticised the government perhaps too strongly, Mrs Harrison would sometimes be on the verge of tears. I would always make up for it later and she would give me a few extra sandwiches or cakes.

Our political differences were literally stitched together one day. The college had announced a fancy dress ball, and as I was scratching my head about a costume, Mrs Harrison said not to worry, as she had an idea. It was now late 1949, Clement Attlee's first Labour Government had been in power for four years, and with the prospect of Britain going to the polls again soon, politics was very topical. Mrs Harrison produced a stack of Conservative leaflets and posters, and sent me off to the local Labour Party to fetch some of their campaign material. She would then sew the whole lot onto a suit, and I could go to the fancy dress ball as "The General Election". The people at Southend Labour Party were pleased to oblige. They were also keen to encourage Indians as at present they only had two among their local membership. Seeing how many leaflets and posters I wanted, they assumed I must be a fervent supporter, so would I like to do some canvassing? I said I would love to, and when the fancy dress ball was over, off I went from house to house in Southend, urging people to support Attlee. And so in a way it was Mrs Harrison, a lifelong Conservative, with her clever idea that I had to thank for getting me into the Labour Party. Over the next couple of months I got completely involved in politics, talking to people on the doorsteps and making many new friends among the trade unionists, activists and supporters. The upcoming election was predicted to be very tight between Labour and Conservative, and on the night of the election on the 23rd of February 1950, sitting down as the results came in over the radio, we were shocked to hear so many of those MPs that we admired and had campaigned for, losing their seats. Attlee clung on to office, but his overall majority was cut down drastically to just five. Churchill commented that another election could not be far off.

Taking the responsibility of being a member of the Labour Party quite seriously, I was invited to chair the Labour League of Youth, comprising the younger membership throughout Southend East and Southend West.

Being such a newcomer to the political scene, I opted instead to be Vice-Chair, letting a more experienced person lead. I enrolled as many of my student and sporting friends as I could into the League, and we arranged a lively programme of debates and lectures, with a variety of guest speakers, convivial picnics and dances.

I was also made a member of Southend Council, which had over 40 other Labour councillors, and sat on my area of Milton Ward's Municipal Committee. When a local election came up, there were three candidates for Milton Ward. By far the most suitable was a 45-year-old electrical engineer called Ellis who had been eminent within the Labour Party elsewhere in the country and had now opened a shop in Southend, and who made a most impressive speech. Then, as we were discussing the candidates, someone proposed my name. Utterly surprised, I stood up and said, 'Look, I'm so sorry, but I can't accept.' The fact was I was too young, being a few months below the minimum age of 21 for a Municipal Councillor. But before I could explain, they shouted: 'No, no, you can't refuse.' I sat down, thinking Ellis would in any case be selected, so it made no difference. A show of hands was called for, to choose him or me. Unbelievably the result was an exact tie, at which point Ellis, being the perfect gentleman, announced he would step aside. I said that was very gracious of him, but apart from anything else I was not old enough for the post. My supporters were disappointed, and frankly so was I now.

With hindsight though, taking on the additional job of a local councillor would have been impossible. My days and evenings were already completely given over to studying, committees, cultural groups and a whole host of sports and social clubs. Some were based in London, including the Indian students organisation, with its communist and socialist groups. As Literary Secretary of the East African Students Union, whose President was Charles Njonjo, it was my job to arrange functions and seminars on Kenyan cultural affairs. Such events could be illuminating in every sense; a Mr Wall, whom I believe was the Conservative back bench spokesman for the colonies, met with our members at the House of Commons one day, only to shock us with his reactionary views on Imperialism and his blatant defence of racialism in East Africa. We were all very angry, struggling to keep our tempers and refrain from shouting at him, including I am glad to say, my friend Charles Njonjo.

On the opposite side of the coin, were people like the journalist Patrick O'Donovan and our good friend Colin Legum, a white South African speaking out against injustice and opposing those from his own privileged background who tried to justify the system. Colin's visit was a very inspiring evening and I was thrilled by the fact that here was someone willing to throw away the advantages he was born with, in the interests of a moral cause. I would always admire such people, who fought as it were, their own side, not out of opportunism, but for the ideals of socialism, democracy and equality in which they believed. I would very definitely put in this category fellows like Colin Legum, along with Fenner Brockway, Michael Scott, Patrick Laurence and Stafford Cripps. I think one of the biggest names on the list would be Dennis Noel Pritt, of whom I would become a great admirer and hear speak many times. There was almost a ferocity in the way Pritt took on the problem of the colonies and the class that exploited not only the indigenous colonial populations, treating them as semi-slaves, but had a similar attitude towards the working people of their own country.

Amid such stimulating activity, unlike the Civil Service, I was never bored! I was though spreading myself too thin, and by the early summer of 1950 my academic work was lagging and my finances strained. To complete the BSc Economics I would have to spend less time and money on extra-curricular activities, train fares and going here there and everywhere. Also, in a matter of weeks, I would turn 21, and be Called to the Bar. It was I felt, time to return to London. When I told Mrs Harrison she was shocked: why did I want to leave, was I not happy in her home? I assured her I was. Was it money then? I said yes, that was one reason. She immediately told me not to worry, she would maintain and support me financially, I could complete my studies and pay her back later, but if not, then never mind, she would be glad to do this. This quite took my breath away, the first time in my life that anyone, other than my family had shown such generosity and concern for me. I was very grateful, but I had to discipline myself now, and really needed to go back to London. Mrs Harrison was in tears the day I left.

I must say I was very lucky with landladies. At Green Lanes, my former landlady had a vacancy and was pleased to welcome me back. So was the Registrar at the LSE, where I resumed my studies, attended lectures at Senate House and worked in the library until 10pm most nights. In August my Call to the Bar arrived, and the proud moment of presenting with my fellow students at Lincoln's Inn to be sworn in as a member of the Utter, or Outer Bar. I sent a telegram to my father, who replied that he was very happy, which was all that mattered to me.

Finding chambers to practise as a barrister was the next requirement, and not likely to be easy in London. Right now there was the BSc Economics to complete, and the following June I took my Bar Finals and fortunately passed. Wanting to do a bit more travelling now, I needed to earn more money first, and took a job with the Hudson Bay Company showing fur coats from their warehouse, earning £1 a day plus a few tips. Adding to this a spot of portering at Euston Station, after a month I had about £60, more than enough for a trip abroad. But where to? One of the communist fringe societies was inviting students to a peace conference in Warsaw, and although I was strongly opposed to the communists, it seemed a harmless opportunity to see behind the Iron Curtain, and a cheap holiday, and some friends and I put our names down. As soon as we heard that young people travelling to Warsaw were being stopped en-route by police and harassed, we changed our minds.

I decided instead to make my own way around France, Germany, Holland, Spain and Portugal, by rail and perhaps a bit of hitchhiking. On the ferry to the Hook of Holland the sea was quite rough and someone said some people on the lower deck were feeling ill. I went down to see if there was anything I could do, and found two Indian girls looking somewhat the worse for wear. We started talking, and it transpired they were from Nairobi. The conversation took their minds off the seasickness, the ferry arrived, and we went our separate ways.

My mother had urged that if ever I were in Portugal, I should visit her uncle, who after retiring as a Monsignor, a senior member of the Catholic Church, in the Philippines had been given the grand title of Vicar General in a little place called Villa Franca. Sadly he had by now died, but I decided to go there anyway. Arriving in Lisbon I ascertained that it was about 25 miles from the city and I could get there by train. I was very surprised to find that the village looked exactly like photographs I had seen of Goa; a high-built road with a sort of bridge directly connected to larger houses, like ours in Goa, with most of the smaller dwellings, the church and sports ground spread out at a distance below. I was quite thrilled that even the architecture of the houses resembled those in Goa.

The warmth of the greeting I received at the church was also an unexpected pleasure. The Sacristan and several other people gathered around me and said that my mother's uncle had been a very popular man who had given a lot to the area, improving the church and cemetery and donating to the school. They also said that he had been a millionaire and, seeming to assume that I had come to collect his money, wanted to know how I planned to spend it. Uncertain how to respond, I said little, other than that I would make enquiries and let them know if I could. They put me up for the night, and the next day I announced I was going for a walk. Taking my few belongings, I wandered happily through the vineyards with their millions of luscious ripening grapes, and eventually got into a little donkey cart which took me on to the next station, and back to Lisbon. My great-uncle's legacy remained as much a mystery to me as to the inhabitants of Villa Franca, though I had greatly enjoyed meeting them, and the beautiful, affectionate welcome they gave me that day, was something I would always remember.

All of a sudden while in Portugal, I ran out of money. I was still collecting the £25 a month from home, and before leaving had arranged for it to be forwarded to me. It had not, however, arrived. With my remaining cash I bought a rail ticket back to London, after which I had just enough to last me until the end of the week. On the Friday I waited patiently at the small pension in Lisbon for the mail, but there was nothing for me. Realising I had better go back straight away, I took a train to San Sebastian. The carriages were all very crowded and I spent the whole night in the third class, without space even to squat on my suitcase, so I lent it to some old ladies and children, who managed to sit on it somehow. I discovered that the working class people in Portugal often travelled with a large, melon-shaped rye loaf, about 2 foot in diameter and wrapped in a bed-sheet, from which they cut slices to share with their children. As the train rattled along, I looked longingly at the bread, hoping forlornly that someone might offer a morsel.

Reaching San Sebastian the next morning I took a walk along the beach, and later, still starving, boarded a train for Paris, where, at a hostel I knew on the Place Pigalle, I felt sure of being able to borrow enough money for a meal. On arrival however I was shocked to find the establishment now only opened at night, which was several hours away. I had had nothing to eat for 48 hours. Sitting down in the square with my head slumped on my suitcase, more tired and hungry than I had ever been in my life, and wondering how I was going to survive, I heard someone say in English: 'Are you not feeling well?' I looked up and saw a young girl. 'I'm fine, just a bit hungry,' I said. 'Come with me,' she replied, 'I'll give you some lunch.' At her flat she cooked sausages, bacon and potatoes, and made delicious coffee.

Never had a meal tasted better. I thanked her profusely. 'Here's my telephone number,' I said as I was leaving, 'promise you will call me when you come to England, and I will repay your kindness.' I never saw her again. It was a moving experience for me, that someone could help a stranger and want nothing in return. Revived, I was soon settled on a train out of Paris and heading for the English Channel. Arriving at Victoria Station, I realised my problems were not, however, over, as I had no money for a Tube ticket to my current lodgings, a long way off up the Northern Line in Archway. A reverse charge call from a phone box to my fellow tenant and friend Turai Singham, brought him promptly to meet me at Archway Station, where he paid my fare.

It was a few days later that a strange coincidence occurred. I was standing outside Lincolns Inn when a group of young people filed out of the building. Noticing something familiar about one of them, I looked more closely and realised it was one of the girls who had been seasick on the Hook of Holland Ferry. 'What are you doing here?' I asked. The girl, whose name was Kanta, told me she was training to be a lawyer. 'Really?' I replied. There were very few female lawyers in those days. Then came another surprise; her brother was none other than A.R. Kapila, a well-known young barrister back in Nairobi. We exchanged a few more words before she went on her way.

I returned to the question of my own career and what I should do next. Should I try to practise law in England now? I would like to have worked towards an MSc or PhD in Economics, but could I afford it? After sending a letter to my parents asking for their advice, the reply came back that I should continue my studies if I wished and not to worry about finance, as they would support me as long as they were alive. This was a fortunate position to be in, and my old friend at the LSE, the Registrar, together with the Registrar of Postgraduate Studies, were willing to accept me straight away for the MSc. The only difficulty was agreeing a suitable subject for research. I was keen on looking at a wide area, for instance, political development in the period following the First World War, while the LSE strongly recommended I do something relating to East Africa, possibly focusing on the Indian community in Kenya. At the time I thought this was very limiting, but later on I understood the problem of postgraduates wanting a grand, sweeping title for their work, whereas the whole point of academic research at this level, was to illuminate, with highly detailed information and statistics, a very specific area. We managed to narrow my chosen subject down, to cover the origins and functioning of political organisations, and political development in East Africa, with the actual title yet to be decided. I was looking forward to starting work. Much of my focus would be on Kenya, including such movements as the troubled Kenyan African Union, struggling, along with the trade union movement, under British Colonial rule, to achieve social and economic justice for ordinary Africans.

Life settled back into a routine of study, part-time work and weekly religious observance. Each Sunday morning a few people from our boarding house, led by Emmanuel, a former Consul General of Chile, now in his sixties, who had divorced his first wife and now had a younger, very sexy one, would take the bus to St Joseph's Catholic Church at Stamford Hill. I had no particular desire to attend but felt that to stop going would be harder. Then something unusual happened at church. After Benediction, the priest asked us not to go home but to come instead to a party. Recently there had been a big scandal about the Maltese Messina brothers, who under the guise of caring Catholics had hung around Euston Station looking for naïve young girls coming from Ireland for the first time, offering them lifts, jobs and accommodation, before ensnaring them into prostitution. Anxious to provide a network that was safe but enjoyable the church was now inviting young people to get together after the services. I was shocked to hear records playing and see boys and girls introduced and encouraged to dance, something the nuns in Zanzibar would never have done. Here in England they had seen how the Methodists attracted their congregations and were taking a leaf out of their book.

While I enjoyed the parties, the Catholic theology seemed more and more ridiculous, its ideas of heaven and hell, purgatory and eternal damnation like something from a children's fairy tale. The nuns in Zanzibar had hoped I might become a priest. I once asked them what would happen to someone like Mahatma Gandhi, who was a very good man but had not been baptised, or to a child who died before committing sin. I was told they have to go into limbo or purgatory. I thought this was very strange, and that God must be very cruel to condemn a person to long, even everlasting, suffering simply for not believing or being born into another religion. So much of the Bible seemed nonsensical. I recalled asking some school friends in what language did God speak to Adam and Eve, to which they had replied Hebrew. Did Hebrew exist back then? And if God had created the universe, where had God come from? More recently I had discussed all these questions and doubts at great length with Meryl Seriwardena and had felt a pressure building within me to give up religion altogether. I was worried though; the old images of hellfire and damnation remained very strong. What would happen to me when I died?

On the 13th of January 1951, I polished my shoes, put on my suit and tie and brushed my hair, as always before church. Emmanuel was already at the door. 'Shall we go?' he said. 'No,' I said, 'I'm not coming today.' He looked at me. 'Then why are you all dressed up, what's wrong?' 'From today,' I replied, 'I am no longer a Catholic, I am no longer a Christian. I believe it is all wrong.' Emmanuel said, 'Don't be ridiculous!' I said, 'I only got dressed because I wanted to convince myself that it is not out of laziness that I am giving up going to church.'

Though still having some concerns, I knew I had to do what I thought was right, not what other people told me. It had nothing to do with being free to go out with women; leaving the church only reconfirmed my idea that I ought not to, in case I slept with them. It was therefore, I believed, a choice made out of strength not weakness. Fearing that my mother who was quite religious might be upset, I had not yet told my family. Instead I wrote to the nuns in Zanzibar informing them of my decision. They must have been shocked, because I got so many letters back saying how sorry they were; they didn't understand, I had been such a good boy. I was also told not to worry and that there were organisations within the Catholic Church set up to help people like me who had problems with their faith. I started getting visitors, on Saturdays, Sundays, sometimes even at night, knocking at the door, wanting to know what was worrying me, and to discuss God and the church. Eventually I told my housemates, 'Look I don't want to talk to these fellows. They don't understand anything I'm saying and just think I'm a heretic. If they call again and ask for Mr de Souza, please tell them I'm out.'

The promise to my father that I would not get married while away was not difficult to keep. If Kanta and I for example were sufficiently drawn to one another and decided to wed, the event would take place in Nairobi. I could see how other possibilities might present themselves though. One of the cleaners at our boarding house was a German girl called Elsa, whom I liked very much. One day I asked if she were married. She told me yes. What does he do? I said. She said he drove round the pubs delivering big barrels of beer off a lorry. Perhaps it was not the right thing to say, but I asked her couldn't she choose someone better? She said she had thought herself lucky; after the war the Germans were starving, and every girl wanted to marry an American, and if they couldn't find one then an Englishman or Frenchman, anything rather than end up as an old lady with nothing. She said she hadn't met people like me, and asked would I have married her. I said I didn't know.

Wars affected the lives of so many women like Elsa. Usually I didn't like the cinema, which I thought was too often about escapism, deluding people with fantasies to make them forget about real issues, but I did enjoy *Gone With The Wind*, the long epic drama about the American Civil War, starring Vivien Leigh. In *Waterloo Bridge*, a soldier and a dancer, also played by Vivien Leigh, meet in London during the First World War and fall in love. When she hears he has been killed in action, she falls on hard times and turns to prostitution. On discovering he was only taken prisoner and is still alive they are reunited, but her guilt and shame overcome her, and after declaring her eternal love for him she kills herself by walking under a truck on the bridge where they met.

London could be a friendless place, and such stories were not that far-fetched. For one thing, getting a job, or dole money, was not as easy as some people believed. One day as I was strolling through the West End, a young girl smiled at me and said hello and asked if I would like to have a cup of tea with her. She was polite and well mannered and so I agreed, and we talked for a while then shook hands and said goodbye. That evening I spotted her outside the Mecca Ballroom where the prostitutes hung out and saw a man come and speak to her. When I next saw her I walked on by, but she came running up to me. 'Why didn't you speak to me like the other day?' she asked, 'when we met you were so nice to me, treated me like a lady.' Putting it delicately, I said that I had seen her outside the Mecca Ballroom. 'Oh no,' she protested, 'I wouldn't be seen dead at a place like that, where the prostitutes go!' I said, 'I'm sorry, perhaps I jumped to the wrong conclusion.' Then, looking upset, she said, 'Well, yes I suppose that's what I am, but my parents had no money, and I didn't have a place to live or food to eat, and then men started taking me to dinner, but they wanted to sleep with me. In the end I thought I might as well charge for this, and that's how I got into it. I never intended for it to happen.' I felt very sad for her. I said, 'I am sorry, I can see you have been brought up in a very straight family, and I wish you well.' The experience helped me to understand the importance of a working welfare system and accessible social services so that no one need sacrifice their dignity to avoid starvation. It also underlined the fundamental moral principles of the National Health Service set up in Britain by Aneurin Bevan, a brilliant speaker and committed socialist, whom I had met on his visit to the LSE.

On another occasion, I had been in the Houses of Parliament in London listening to the speeches, and on coming out went to use the nearby public convenience. While I was in there a respectable looking man came up and asked me, 'Are you Indian?' I told him, yes originally. He then asked if I could get him back to India. There he had been a big man, a railway inspector with his own office, a house, servants and food, all paid for by the government. 'Now I am in Britain,' he said, 'I wash the toilets. I want to get out, I cannot stay here any longer, please take me away.' I said, 'I am sorry I am just a student, I don't know where to take you.' I did feel sorry for him, as one sympathises with anyone who feels they have come down in life.

On the other hand some of the Anglo-Indians were very arrogant. We had a couple of them in our boarding house and they hated we Indians and Goans because, as they saw it, we had no European blood in our veins. This incidentally might not have been true, as, going back far enough, one of our ancestors might have married a Portuguese soldier for example, making us perhaps 10 percent or 20 percent European. The fact is none of it should matter, but in those days, to a great many people it did. Over the next few months I began to find it hard to concentrate. Was it something to do with giving up the Catholic faith? No, I felt very sure about that. I realised what it was; my father, from whom I was used to receiving regular letters, seemed to have stopped writing. However busy, he had always found time to send me at least a few lines, but now there was nothing, and as the weeks went on I became concerned. Then a family friend just arrived from

Kenya came to see me. 'I'm sorry Fitz,' he confided, 'but I have heard your father is not at all well.'

International Club, Southend-on-Sea, January 1950

Graduation as a barrister at Lincoln's Inn, 1950

In wig and gown

Chapter Six

Return to Kenya

1952

My father had developed diabetes, a controllable condition, and with proper care and monitoring, not life-threatening. Inevitably though, I thought of Meryl Seriwardena, the injections, and the awareness of mortality. I came to a swift decision, that I would put my studies on hold and return home. A telegram to my sister Iva brought money for my fare, and I notified my parents that I would be sailing on the next available ship.

It was the newly built SS Kenya, on her maiden voyage in March 1952. Discovering that a brief stop at Aden was scheduled, I had written to Alex Sequeira to let him know. As we dropped anchor, a motor launch flying the British flag came alongside. Standing by the flag was Alex. I thought good god, he is a changed man he looks about 20 years younger. As Secretary to the Parliament, he was quite a big figure in Aden, and drove me all around, showing me the whole place and introducing his wife, a former teacher.

In my haste to get home I had omitted to send a telegram with my estimated arrival time, and hence there was no one to meet me at Nairobi Railway Station. The 6pm train to Konza had already left, but in any case I would have had to wait there for the morning train to Kajiado, where it was another 24 or 48 hours, often even longer, until the connection to Magadi. However, I had only a couple of pounds in my pocket, and nowhere to spend the night in Nairobi either. Abdul Bhaijee, a friend I had shared a flat with in London, had told me I could stay at his family's home, but I wasn't very keen, thinking that as Muslims they would be in purdah, like the Bohra community in Zanzibar, and it might be embarrassing for them to have a total outsider in their midst. They had also been pushing Abdul to interest me in his sister, a request he was reluctant about, and I did not wish to offend the Bhaijees by accepting their hospitality while declining their daughter. After sitting on my suitcase for ten minutes considering what to do, I telephoned Abdul's father, who promptly came in a car and took me to his hardware shop, on what was then Government Road. Mr Bhaijee was about 55, and had two daughters, including the one he hoped I might marry, living at home with him and his wife. He was adamant that I stay with them, insisting there would be no problems at all and they would be happy to look after me, their son having already written glowing accounts of me, and what a great friend I was. Mr Bhaijee pressed me very hard. Thanking him for the lift from the station, I said he was very kind, but could I think about it please?

In fact I was thinking about my father and when I was going to see him, and was anxious to get word to my family as soon as possible to tell them where I was. I was also thinking about a letter I had received while in London from a Goan journalist, born in Nairobi, who was prominent in the East African Indian National Congress. His name was Pio Gama Pinto. In 1944, aged 17 he had staged a protest in Bombay against Portugal's control of Goa, his political activism later landing him in trouble, and to avoid the threat of deportation to a Portuguese concentration camp in Cape Verde, he had returned to Kenya. Pio had asked me to bring him some political books from London. His office was now in the Desai Memorial Library, just a short walk from Mr Bhaijee's shop. I had also heard that he had until recently been in Magadi, being treated by my father for a chest infection. My father, worried it might develop into pneumonia, had urged his patient to stay where he could observe him, but Pio could not wait, he had things to do in Nairobi.

Although it was the first time we had met, Pio, a couple of years my senior, greeted me with great warmth and affection, hugging me as if we had known each other for ages. We talked on a range of subjects, but the focus returned always to politics, specifically the situation in Kenya. Pio was both concerned and excited about what was happening in the country and the nationalist movement, with whose aims it seemed he was seriously engaged. He was also eager for people to come and help him, and asked if I was interested in getting involved. Moved and inspired by the energy and obvious commitment of this bright young man, I readily agreed.

At about 5pm another gentleman walked into the office, whom Pio introduced as Mr Nazareth. Realising this was the highly reputed barrister J. M. Nazareth, I asked him in some awe, 'Not *the* J.M. Nazareth?' He replied, 'Well I don't know what you mean by *the*, but I'm a Nazareth.' He then joined the discussion – of the colour bar, the intransigence of the British over land appropriation in the White Highlands and elsewhere, and the general social and economic inequity to which the indigenous Africans were subjected. It was felt that if the British did not make concessions, confrontation was inevitable, and in the ensuing backlash many lives would be lost, the national movement possibly annihilated and Kenya's political and economic progress put back years. We concurred that to avoid such a fate, the Indian community should throw its lot in with the movement and try to guide it on the path of non-violent change.

Nazareth left us, and at about 7pm Pio and I went out to have a meal. I asked where he was staying, and he told me he shared some servants' quarters with two other people in Pangani. I said rather boldly, 'Well you'll be four now.' He smiled. 'You are most welcome. I've only got one bed, but you can have it. I'll use a spare mattress on the floor.' I said I couldn't possibly take his bed, but he was insistent. I phoned Mr Bhaijee to tell him I would be staying the night with Mr Pinto. He sounded disappointed, but said to call at his shop if I needed assistance in any way, and that he would be happy to give me a car or a driver, which was a great comfort since none of us had our own transport. I also sent a message to my father with my good wishes explaining that I was presently stranded in Nairobi but would get home as soon as I could.

Several Goan bachelors lived two or three to a room alongside Pio, cooking together and sharing meals, and having one servant between them. In the morning the servant made hot water in a 4-gallon tin, and in a makeshift bathroom we would take turns to wash with a little mug, while fresh hot water was prepared. Most Goans, such as the government clerks who took the 8am bus from Pangani, to avoid the morning bath queue, preferred to wash in the evening, but neither Pio nor I were in a rush, and after washing and dressing we got to the bus stop at about 8.30am, to return to his office in the Desai Memorial Hall Library.

Waiting with us that morning was a very athletic and handsome young gentleman with slightly curly hair and a Goan accent. Indeed I assumed he was Goan, and everyone treated him as such. Very amiable and with a nice sense of humour, his name was Joseph Zuzarte, and it transpired he was of Goan/Maasai parentage, had been to Bangalore and Goa and knew a lot about Goans. He worked for the Overseas Touring Company, the agent at that time, I believe, for Morris Cars.

For the equivalent of about sixpence we had breakfast of tea and a samosa at the Green Hotel, then on Abdullah Street. Owned by Hyder Teja, an Indian from Zanzibar, the ten-room hotel was quite popular with Goans, who shared four or five to a room. Hyder, a member of the Ismaili community, was very charming and friendly, allowing everyone a lot of credit. Later Pio took me to Kiburi House on Grogan Road, which I think belonged to the East African Fuel and Bark Supply Company, a limited company but on semi-cooperative lines. The premises were small, a shop with tiny office rooms above, but they were in what was probably the first commercial building to be owned by a group of Africans in this way. Each office was rented by a trade union, and Pio's closest friends among them here were J.D. Kali and Bildad Kaggia. He knew all the other trade unionists, including Stephen Ngobi, Fred Kubai and a few others, and I could see they all had a lot of friendship and affection for each other. Pio would spend about two hours each day at Kiburi House, discussing political developments and how to further the trade union movement and civil rights.

In Nairobi there was almost total apartheid, with front-row bus seats, for example, marked for Europeans only, the middle for Asians, while Africans were restricted to 'second class' behind a big barrier at the back, and paid less for their tickets. In churches the seats were not always labelled, but a similar system was the norm. I had seen priests before asking Asians to vacate their places for Europeans, which had made me very angry, and had decided not to attend church in Kenya at all. In terms of living space, over 75 percent of Nairobi's residential areas were reserved for the 1,000-odd European families, and 20 percent for Asians. Into the remaining fraction of the city, comprising Pumwani, Starehe and bits of Shaurimoyo and Kariokor, the old quarters of the Carrier Corps from the First World War, were crowded the Africans.

I stayed with Pio for a few days, taking turns for the bed. Having got my message, my father had arranged for someone to come and take me from Nairobi to Magadi by car. Our reunion, after five years apart, was an emotional one, and my father, mother and sister Iva now arrived from Goa, were waiting eagerly to see me, and we all hugged one another. I was relieved to see that my father, though tiring easily and obviously still recuperating after time in hospital, was just the same. He asked what I planned to do now. I said I would try to find a pupillage with a lawyer in Nairobi, after which I could practise. That meant finding accommodation there too of course, which could be expensive, for though government controls kept the rents low, landlords compensated by demanding a lump sum as key money, or 'pugree' in Hindi, before granting a tenancy – an illegal but very widespread practice.

Meanwhile though, I was very happy to catch up on some time with my family. My father had been working hard, probably too hard in light of his illness, treating Europeans, Asians and Africans. Italian former prisoners of war also kept turning up at the surgery, and curious as to what could be wrong with those healthy-looking young fellows, I stole a look at their medical cards one day and saw they had all contracted venereal disease. The Italian soldiers had earned a reputation after the war for falling in love with Ethiopian girls. My legacy was one of the unwanted service rifles and ammunition they brought in lieu of payment, which I took out to hunt wild animals. I thought I had better do things properly, so went along to the District Commissioner's office in Nairobi to ask about getting a gun licence. The D.C. was always treated like a little god, and whenever he visited Magadi they would throw a party for him. When I explained what I wanted he asked me in a very blunt manner, did I know it was illegal to walk about the streets of Nairobi carrying a gun? I replied, 'I don't know about that, but unless my eyes deceive me, I have seen hundreds of people walking around with guns in holsters, and in their hands for that matter.' He looked at me, a 20-something Indian boy standing there in his office questioning him. 'You are an insolent young man,' he said, 'get out.' I think I then said something like, 'Look, I can get out of your office, it doesn't matter; it doesn't alter the facts.' At this he became really angry, 'Nobody speaks to me like that,' he shouted, 'I can have you thrown out.' But this was typical of the D.C.s in general. Nobody went against them, as they had the power over all the traders and most other people within their area of jurisdiction. Not all Europeans held Asians and Africans in contempt however.

Though not a surgeon, my father was skilled and versatile and would always do his best for any patient. He told me how his first visit to a morgue as a medical student had turned his stomach, and how amazed he was to see the morticians cut up the cadavers and then cheerfully drink tea, standing their cups on the slab. Now, watching him deftly clean and cut out wounds and pus, it was my stomach that heaved, forcing me to turn away and vomit. My father was also very courageous. Once when we were at the hospital, a patient stripped off all his clothes and began waving a knife. People were screaming and running away, but my father, who did not even know him, and without so much as a stick for protection, walked up and asked him slowly and calmly to hand over the knife saying that everything would be all right. It was a question of showing authority, but would the man accept it? I held my breath, terrified of what might happen. To everyone's amazement and relief, however, the man did as requested and gave up the knife, whereupon they all cried out to kill him. My father said no, he was not to be touched, the man had put his trust in him, and it had to be returned.

Africans in need of medical assistance were continuing to walk long distances to see Dr de Souza, as he was still the only medical man for miles, including part of the Maasai lands and almost as far as Tanganyika. Since the onset of his diabetes, however, he did not always have the energy to drive out on calls, and so, as before, I offered to either accompany him as back-up or take his 'ambulance', the rickety old 1936 black box Chevrolet, out into the bush alone. I would never forget one particular patient. To safeguard their cattle at night in their 'manyatta', their homestead, the Maasai corralled them in simple brushwood fences. If a lion did manage to leap over, they would leave it to gorge on one cow. Then, after a night of ritual singing and dancing, imbibing alcohol and narcotic plants, they would draw lots for one of them to go in and kill the lion. Though the Maasai were highly skilled with their spears, this was obviously very dangerous, particularly with a wounded lion, and could go either way. One day a tribesman came to our house seeking urgent help for his friend who had been mauled. I took my father's Chevrolet and followed him. Spear in one hand and holding up his shuka, his loose skirt-like clothing, in the other, he ran nimbly over the rough ground, never once tiring, slipping or hurting his bare feet on the sharp rocks. Cleverly avoiding steep gradients in which the vehicle might get stuck, he took me on a safe but circuitous route of probably 20 miles to reach the injured man. On arriving I found a fellow with his intestines literally hanging out. Remarkably though, he was conscious and walked to the car holding his innards, smelling to high heaven, making me quite uncomfortable as he got in. I was sure he would not live.

We eventually got him to Magadi Hospital, visited him for several days, and, even to my father's surprise he eventually recovered. Few survived such attacks, and those who had been mauled were often found with a black buzzing patch of hundreds of flies – believed to bring money and good luck – stuck to their open wounds, or, most horrific of all, were left in the corral to be finished off by the lion. These tribesmen were incredible though. When the British Army was holding tug-of-war and running events in a bid to recruit Africans one day, a Maasai who happened to be standing nearby ran over and joined in one of the races, reaching the tape way ahead of the others. We all laughed and cheered, especially as, lifting up his shuka, he had run virtually naked in front of everyone, including several ladies.

Superstition had a strong hold over many Africans, and death would often be blamed on someone having put a witchdoctor's curse on the deceased, with retribution then sought on the alleged perpetrator. It was from the window of our house that soon after a chief called Edmund, whom my father had attempted to treat for a peculiar wasting disease, had died, I saw a huge crowd of Africans chasing and throwing stones at another man. As he ran, a stone hit him and he stumbled and fell and I thought he was surely dead, only to see him get up again and to my shock, run to our fence. My father immediately let him through the gate and locked it again, and the mob drifted away. The man was apparently the assistant chief. There was a theory that the mysterious wasting disease that had killed Chief Edmund was caused by eating monkeys, a delicacy in the Congo, or that it was a forerunner of Aids.

I think some description of Magadi would be important at this point. Situated by Lake Magadi in the Great Rift Valley, about 75 miles south of Nairobi, the soda factory was built by the Germans in 1910 and taken over by the British after the First World War. The vast quantities of soda ash lay in a sort of underground mountain from which water would seep into the nearby lake, on the surface of which a salt crust was formed. This crust, three to four feet thick, was solid enough for lorries to drive safely across it, carrying material and supplies to and from the factory. A stretch of railway had also been built from Magadi to Kajiado, joining the line to Konza, Nairobi and Mombasa, from where the soda ash was shipped to South Africa and elsewhere.

By the time of my father's appointment as Medical Officer, the Magadi Soda Works was owned by Imperial Chemical Industries, a European conglomerate formed in 1926 from four companies including Nobel Explosives, the dynamite manufacturer whose founder gave his name to the Nobel Peace Prize. The general manager and his 50 or so subordinates, all Europeans, lived in a row of houses at the top of the ridge, with a beautiful view of the lake and pleasant breezes. Each home had five or six bedrooms and an acre or so of garden. They had their own club, a golf course, tennis court and small swimming pool, and no Indians or Africans were permitted to use or enter these facilities at any time.

The Indians were divided into two categories, the 25 to 30 more senior staff given two-bedroom semi-detached bungalows with gardens of a quarter of an acre at most, while the electricians, masons, carpenters and mechanics –

the 'fundis' as we called them – lived in corrugated iron and stone rooms called landis. Married couples had two rooms with a little courtyard out back; single fundis lived two or three to a room. Cooking, eating and sleeping all had to be done within, and corrugated iron sheets fixed together served as a bathroom, with buckets for toilets situated about 40 feet away. A club for Indians was situated near the seniors' bungalows.

Further down the hill, close to the factory and almost level with the lake were about 200 more landis for the Africans. Unlike those of the Indians, these makeshift tin dwellings with sloped roofs had no concrete floors and stood simply on the bare mud. They were also very overcrowded, each with 15 to 20 people, forced to cook and often sleep in the yard. Magadi being one of the hottest places in Africa, often reaching 105° Fahrenheit in the shade, this was perhaps a necessity, though from lying overnight on the soda ash, many Africans developed painful sores, which a predecessor of my father's, a Dr White, was alleged to have treated by amputation.

The temperature in Magadi was often too much for me and I soon felt ill if I left my head uncovered. Night-times could be suffocating and the servants often put beds for us on the veranda where, drifting in and out of sleep, I would hear hyenas skulking by. The intense heat baked the ground, the air and the tin sheets of the African huts, which burnt the skin if touched. There were lots of women and children living here, and how they managed I don't know. No one seemed to complain, they just accepted it. Their only relief was the African bar in the evenings, drinking their native brew amid noisy song and dance.

The whole of Magadi was run, like most of Kenya, on a strict apartheid basis. The town's one shop, Said Omer and Brothers, owned by an Indian, was no exception. This large bungalow sold everything from food – meat, rice, maize, ugali, vegetables and tinned goods – to clothes, fabric, utensils and assorted hardware and household essentials. The two larger doors at the front of the building served the Europeans, while the 3,000 or so Africans in Magadi had to crowd in to a narrow counter at the rear, a scene of regular chaos, screaming and shouting as people struggled to obtain what they needed.

Whether the shop owner chose this segregation or the Soda Company instructed him, I do not know. Possibly he just assumed it was the way to do things, but whatever the reason, the rules were rigidly enforced and any Indian or African entering the front doors would simply be ignored. One day I did go in the front and was shouted at. I retorted, 'Go to hell,' and stayed there until I was served, probably because they knew I was Dr de Souza's son. The Africans, who rarely used or understood money, traded in goats or sheep, and were swindled by the shop, getting far less in goods than the equivalent going rate for their livestock.

Returning to Kenya after five years amid the decency and relative equality of Britain, it was quite disgusting and intolerable to see such officially imposed racialism as a part of everyday life, and the way the Europeans shouted at the Indians, the fundis, and, most harshly, the Africans, made my blood boil. It was a far cry too from the mixed but harmonious community I had known as a child in Zanzibar.

My father had been given a house attached to the company hospital, situated between the European and Indian quarters. The reason for this exceptional proximity to Europeans was, apparently, that the dwelling had been built originally for a European medical officer. It was quite modest – two bedrooms, bathroom, kitchen, toilet and a small open veranda at the front and rear. In the half-acre garden, to keep busy and provide food, my mother kept a profusion of ducks, geese and guinea fowl, and grew vegetables on the surrounding land.

Apart from the searing heat, it was, or could have been an idyllic, contented life, if one had no social conscience, or could swallow one's pride. For instance, all the Europeans were very glad of my father's medical expertise for themselves and their families, but never invited him to dinner as they did other colleagues, or for so much as a drink. Even Doctor Anderson, a respected consultant surgeon who came to Magadi once a week from Nairobi Hospital, and was a devout Christian in the Oxford Movement, kept my father at a distance socially. I did not hold it against him, he was a very good and kind person, but this was the convention.

Other forms of discrimination were more blatant, like the tennis matches at Magadi between Europeans and Indians. My father had taught me the game, and like him I had become a keen player. But on the occasion of my first match I had been shocked that we weren't allowed into the clubhouse even for the toilets, but had to use a makeshift latrine outside, screened with sackcloth and with not even a chair to sit on. I told my father I was never taking part there again and nor should he. He replied that it was a great honour to be invited, and though he didn't like the segregation, he felt that being an employee, there was little he could do and that the company might hold it against him if he refused.

One day in Magadi my mother fell ill. She was taken to Nairobi and admitted to the Native Civil Hospital (now the Kenyatta Hospital) where they diagnosed kidney disease. This wooden hospital with mud floors was I think for Africans and Asians, and another example of segregated, poorer conditions for non-Europeans. In time though my mother became well again and returned home, much to our relief.

In the end my father stopped going to the Magadi company tennis matches, which I was glad about, but the sense of indignation about the enforced racial policies would not leave me, and ever since as a young boy reading Mahatma Gandhi's books, and all through my time in England, the impulse to challenge the injustice in Kenya, suffered most acutely by the Africans, had been growing. Gandhi was now dead, but his ideas of equality and freedom seemed more resonant than ever. India had achieved independence, though at terrible cost during Partition, which some had blamed on Gandhi. If Kenya's people could become free and have their rights restored without bloodshed, it would be wonderful indeed. Pio Pinto and his friends, who like Gandhi believed firmly in non-violence, gave one hope that it could be done. Meeting Pio had re-ignited my earnest desire to work towards such change, and made it the single most important thing in my life.

The other priority of course was to obtain a pupillage, which I could not put off indefinitely. The first step towards fulfilling both these ambitions was to get myself some kind of accommodation in Nairobi, and having been very impressed that Gandhi had chosen to live in the Bangi Colonies in India, among the poor, I decided to follow his example and go and live with the Africans in Pumwani, one of the oldest parts of Nairobi. When I told my father he looked at me curiously and said, 'Have you seen the place?' I admitted I had not, but said that I would go anyway, having made friends with some Africans who had invited me to stay with them there.

When I arrived I understood my father's reservations. The conditions at Pumwani were quite startling; with their unplastered wattle and mud walls, doors made from old packing cases and roofs of thatch or flattened out 4-gallon kerosene tins, these makeshift huts comprised tiny rooms crammed with people. The floors were mud, and with no windows, the atmosphere was dark and depressing even in the daytime. Shared latrines were several hundred yards from the huts, along with a solitary municipal water tap where the residents filled up the old kerosene tins, which were adapted for a multitude of uses from construction to kitchen utensils. When my friends had welcomed me in, and I stood there with my trunk and asked where I should put my clothes, they looked bemused. Of course, there was no such thing as a wardrobe or any furniture at all, not even beds, and everyone slept on the ground.

I thought that if I could find a space that had at least a separate entrance, I might endure it here. The real horror though came at night, when I realised that there was absolutely no street lighting of any kind, and I had to find my way through an endless maze of narrow, muddy alleyways, full of drunks and prostitutes and an overpowering stench from people relieving themselves. That said, there seemed little crime as such, perhaps because few had anything to steal. It was hard to believe that some of the people living here were office workers, though many of them did manage to move out, to Kariokor or Starehe, and build slightly better homes.

Talking of Starehe, a YMCA had been opened recently there and the caretaker, a very charming person called Fred Ng'ang'a, had invited Pio, Haroon Ahmed, Rawal and a few other friends, including myself. This at least gave us a place to congregate once a week or so, and it was interesting and encouraging for me to see how progressive, intelligent and forward-looking they were; young people full of dynamic ideas.

Most of us had the same problem of how to make both ends meet, but it was good for our morale to get together. In Nairobi, finding a place to sleep, eat and wash, the simplest of needs, was a big problem for many of us. At about this time I met another young man in the same situation, though facing an added disadvantage. Argwings Kodhek, six years my senior, born in 1922, had been studying for the Bar in London when he was taken ill with TB. In hospital he had struck up a friendship with one of the nurses, a young Irish girl called Mavis. When I met Mavis, she told me how she thought Argwings had a delightful sense of humour and that he was always very friendly and affectionate. After she had been nursing him for six months, he proposed to her. She said she had never imagined she would be able to marry a barrister, or dreamed that she might live abroad, but she liked him a great deal and accepted. Getting married proved to be not so simple however. In those days, for a black African to marry a white woman was highly unusual, though there was of course no law against interracial marriage; the couple asked both

Catholic priests and Protestant ministers, and approached several parishes in London, which all said no. Eventually, they found a church that would agree to conduct their ceremony. If I remember rightly, this was around the same time that Seretse Khama, the grandson of the King of Bechuanaland, caused great furore in both his home country and among people in the British Government for marrying Ruth Davis, an English clerk at Lloyds' of London.

Having become man and wife, Argwings and Mavis were very happy, and he being qualified, the plan was for him to return to Kenya and begin practising law, and for Mavis to follow him out after a month or two. The young bride's voyage from England turned into an ordeal however, with other passengers subjecting her to repeated verbal abuse and insults, saying that she was now a nigger since she had married one. She was naturally very upset at such treatment and would sit for much of the time in her cabin crying. She said that when the ship then arrived at Mombasa, one white settler came up and offered her 20,000 Kenya shillings, about a thousand pounds, if she would call it a day and go back to England immediately.

Mavis was so shocked and disorientated by this experience that on going ashore she refused to meet her husband as arranged and instead checked into a hotel, locked herself into her room and cried. Two days later she emerged and, on seeing Argwings was so happy, realised that she loved him a great deal and would accept all sorts of problems that might have to be suffered for his sake. Reunited, the couple boarded the train from Mombasa to Nairobi. Although a married couple, they would not have been able to afford the fare for one of the 'special first' sleeper carriages and therefore, as obliged by regulations, most likely travelled in separate male and female compartments. Arriving in Nairobi, Mr and Mrs Kodhek set about trying to find accommodation. It was not going to be easy: Argwings was barred from living in the European areas and Mavis from the African, which she would in any case, I imagine, have been less than keen to do. No hotel would take them and it looked as if they would be sleeping on the street that night, until our very good friend D.K. Sharda, then one of the leaders of the younger Indian group, which I will come to later, invited them to come and stay with him for a week.

They ended up staying three months, not because they wanted to take advantage of their host's hospitality, but because they simply could not find anywhere else, which he understood very well. Then one day Mavis got talking to an elderly English lady in a shop and the two of them became very friendly. The lady took pity on Mavis and Argwings and offered them a rondavel normally used for servants in Kabete. They accepted gratefully and were so happy to finally have somewhere of their own. After that they obtained a place in Baba Ndogo Estate at Ruaraka. I remember Mavis was very jealous of her husband associating with African girls and would not allow him to meet them even for a few minutes.

Many of the inhabitants of Ruaraka were impoverished whites, and Francis D'Silva, a Goan, owned quite a large area of land here. I had first met him when I had stayed in River Road with Dr Dias, who was a good friend of his. D'Silva had an English friend called Stanley Good, on whom he depended totally. Good, who had been in the army in India, would attend auctions on D'Silva's behalf and look out for old farms to buy up from the poorer English. These tended to be smallish poultry farms – chickens, geese and turkeys – and were also where some of the English men kept their mistresses, usually African, sometimes Seychellois.

The farms were generally of about ten acres, and D'Silva had by increments acquired about 40 acres. He had then proceeded to open some quarries and build some bungalows, which was a bit of an exaggeration for such rough-and-ready structures with unplastered walls, mostly of mud rather than cement, and roofed with second- or third-hand corrugated iron sheets, or in some cases even the flattened out 4-gallon kerosene tins. The layout was like most Indian accommodation – single storey with two or three rooms, a courtyard and verandas back and front, with the added touch of electric lighting from a generator. As I recall, D'Silva had put up about 20 to 30 such dwellings and on the surrounding land planted a huge amount of mangoes, and called the estate 'Mango Farm'. Access was something of a problem, as, after leaving the main road to Thika you had to travel along a mile or so of very rough, muddy road, which in the rainy season sprang potholes a foot deep, allowing only the big American cars to crawl through at about two miles an hour. On finally arriving at Mango Farm, one would usually see lots of Indian children playing outside. A relative of one of the clerks at Magadi, M.T. Patel was among those who had moved into the bungalows, and for many other Indians the accommodation D'Silva provided was a tremendous change for the better. I am sure though that this influx must have angered a lot of the Europeans living nearby, the poor whites being the most racist of all.

Francis D'Silva had, I believe, originally been a clerk in the District Commissioner's office. During or after the war he had surmised there was a lot of money to be made in army surplus and begun buying up uniforms and equipment – hundreds of deckchairs, tents, tyres, generators, electric pumps, machinery and any other items that looked useful at auction, and selling them to second-hand shops. Thus he was able to build up some working capital, and I might add that in acquiring land with it as he did, he was one of the few Asians who had successfully got round the White Highlands Act, which normally prevented them from moving into such areas. His secret lay in a simple piece of subterfuge, in the shape of Stanley Good. A short, stumpy little fellow in his late sixties, Good had no money of his own and had been almost destitute when D'Silva took him in and gave him a room in his house. When a farm was heard to be coming up for sale, Stanley Good would put on his old military uniform, hat and medals, and D'Silva would drive him into town where

Good would make his way alone to the Land Office, a wood and iron building at the end of Government Road. There he would impress upon the officials how he had fought for the British Empire in India and how it was only right and proper that he should buy the farm, and would then negotiate a good price. The money was of course provided by D'Silva and the properties became to all intents and purposes his, but to avoid any possible comeback the deeds were all kept in Good's name. It was, however, quite widely known that the land comprising Mango Farm belonged in all but name to D'Silva, an Asian who was doing quite well out of acreage once owned by Europeans. This must have caused further resentment among the more racist of the poor whites in Ruaraka. After I learned about the situation, I used to ask D'Silva what he thought might happen if one day his friend changed his mind and decided to take over all the property to which he had title. D'Silva would always reply no, no, Stanley was a very good man, and would never do that to him. Having spent many an evening sitting and talking with Stanley Good and finding him a very nice person, I could certainly see no indication that he might renege on their arrangement.

There was another Englishman living at Mango Farm, an elderly doctor, who it was said had been struck off by the medical board and spent two years in prison. People sometimes mentioned his past in vague whispers, but no one talked openly about it. It was said by some that he had performed an abortion on an English woman, an illegal practice in Kenya, as it still was then in Britain. It was further rumoured that in this case the mother had died from the procedure, which if true might explain why the doctor was completely boycotted by the Europeans. Francis D'Silva, however, had taken him under his wing and given him a room. Being almost 80 years old, and having practised for many years, the old doctor used to tell us lots of stories about Kenya in the old days. Despite his advancing years, he was still very active, a thin and wiry figure, and still knew his medicine very well. He would treat people in the neighbourhood for a variety of ailments, and they would pay him a little. I suppose it was all unofficial, but very useful for the residents of Mango Farm, being rather cut off from the city to have someone with medical experience on hand that could help them. He seemed very conscientious in looking after everybody, and really was a very fine person. Who knows, the poor woman who died may perhaps have been in dire straits and he had acted from the best of intentions.

My stay at Pumwani did not last long. In the end I was advised that it was illegal for me to live in an African area. I must confess I was relieved, as I don't think I could have lasted long there. Pio came to the rescue, putting me up for a few nights, then a good friend of our family, an ex-postmaster from Magadi called Shantilal Amin, invited me to stay with him and his family in his current accommodation on what was then Park Road. With nine children, Shantilal's small semi-detached government house was very full already, he and his boys using one of the two bedrooms, his wife and daughters the other, but he insisted on putting a bed in the dining room for me even though they all slept on the floor. It was very kind of him, a generosity and hospitality I will never forget.

I searched desperately for a place of my own, but although some new houses were now being put up in Nairobi, landlords were demanding around 10,000 shillings in illegal pugree for even a single room, and my father's salary was only about 1,600 shillings a month. Then a friend called G.L. Vidyarthi, a staunch nationalist and proprietor of the *Colonial Times*, who had been imprisoned for his political activities, offered me one of the properties he had recently built on First Avenue, Parklands. The rent of 300 shillings a month was average, but he would not ask for pugree, provided that whenever I decided to vacate, I would not pass the occupancy on to anyone else.

I was more than happy to agree, and thanking Shantilal and his family for looking after me, I moved to the luxury of a three-roomed bungalow with a shared courtyard and the usual toilets and bathroom outside. My father would send me about 1,000 shillings a month, which left very little for him and my mother and sister to live on. But they were doing everything possible to help me, my mother even coming from Magadi whenever she could to cook for me, as I didn't have a servant. I had no fridge and little furniture, but we bought two divan beds at auction for about 50 shillings so my mother could stay over.

My routine now was to take the bus into town each day, meet with Pio and work on political campaigning, usually until 9pm or 10pm in the evening. Some nights I would walk all the way back home, past Parklands Police Station, then the little road that is now part of M.P. Shah Hospital, and across to First Avenue, Parklands, the way pitch black with no streetlights, with roaming dogs often attacking.

With bus fares and food, and still no paid job, I was soon finding it difficult to afford the 300 shillings rent. At a party one evening, I met a Mr and Mrs Rebello who said they had a spare room that I should come and look at. It turned out to be very large, was only 80 shillings a month, and in due course I moved in. In the flat next door lived an Indian lady, Umadevi Chaudri, and a man called Pravin Rawal, a nationalist who worked for a pharmacist in town. They weren't lovers or anything, just very good friends.

We soon became well acquainted and it was thanks to them that I met some very interesting people who would play an important part in my life, in particular Haroon Ahmed, then editor of the *Colonial Times*, who came over every evening, when we would discuss local and world politics at great length. Haroon, a Muslim, had, like Vidyarthi, been imprisoned for some of his anti-imperialist articles, and introduced me to all his friends in the trade union and nationalist world. Sometimes we took a drive out beyond Naivasha Road, a couple of miles further on, off the beaten track to Kijabe where the hot springs lay, and his father, an elderly Goan who spoke no English, ran their small family shop.

As the nationalist struggle in Kenya grew louder and the British largely dug in their heels, everyday life threw up its share of dramas. A rather unpleasant one occurred suddenly before my eyes one day when, while sitting in the communal courtyard, I saw the 16-year-old daughter of another neighbour pouring what appeared to be water over herself. I thought it even odder that she was all dressed up in a sari. When she took some paper and a matchbox and began scratching at it, I realised with horror that it was kerosene she had poured and she was about to commit suicide. Rushing up I grabbed the matches from her, but only just in time. She broke down in tears, saying her mother was dead, that her father got drunk and beat her, and she no longer wanted to live. The other residents and myself told the father off very severely and made him promise not to drink or harm her again. Later it occurred to me that he might have been abusing her sexually.

A happier story began when my next-door neighbour Umadevi Chaudri advertised a spare room to rent. The first person to respond, pulling up in an old Austin, introduced himself as Victor Haslaeur, a Swiss. Umadevi told him frankly, 'I'm sorry, but you won't be happy here, we are all Indians.' The Swiss asked, 'Are you a racialist?' She replied that she really was not but was only thinking of him. Victor insisted he wanted the room however, moved in, and he and Umadevi got on well, so well in fact that they eventually got married. Many years later after Victor died, his son would visit me. I would never forget that I was in Victor's company when I received the first ominous sign of what was unfolding in Kenya. We were sat in the garden talking when Victor suddenly put his fingers to his lips, grabbed my shoulders and pulled me down behind the wall. 'They're going to kill someone,' he whispered. There was a sound of footsteps and peering up I saw a group of ten or more Africans padding softly by, armed with machetes, their weapons and eyes glinting with menace.

The long, fragmented train journey between Nairobi and Magadi made it hard to visit my family often. The only alternative was to get a lift by road, and with my father too busy, and few Indians having reliable vehicles, that usually meant asking one of the Europeans, who had company cars, mostly similar Chevrolet saloons of the black box type used by Chicago gangsters. Groups of them often went into Nairobi for the weekend, and when a lift had been arranged, for say 7pm on the Sunday or Monday evening, I would wait at the Stanley Hotel. The place being 'whites only', I had to stand on the veranda or the terrace, sometimes until 11pm for whoever was taking me to appear, and the nights in Nairobi could be very cold, especially when wearing only shorts and a shirt.

I still got to Magadi far quicker than by train, though the journey could be arduous if you got stuck in potholes or mud. More serious were the rhinos, which more than once had ripped mudguards from the car I was in and been known to shunt vehicles off the road. What would be really useful, both for family visits and getting around to meetings in Nairobi, was my own transport. Sajjad Ali Gulam Ali, my old friend from Zanzibar and with whom I had shared many happy times in the UK when we were studying, had come to visit and we decided to go and see my parents in Magadi. It was there that I saw the beautiful 1939 Morris 8, registration D9460, being driven proudly around town by the Indian mechanic who had lovingly restored it. My father, who was interested in cars, asked what he had paid for it and would he consider selling? The mechanic said 2,500 shillings. My father replied that he would give him 3,000 to cover the restoration. No, no, said the mechanic graciously, for my father, he would only ask the cost price. Eventually a deal was struck for 3,000, to be paid in instalments. My father then promptly handed me the keys and announced, 'Take care of it, it's yours.'

After a week I was keen to return to Nairobi, to my work with the nationalist cause, and hopefully now find a law firm to start in my profession. Naturally I was eager to take my car, but although having driven my father several times, I had never done the whole 75 miles and wanted to make an early start, so at 5am Sajjad and I loaded suitcases and bedding into the Morris and set off. On reaching Rhino Hill, a notoriously steep gradient frequented by the beasts, all went well until we had climbed to about 15 feet from the top, when the engine suddenly stalled. Reversing back almost half a mile, I then came up faster, hoping the momentum would carry us over, but again the hill proved too much.

On the third attempt I drove at tremendous speed, only to manage another 5 feet or so – so near and yet so far! Sajjad and I then got out and tried to push the remaining distance, but the weight, angle of the road and growing heat of the day were against us. Keeping an anxious lookout for rhinos, we made five further attempts before removing our luggage and the spare wheel and trying in reverse. The lighter load made all the difference, the Morris chugging steadily backwards over the brow of the hill. Cheering heartily, we had descended several yards before remembering our suitcases and the spare wheels. Trudging up and down on foot, it took several trips to collect everything, by which time we were totally exhausted.

It was by now about 2pm in the afternoon, and we drove on until we came to the Ngong Hills where another steep gradient awaited. The Morris gave up about 30 feet from the crest, but this time we were a bit cleverer, and putting a stone behind the wheel, offloaded the cases and tyres straightaway. In those days there was absolutely no danger of your belongings being stolen, for rarely was there a soul about. As we got to the top however, the car stopped again, the engine boiling hot. Worried we might be stuck overnight, we went in search of some water for the radiator and after almost giving up hope came across a Maasai manyatta. The Maasai were very kind and from a small stream filled a karahi for us.

To our surprise they then introduced us to their daughters, making it plain that they wished us to spend the night with them and that it would be a great honour if we were to produce children. This I learned was not uncommon in Kenya, the sharing of the reproductive seed to bring families propitiously together. Sajjad and I were quite taken aback, and even had I been mature and able enough, I did not want to have sex until I was married. It was quite awkward, as we did not wish to give offence. Then they saw the Morris and gave a look of recognition. Perhaps they had realised I was Dr de Souza's son, but for whatever reason we seemed to be off the hook now and giving the car a helpful push, they waved us cheerfully off.

It was cold and dark when at about 6.30pm we finally saw the lights of Nairobi. Sajjad went to stay with Abdul Bhaijee, I to Mr and Mrs Rebello. Noting our fatigue and mud splattered clothes they asked if we had been on safari to Uganda or maybe Sudan. It felt like it, and we were glad the journey was over.

For me, there was soon something else to celebrate; visiting the offices of advocates Madan and Shah I was told, 'We will put a table and chair here for you.' My life as a lawyer was about to begin.

RETURN TO KENYA - 1952

Sajjad Ali and myself in Paris in the winter

Sajjad later with my mother and me in Nairobi

Chapter Seven

A Little Background about Asian Migration to Kenya and the Goan Identity

Before describing further this new chapter of my life as a lawyer in Nairobi, I think I should say a little about the context within which Indians, including Goans, had come to live in Kenya.

In the 1890s, 350 Indians arrived on African shores in a dhow. Brought by the British from Karachi, they had each paid 35 rupees for their passage on a vessel so crowded they were each allotted just nine square feet on deck for the duration of the voyage. They would now begin work on the grand project of constructing what would eventually be a 660-mile railway line, running from the Indian Ocean port of Mombasa in British East Africa, all the way to the eastern shore of Lake Victoria in Uganda. In 1895 the first section of track was laid at the Kilindini Harbour, Mombasa. Week by week, month by month, the line stretched slowly westwards, into the interior. The work was hard and the days long, hacking a route amid dense undergrowth, breaking through rocky hillsides with hammers and bare hands, and sleeping exhausted each night in huddled tents. There was also danger, not least from the proximity of man-eating lions. The notorious Tsavo incident occurred during the building of a bridge over the river, when, according to varying reports, two lions left between 20 and 135 men dead. There were also mosquitoes and disease to contend with, and locals that objected vehemently to the railway coming across their land; sometimes there was more than intrusion: when two Maasai girls were found to have been raped their tribe attacked the railway workers' caravan, killing around 500.

By 1900 the caravan came to a large area of swampland, which its inhabitants the Maasai called Ewaso Nyirobi, meaning 'cool waters'. A supply depot and station were established, and after the engineers had drained the ground houses began to be put up. Being at a midway point between Mombasa and Kampala, with multiple rivers supplying fresh water, and at an elevation cool enough to prevent malaria-carrying mosquitoes, the location gradually attracted European settlers and became known as Nairobi. The completion of the rest of the railway took approximately five years, arriving at Lake Victoria in 1901. In 1913 a branch line to Thika was added, followed by extensions to Magadi in 1915, Kitale 1926 and Naro Moro 1927. In 1929, the year of my birth, a line from Tororo to Soroti was opened, and the network became known as Kenya and Uganda Railways and Harbours. With further expansion, by 1931 one could even change at Nakuru to go all the way to the Ugandan capital Kampala.

Of the 32,000 men who had achieved the huge feat from Mombasa to Lake Victoria, between them laying over a million sleepers, nearly 2,500 had died during the construction. The majority returned to India, while almost 7,000 decided to stay on, some perhaps still hoping for the land they had been promised. They and their children and grandchildren would become the Indian and Goan community, of which I would be a part when I first came from Zanzibar to Kenya just over 40 years later, travelling along some of the miles and miles of track the Indians had sweated to put down, from Mombasa to Kajiado, to Nairobi, then to join my family in Magadi where my father was the company doctor. Until then, having grown up on the island of Zanzibar I had never seen a real train, and can remember still my first sight of the engine when I arrived in Mombasa in the 1940s: the noise, the clouds of steam puffing from the chimneys, the incredible size and power of the piston rods.

From its inception, Nairobi and its new population were to be divided by the British along racial lines. Governor John Ainsworth, who had arrived as a young man in the early 1900s, split Nairobi into seven districts, making no provision at all for the indigenous Africans. To run the essential services, and for the maintenance of law and order, Indians prepared to stay on were recruited, and for those already in business or looking to start, Kenya was seen as a place of possibilities, somewhere in which despite the harsh landscape and economic uncertainties, one might perhaps settle and make a living, even prosper. Among the Goans who arrived in Nairobi in the early 1900s was Joaquim Antonio Nazareth, from the village of Moira. Joachim's brother Raphael had arrived a few years earlier and started his own bakery, obtaining a six-year contract from the British to supply bread and cakes to the Uganda Railway, for whom he had initially worked as a clerk. The Nazareth brothers worked together in the bakery, later branching out into other business ventures, including a soda water bottling factory and a store on Government Road.

By this time Joachim and his wife, living in a wood and iron house on River Road, had four children. The youngest, born in 1908, John Maximian Nazareth, fell ill one day with typhoid, his young life hanging in the balance. Tended by a European nurse, the child recovered and would go on to study in Bombay and then train as a lawyer at the Inns of Court in London, being Called to the Bar in 1933. This was the man I had already heard so much about and who, in 1952, I had been surprised at being introduced to him by Pio shortly after our first meeting: 'not *the* J.M. Nazareth,' as I put it that day in the Desai Memorial Library. A distinguished lawyer and Queen's Counsel, as I recall Nazareth only took civil cases, often involving charges of defamation. He served as president of the East African Indian Congress from 1950 to 1952, was elected to the Kenya Legislative Council from 1956 to 1960, representing the Western Electoral Area, and was a puisne judge of the Supreme Court in 1953, becoming president of the Kenya Law Society in 1954. He also became President of the Gandhi Memorial Academy Society and Chairman of the Gandhi Smarak Nidhi Trust at the University of Nairobi.

Certain individuals in the Indian business community, with the right connections, were given a head start and the chance to prosper on a larger scale. A.M. Jeevanjee, who had supplied the Imperial British East Africa Company with the thousands of railway workers from India, had made big profits from the contract. The story goes that after arriving at what would become Nairobi he received a further reward when Ainsworth told him he could have an area of land stretching as far as he could run, presumably within a certain time. In the event, Jeevanjee persuaded Ainsworth to let his Pathan servant run on his behalf, and thus gained all the land between what is now Biashara Street and the Jeevanjee Gardens, named after him. Jeevanjee was also given the opportunity to build much of the physical infrastructure of the city including government offices, railways stations, post offices and a wood and corrugated iron police station and jail.

While the British occupied the key positions in these institutions, the clerical and supporting staff continued to comprise mainly Indians, and in the early days all the records were kept in Urdu. In 1902, Jeevanjee started the first newspaper in Kenya, the *African Standard*, published weekly in Mombasa. When he sold it three years later to two British businessmen, it became the *East African Standard*, a daily paper, headquartered from 1910 in Nairobi, and at this time was staunchly pro-colonial in its editorial content. As for Jeevanjee, some people have estimated that at one time he owned half of Mombasa, and even more of Nairobi. In 1910 he was elected to Kenya's Legislative Council, becoming the first non-white to do so.

Kenya's National Museum, then named the Coryndon after a former governor, had been somewhat ahead of the times when in 1941 it opened its doors to all races thanks to its new curator Canon Leakey. Others had objected to the move, claiming Africans were 'smelly' and

Asians 'over-scented'. Lady Delamere allegedly remarked that 'to be within measurable distance of an Indian coolie is very disagreeable.' Canon Leakey no doubt saw the irony of this, as the museum's forerunner had been established in 1911 with a donation from an Ismaili from India, Alidina Visram, who in 1863 at the age of 12 had sailed to Zanzibar and thence to Africa.

Another Asian who had become a fixture in the community was Rosendo Ribeiro, a Goan who had initially practised medicine in Ponda, before sailing to Mombasa in 1898. The coastal region being plagued by malaria, Dr Ribeiro had followed the 'iron snake' of the railway to Nairobi and lived for two years in a tent, compounding medicines with his assistant C. Pinto and, rather like my father later on, settled for payment in kind, often in the form of chickens. Eventually the government gave him some land near the station and he built a dak bungalow, establishing his reputation as the first doctor in Nairobi. Alongside his medical practice he opened a pharmacy in Victoria Street called R.Ayres and Co., patenting his own anti-malaria tablets.

In 1908 Dr Ribeiro went to Goa for an extended holiday, where he married Margareta Lourenco, youngest daughter of a successful lawyer. Returning to Nairobi with his bride, Ribeiro had soon started a family. Elegantly attired in a three-piece suit with gold watch chain and homburg hat, the doctor cut a charismatic figure, not least for the zebra he had bought in 1907, tamed himself, and rode regularly around the streets of Nairobi making house calls to his patients. Despite some bizarre and highly apocryphal stories that the doctor displayed the removed parts of circumcised Kikuyu women in his surgery, and that he fed his rose bushes on human blood, he appeared to be prospering, engaging a live-in tailor and nannies to attend to the children and issuing invitations to dances at his home.

When I had first arrived in Kenya in my teens in the 1940s, Dr Ribeiro was in his seventies and still riding his zebra, well known and respected as a former diplomat as well as a doctor, having held the title of Portugal's Vice-Consul in Nairobi from 1914 to 1922. Reputedly the first person to diagnose bubonic plague in Kenya, Rosendo Ribeiro was awarded the OBE. I recall when he invited our family to dinner one evening at his fine house in Victoria Street, he apologised discreetly to us for not using the best cutlery as his wife had locked it away.

Dr Ribeiro on his zebra

From the early 1900s, as Goans married and started families in and around Nairobi, their numbers swelled. With this expansion came the growth of civic institutions and a certain amount of rivalry between the various business and community leaders. Official political status for Goans was confined to representation on the town council, and support for popular local causes and good works could help a candidate gain the one seat available. The Nazareth brothers (father and uncle of J.M. Nazareth), who employed large numbers of people, paid for street lights and other neighbourhood improvements, and in 1911 sponsored a Silver Cup for the Asian football tournaments. One or both Nazareths, Dr Ribeiro and J.M. Campos became regular rivals in the town council elections.

Goan clubs, large and small, proliferated in the early days of Nairobi. These associations fostered communal spirit, but there was also dissent. Elements within the Goan Institute were unashamedly elitist, restricting membership to those in commercial and professional occupations, and in 1905 butlers, cooks and tailors were barred. In 1911 the Institute passed a resolution which declared that 'In every part of the world, the direction of communal, social and political affairs of a nucleus of individuals, of a community, and of a nation is always entrusted to the upper class...' The Goan Institute's first president was the businessman J.M. Campos, but when a newspaper article referred to him as 'President of the Goan community', there were angry letters stating that the Institute represented barely one quarter of Nairobi's 500 Goans. Dr Rosendo Ribeiro had already been voted for as an alternative leader for the excluded majority, and to cater for their needs a broader-based movement, the Goan Union, already active in Bombay, opened a chapter in Nairobi, offering moral and practical support, including assistance with welfare, medical and legal matters. This organisation, open to all occupations, was looked down upon by some of the leading lights of the Goan Institute, notably P.X. de Gama Rose, who allegedly described the Goan Union as a lot of illiterate servants not equipped to engage socially or politically with the educated classes. I believe de Gama Rose had married a European, and talked a lot about his time at Oxford University. More generally, I do remember so-called lower-class Goans really being thought of as dirt, complete outcasts.

The rivalry between the two Goan associations led them in 1911 to clash over which should be the official organiser for the celebrations marking George V's coronation. The eagerness on both sides to participate in the event indicated that East Africa's Goans were in general pro-British and tended to run their clubs on the traditional European model. However, one key difference between the Goan Institute and the Goan Union was that while the former conducted its communications in English, the latter passed resolutions in the vernacular Goan language of Konkani. In the light of this choice of language, and reading their 1911 resolution further, it suggests the Goan Institute members automatically equated the use of English with being educated, and by virtue of identification with the British, with status, '...an educated man is better fitted to judge and appreciate the pros and contras of a question... affecting the interests of the community he belongs to, than an ignorant man.'

In terms of their leadership, the two groups were not completely separate, with Institute member Dr Ribeiro, for example, serving on the committee of the Union, and J.M. Campos, the Institute's first president, working enthusiastically on behalf of the Union. Others were much more polarised in their allegiance, with some like F.X. de Gama Rose of the Institute set on denigrating the Goan Union. At one point J.A. Nazareth wrote a strong letter to the newspaper in Nairobi, objecting to the hostility on both sides and calling for a special conference to try to resolve it. To add to the mix, two more groups arose, the Railway Goan Sports Club, catering for railway employees, and the Nairobi Goan Tailors Society.

While the Goan Institute and the Railway Club interacted with joint events, the Tailors Society, for reasons of caste and class, remained apart. The Goan Institute continued to be exclusive, but at the same time its influence dwindled until the arrival in 1919 of Dr A.C.L de Souza, whom I have mentioned earlier. While the Goan Union all but disappeared from Kenya, Dr de Souza and his wife Mary reinvigorated the Institute to become the main focus of Goan civic affairs in Nairobi, popular with young and old alike, a welcoming club where children and young people could spend countless happy hours playing carom and table tennis, and learning to dance, as I had done in the similar club in Zanzibar.

For my mother, Goa was probably the place she felt most at home. My father too had often talked about returning there. I remember when we lived in Nairobi, how he would sometimes pace up and down at night, talking about going back and restoring the fortunes and proud reputation of the family liquor business, for which our ancestors had won medals and plaudits. I had said at one point that I did not think we should earn money from such a trade.

I had left Goa as a young child, but growing up I was aware of a rich heritage, the Indian and the European, the Hindu and the Christian. On returning to Goa for the first time in 1959, after 30 years, I was surprised at how many things I saw fitted with my memories. I found the caste system was very strong. I remember when I arrived all these fellows of the lower caste came to see me, about 30 or 40 of them. My mother said we were supposed to give them some food and liquor, so we made some toasted grams and they all ate and drank feni and sang praises to me. Hearing all this I decided to make a speech, which I had been thinking about for a long time. 'Listen,' I told them, 'all this caste system is rubbish; we are no more bhatkars than you are mundkars.' Bhatkar meant landlord, and mundkars were originally people with no property rights, whose houses could be pulled down and the materials taken by the landowner. After Indian independence the law had changed so that if you had lived somewhere for three years you could buy the land and house, which was right I think.

After I had made the speech, the fellows cheered me. Noticing they were all still standing, I said, 'You must all sit down with us,' and told my mother to have chairs brought out. Not one of them would sit. I said, 'Look, I'm telling you, you've got to sit down we are all equal.' 'Yes, thank you,' they replied, 'but we cannot sit, our fathers would object.' I said, 'Your fathers are not here.' But they told me it would also bring a curse: that I was after all more than a landlord and an employer – I was their bhatkar: their philosopher, their guide.

What makes a Goan? Being born and bred in Goa was always the natural and obvious qualification. I mentioned earlier however that many, perhaps most Goans, considered themselves to be Portuguese rather than Indian, Christian rather than Hindu. I sometimes used to ask such people, 'Who made you Portuguese?' to which they replied, 'The law.' There was some truth in this, and it may have been Salazar that allowed the Christians access to better schools and other advantages, prompting Goan families to convert.

Further back in history, Christianity and the Portuguese identity was also spread by soldiers sent out to bolster Goa's military strength. In the days before the Suez Canal, the voyage from Portugal might take several months via the Cape of Good Hope. When the young soldiers arrived and saw the young local girls swimming, friendships and often romance would blossom. When the Portuguese Governor of Goa got to hear of this, he decreed that any soldier seen talking to one of the girls be arrested and taken with her to the nearest church, where she would then have to convert to Christianity and the two of them be married.

The Governor further advised his superiors in Lisbon that over time this policy would swell the Goan population that was loyal to Portugal, and provide a stream of like-minded, willing administrators and civil servants. The Portuguese Government, in a quite Machiavellian way, urged him to continue winning over the indigenous population with similar enticements, such as land and other rewards. The impact on Goa was thus two-fold, expanding the influence of the Catholic Church and the imperial power of Portugal.

Many Goans of course also went to Bombay to work for the British. Alongside them were locals referred to as East Indians, which for a long time I couldn't understand, Bombay being on the west coast. The name in fact related to their employers, the British East India Company. These East Indians, who had been given chunks of land around Bombay by the British and were often quite rich, considered themselves very superior to Goans. We had this hierarchy in Bombay at that time: first were the British, who were considered aristocrats, regarding those who consorted too much with the locals as second-class citizens. The offspring of those who assimilated biologically were called Anglo-Indians, and in time this became more acceptable. Below the Anglos were the East Indians, then the Christian Indians such as Goans, and lastly the non-Christian Indians.

With assimilation the number of Anglo-Indians grew. Having held steady jobs in administration or on the railways, when independence came in 1947, considering themselves British, they left in droves for Britain, expecting to find similar positions there. Few however were offered work, and many eventually found their way to Australia. It was very sad for them, because even if dark as charcoal they invariably talked of being British. They were also quite anti-Indian. An Anglo-Indian woman I met in London told me that when she fell in love with a Goan boy her mother threatened to disown her. As a result she had married a man 30 years older than herself and had a miserable life.

Like the majority of Indian couples, my parents too of course had entered an arranged marriage, but they had been of a more similar age and had enjoyed a happy relationship. As a young man, however, my father had been very much in love with another girl and they had meant a lot to each other and wanted to marry. It must have been very painful for both of them when he had to give her up because of social pressures.

Goans lived and settled in other parts of Africa too. One of my father's brothers, my Uncle Joobhoi, became a Catholic priest and was sent by the church to Mozambique, which like Goa was a Portuguese colony in those days. Then, when he saw how unfairly the Portuguese authorities and the priesthood were treating the local population, especially the mixed-race people of Mozambique, he left the church and started a political newspaper, attacking Portuguese rule. It wasn't long before they arrested him. He was obviously a very strong-willed man and he took a lot of risks, someone whom they would call today a freedom fighter. A lot of Goans, however, wanted to go and settle in Mozambique and they must have thought my uncle was mad for supporting these people as he did, and I believe he became something of an outcast among the Goan community because of it. There were to be similar attitudes towards myself among some of the Kenyan Asians during the independence struggle.

In October 2015, my wife Romola and I were invited to a very interesting talk at the Kenya High Commission in London. The speaker was Sharad Rao, born in Nairobi in 1936 and now Chairman of the Kenya Judges and Magistrates Vetting Board. The subject of the talk was 'Kenya Then and Now – Asians' Contribution to the Politics and Development of Kenya'. Sharad had been Called to the Bar at Lincoln's Inn a few years after me, in 1959. Back in Kenya, still under British rule, as Sharad observed, 'The big law firms were all European… and it was their stated policy not to accept Asian or African lawyers, even for articles.' He also reminded us that racial segregation was enforced not only in transport, housing, jobs, public toilet facilities, etc., but also in vital services like hospitals. I was to experience this at first-hand in pre-independence days, when I had an accident in my car.

In 2015, the number of Asians remaining in Kenya was I believe fewer than 80,000, under 0.2 percent of the country's 47 million or so inhabitants. Furthermore, Kenya's civil service, once an Indian preserve, is I understand now staffed almost entirely by Africans. Yet Asians, who opened up many of the most isolated parts of the country, bringing infrastructure, services and development, remain an indelible part of the country's history, and despite the Africanisation programme, a number of those who took Kenyan citizenship after 1968 went on to high achievement in the law, police and civil service. The Asian community's philanthropic work in Kenya, past and present, includes the Platinum Jubilee Hospital built in 1958, now known as the Aga Khan Hospital, the M.P. Shah Hospital in Nairobi, and in Mombasa the Pandya Memorial Hospital. In addition, Asian charitable foundations help with food and education for those in need. I feel proud to have been one of the many involved in these efforts. Sharad pointed out that the Kenyan Lions Club flourished among the Asian community, largely because the Rotary Clubs and Masonic Lodges had excluded them. The Lions have done good work for charity, notably the Eye Hospital treating cataracts, and the Jaipur Foot Hospital providing many thousands of free artificial limbs.

Today, the numerous philanthropic programmes supported or set up by Kenyan Asians benefit largely the African population. Among the most prominent of such institutions is Nairobi University, and it is here that you can see a tribute to possibly the most important Asian contribution to the development of East Africa. Standing on the second floor of one of the campus buildings, it is a bronze statue of a man wearing a simple dhoti and walking with staff in hand. It is Mahatma Gandhi, whose political theories and example were the inspiration for so many who fought for a fairer world. In the days before television or computers, however, knowledge and ideas could only be spread by word of mouth, or for those fortunate enough to have learned to read – the 'white man's magic' as Kenyatta described it – through books.

An Indian man, Ambu Patel, played a significant part in bringing important written works to the people of East Africa. Arriving first in 1955 aged 26, Ambu had trained in India and London as a bookbinder and later set up his own company in Nairobi producing and selling books, including titles on Gandhi. Fiercely critical of colonialism, he wrote articles for the press, formed the 'Release Jomo' committee, and employed and looked after Kenyatta's daughter Margaret when her father was in detention. Ambu gave Kenyatta the leather jacket that became a trademark look for the leader, and I recall something else, a series of photographs he had taken of Kenyatta over some time, which he had compiled into an album as a tribute to his achievements and shown to him around the time of independence. One day, some friends and I found Ambu in a state of great agitation because he could not locate the photographs; it seemed they had either gone astray or there had been some misunderstanding and they had been assumed to be a gift. Ambu had probably planned to use the photographs in a biography of Kenyatta and had no negatives or copies. In 1963, Ambu did publish his book, entitled *The Struggle for the Release of Jomo and his Colleagues*. Ambu Patel was also a great devotee of Mahatma Gandhi, and thanks to publishers and booksellers, many more people were able to learn about Gandhi's life and ideas and to pass that invaluable knowledge to their children, as my father did.

Chapter Eight

The Fight for Justice and a Dramatic Turn of Events in Kenya in Late 1952

My career as a lawyer was to begin at Madan and Shah Advocates, on the first floor of Badru House above two shops on Government Road, Nairobi. The renowned J. M. Nazareth, who had become a QC early on in his career and might reasonably be called the most successful lawyer in East Africa, whom I had first met with Pio, was a senior partner. Later on I would often go to ask his opinion on a particular case, though I would not always agree with his answer and sometimes he would then concede. I was particularly lucky, as my table and chair were in a room shared with Satish Gautama. Apart from being one of the ablest lawyers I have ever met, Satish was the most affectionate and friendly person, destined to be a lifelong friend, and with his wife Sushila, a tower of strength, coming to my assistance whenever I needed it most.

Madan and Shah had paid a predecessor, a Sikh pupil called G.S. Sandhu, 1,000 shillings a month, but I was offered nothing. Later I found out that this was Nazareth's decision, on the premise that articled clerks in England frequently paid their first employer in order to gain experience. I was very upset about it but I suppose Nazareth must have thought I had family money.

A fellow associate, Hirabhai Patel, was in a similar position. His father had started a business hiring out bicycles, and for several months the family were kind enough to give me lunch every day at their home in an area of Nairobi near Grogan Road. Many years earlier Colonel Grogan had wanted to marry a lovely girl called Gertrude.

Her mother, sceptical of his character, was alleged to have asked him, 'Have you done anything spectacular?' Keen to impress, he pledged to walk the length of Africa from Cape Town to Cairo. The journey, some of which he understandably cheated on by taking trains, as well as boats along the Nile, took him several months. He also bought a neglected stretch of mosquito-ridden land in Nairobi from the government for peanuts, built houses, and after obtaining permission to sell them to Indians, made a lot of money on the deal. This was now Grogan Road. I would one day meet the elderly Colonel Grogan, an amiable soul, but obviously a tenacious character in his prime.

Most evenings from 5pm I would join Pio and others in the national movement at the Desai Memorial Library. The Library and attached Memorial Hall had a political and historical significance, having been created by a trust under Dr A.C.L. de Souza (no relation of mine), a staunch nationalist and fighter for freedom and equality in Kenya. A Goan, his wife also a doctor, de Souza was founder and editor behind the *Colonial Times*, the paper officially owned for many years by G.L. Vidyarthi. Many Indian associations were like this, fronted by very rich men, while behind the scenes it was the younger people who really ran them. The Indian movement in Kenya was for many years led publicly by the Jeevanjee brothers and the Virjee family, while all their speeches in the Indian National Congress were written by a young law clerk named M.A. Desai, who was the backbone of the movement. Desai went from town to town preaching to the Indians to wake up, fight for equality and join hands with the Africans, very much like what Pinto was now doing. Being a Gujarati I suppose Desai could understand them and campaigned amongst them for many years. Sadly in 1926 he died, I believe of blackwater fever, and was either cremated in Nairobi, or his ashes were taken there. A.C.L. de Souza, who had been a great friend, collected a vast amount of money and erected the Desai Memorial Library and Hall on Victoria Street, Nairobi. This magnificent building with its beautiful Greek pillars was intended as a permanent monument to a man of great principle who had devoted his life to the cause of social justice.

When I arrived back in Kenya in 1952, however, the committee set up by A.C.L. de Souza to keep Desai's spirit and work alive had not met for several years and the library had fallen into neglect. I decided to do something about it and set about trying to tidy and organise the books. It proved quite a task. Then one day Pio told me of two young people who had been expelled from Makerere University for leading a strike about the quality of the food there and asked if I could find them a job. Josephat Karanja and Isaac Omolo Okero thus came and helped bring the Desai Memorial Library to life again, working under me for 180 shillings a month each. Salaries regrettably being then based on race, this was a generous sum for an African. The two of them did a good job, creating an inventory of all the books and reorganising the allocation system. When Indian scholarships became available I went to see Apa Pant, the first Indian Commissioner to Kenya, who had started a scholarship scheme, and requested that both young men be sent to India to study Librarianship, and was delighted when they were accepted. Josephat would eventually rise to be the fifth Vice-President of Kenya, and Isaac the Chairman of Kenya Airways.

Apa Pant was also very supportive of our work in the national movement, inviting 20 to 40 Africans and others to his house for big dinner parties, often twice a week. After a good meal we would all sit in the lounge on chairs or the floor and he would invite discussion on the political situation. We were really interested in awakening people to the necessity of Indian and African cooperation, and of course that of the more enlightened and progressive Europeans if we could. I don't know if the government knew what we were discussing, but it was all quite open with no subterfuge or underground activity involved. There was probably little the authorities could do about it, given Apa Pant's status. A barrister, he had studied at Oxford, played polo and was Prince of the small Indian state of Aundh, so knew lots of Europeans in the highest places, some probably at university with him. He was a fantastic person, getting on equally well with the English dukes, lords and knights – several of whom had acquired, or to be more accurate, appropriated, large swathes of land in Kenya – and the poorest of the poor. Most Fridays we would also be given lunch at his house, and together weigh up the political events of the week.

Apa Pant's one great quality above all was that he was a very eloquent speaker. He was also a very affectionate, determined and idealistic person who wanted to work for the principles of non-violence and independence for all countries and believed fervently in the equality of all races, irrespective of colour or creed. One of his key contributions in East Africa was to form a very efficient office in India House, where the High Commission was based, with excellent, committed staff. Two people in particular, whom he recruited in their youth, were John Kiereini, who would later become Chief Secretary of the Kenyan Government, and John Kamau, who led the national movement within the churches. Both men were in my view an influence for good on the civil service and the religious organisations respectively, leading the moderates within these spheres towards the goals of independence and equality in Kenya. This side of Apa Pant has often been forgotten, that he was not only a great orator who could inspire an audience, but also a skilful bureaucrat, able to organise liaison with governments in India and elsewhere and pull strings where necessary to steer Kenya's Indian community into constructive and peaceful political action.

Apa Pant's assistant to begin with was Raja Rameshwar Rao, also a Raja but much more moderate and, I thought at the time, more interested in good living than serious politics. Rao was succeeded by Ishi Rehman, a Muslim, Oxford graduate and barrister, a friend of Nehru, and whose father I believe was Prime Minister of Hyderabad, and his two brothers high-ranking officers in the Pakistani Army. Ishi was a staunch nationalist and gave great support; in fact he was even more left wing and aggressive than Apa Pant. Ishi held his own house parties where his wife, being half Russian, half Indonesian, was probably fiercer in her condemnation of racialism and the colour bar than anyone. For months on end, every night she cooked grand Indonesian dinners for us all and anyone could walk into her home and be made welcome. About three-quarters of the guests were Africans, some of them probably police informers; but lots of liquor was served as the discussions got under way. I often wondered how many thousands of pounds they spent on those marvellous evenings. I was told that Mrs Rehman was a millionaire in her own right and that her husband was rich too.

Apa Pant (second from left) and his wife Nalini. Apa Pant was Indian Commissioner to Kenya and also Prince of a state called Aundh in India

Someone else who would help us was J.M. Desai, an agent for National Mutual Life Insurance Association of Australasia, which had branches all over Kenya and was the owner of Kettles, Roy and Wilson. Like the Rehman's, his money was a blessing, enabling us in particular to get around to meetings, as the few of us who did own a car could rarely afford the petrol. J.M. Desai would entertain or accommodate anyone at our request, amongst them political people from England including later on Fenner Brockway, Labour MP for Eton and Slough at the time and one of the founders of the Congress of Peoples against Imperialism, and Leslie Hale, Labour Party MP for Oldham also involved in the anti-colonial movement. Both were later to be made peers of the realm and join the House of Lords. For this hospitality Desai incurred the wrath of the government and was exposed to great risks, his courage and generosity motivated by his determination to fight racialism in Kenya. As one of the very few Indians with money who were willing to come forward, he played a very important part in the movement in those days.

That spring of 1952 I had returned from England an idealist, determined to fight for equality for all Kenyans, for the rights of the underdog and the underprivileged, to oppose colonialism and bring about socialism, fairness and independence for the country. Nothing would shake my commitment to these aims and I was prepared to sacrifice whatever might be necessary to pursue them, and though not a pacifist, to do so as far as humanly possible through non-violent means. My own contribution might be small but I was very intent on making it. Others had been leading the way, and in the forefront was Pio. His charm, warmth and affection, tremendous sense of humour and willingness to share whatever he had, to engage on the same level with people regardless of race, colour or religion was an object lesson to us all.

Alongside J.M. Nazareth, a number of other politically aware Indians would play a valuable part in the struggle for freedom and equality in Kenya. My good friend

Chanan Singh started out as a junior workshop fitter with the railways, studied at night to obtain a politics and economics degree and became a barrister via correspondence course, all without leaving Kenya. In India it was very unusual for a manual worker to become a doctor or lawyer, but Chanan Singh was extremely intelligent and far-sighted, his achievement particularly impressive in that he came from a community more interested in repairing cars than getting involved in politics.

Another of my good friends at the time was K.D. Trivedi who, after working for many years in the Attorney General's office, retired at 55 and trained as a lawyer in England where we were fellow students, our 40-year difference in age no obstacle to establishing a firm friendship, which we kept up in Kenya. R.B. Bhandari, who I think started life as a railway guard, came from a very respectable family and was brought up by his mother in difficult circumstances after his father died young. Another very affectionate, warm-hearted, loving person, Bhandari was highly intelligent, very very modest and one of the nicest people I have ever met in my life. K.P. Shah was a young Gujarati who sold clothes for his living. From a little shop and a handful of shirts, who would have foreseen that one day he would be a millionaire. Neither must we forget the very eloquent lawyer and brilliant Sanskrit scholar Arvind Jamidar, or Haroon Ahmed, philosopher, Urdu singer and poet, who, beneath his love of the good life, was a serious and determined person.

These were a few of the 25 or so intelligent, mostly younger Indians who from the early 1950s onwards formed the Kenya League, its key objective to motivate and, importantly, unite the Indian community. The British had been trying to do the opposite, offering five Indian seats in the Kenyan Parliament, two of them designated for Muslims, three for non-Muslims, a proposal more or less accepted by the Indian leadership of Chunilal Madan and A.B. Patel. Others of us resisted as we believed that once religion became a criterion of politics, not only would it be divisive, but also sow the seeds of future conflict between Muslims and Indians, the latter usually referring to Hindus.

The Kenya League's mentor was really D.K. Sharda, to whom I referred earlier, a former schoolteacher who lived very modestly and started a weekly newspaper with J.M. Nazareth called *The Tribune*, with Sharda the editor and Nazareth contributing regular and very interesting articles. Weekly meetings were held in a large boardroom with 30 to 40 chairs and a few tables, at the offices of the East African Indian Congress. From about 5pm until 9pm, over tea and bhajias bought from our one shilling per head kitty from the Green Hotel, we would thrash out how the organisational and financial strength of the Indian community could best unite with the numerical superiority, growing awareness and ferocity of the Africans. We believed passionately that such a combined force would be impossible to hold back and that when it happened, social and political equality would inevitably follow.

The Kenya League was our main platform for addressing meetings of the Indian associations. These existed in almost every town across Kenya. For a small nominal subscription of one or two shillings, Indians could attend meetings, elect a committee and choose delegates to send to the Indian Congress within Kenya. This Congress was to a certain extent modelled on its Indian counterpart and I would not be surprised if those who formed it in 1914 had in mind that it would receive support and patronage from that quarter; certainly the leaders in Kenya regularly appealed to Congress in India, which had on occasion sent some very prominent people to advise, lead and represent the Indian community and Congress in discussions with the Colonial Office in Kenya, as well as the British Government in London. Among these leaders were H.N. Kunzru, Sir Maharaj Singh and Sarojini Naidu, for a while Mahatma Gandhi's private secretary and known as the 'Nightingale of India' for her eloquent speeches. Sarojini was witty too, once remarking on an army of cleaners toiling to prepare a railway station for her employer's arrival, 'See how much it costs to keep Gandhi poor!'

We set about joining the various local Indian associations, trying where possible to infiltrate their executive committees and take them over. In Kisumu, thought to be very strongly on the side of the younger generation, we succeeded, as we did in Nakuru, up to a point. In hotly contested elections there was often an agreement to share seats according to the number of people present. In most of the associations the younger element tended to make up a quarter or a third of the executive committee.

The most backward as far as we were concerned was Mombasa, being strongly controlled by A.B. Patel, then the undoubted leader of the Indian community. Patel was a lawyer who had been brought over from India by J.B. Pandya, head of the Chamber of Commerce and basically a shopkeeper. The shop-keeping class in East Africa was the most moderate, conservative, reactionary, call it what you will. They believed in making all the right noises and passing resolutions, but believed much more in making money. They gave small sums to the movement, as little as they could get away with, their underlying view being that the less politics you did, the better. When it came to the crunch they certainly didn't want to sacrifice anything, particularly their profit margins. To them we were the starry-eyed idealists, extremists or communists – often labelled 'fellow travellers' – younger Indian intellectuals, doctors, lawyers, business people who had been to college or been part of the National Congress in India, or been involved in the Quit India movement in the 1940s. As far as I knew there were only two actual communists amongst us – Makan Singh and Rao. I had never been a communist and did not believe in dictatorship, but social democracy.

Pio, other friends and myself often went for a bite to eat at the Blue Room. Bought from Europeans a couple of years earlier by an Ismaili who had opened it to all races, this restaurant was the only place of its kind in Nairobi that served Indians and Africans. You could get a good chicken biryani for four or five shillings and with nowhere else for us to go, it became a sort of headquarters for all the meetings, gossip and little discussions that we had going on at this time. Most of us would put a shilling or so each into a bag and leave it behind the counter to pay for any African who couldn't afford a meal. Among the regulars was a very affable and friendly fellow who, if we were already seated, would come to our table and say, 'Hello, hello!' shaking our hands warmly, or if he was there when we arrived, we would go to his table and do likewise. He was a very charming person and we liked him very much. His name, already well-known, was Jomo Kenyatta.

Born into the Kikuyu tribe in around 1891, Kenyatta had, in his own words 'learned the white man's magic' of literacy early on. From 1929, when he was sent to Britain by the Kikuyu Central Association to campaign for 'Uhuru' and the return of appropriated tribal land, especially Kikuyu land, he studied at the Quaker college in Birmingham then briefly in the Soviet Union, which at the time supported the African anti-colonial movement. After completing a PhD in social anthropology at the LSE, he had returned to Kenya in 1946, becoming Principal of the Kenya Teachers College, urging hard work and honesty while continuing to call for land reform. In 1947 his appointment as President of the Kenya African National Union had drawn death threats from white settlers.

The land issue was, like the colour bar, a fundamental injustice. English aristocrats had been known to come out to Kenya, point to a pair of distant hills and demand that their lawyers draw up title deeds in their name for the thousands of square acres that lay between the two points. Much of this land already belonged to the Kikuyu people, who had no concept of written ownership. They also believed that their souls and those of their ancestors resided in the trees. Once the land was stolen, those souls were imprisoned in the trees and freeing them again could only come about by freeing the trees. The Europeans did not seem aware of this concept, which to them probably sounded nonsense but to the Kikuyu was sacred. The land itself was important too of course, even if it was sometimes poorly managed, though this was a matter of opinion and really no one else's business. Our fervent hope in the nationalist movement was that the trees and the land could be restored to their rightful owners peacefully.

That year of 1952 was the first time I went on an aeroplane. It began with a phone call from Geneva: 'Fitz, this is John Ennals.' My first thought on hearing the name was strawberries. English brothers John, Martin and David Ennals, who had been prominent in the National Union of Students during my time in London, had run the casual employment agency, one summer setting me up with the rather pleasant job picking fruit in Cambridgeshire. John was now Secretary General of the World Federation of United Nations Associations in Geneva and somehow had tracked me down to the offices of Madan and Shah, Nairobi. He was presently involved in a forthcoming conference on education being held in Mogadishu and wanted to know if I could organise a delegation from Kenya. I said I felt honoured to be invited, but having not been back in Kenya long, I did not represent the country as such. At the same time I was not diffident about what ideas I might offer.

John promptly appointed me as one of the representatives, and with J.M. Nazareth as President and myself as Secretary, we formed our own United Nations Association in Kenya. Joining us at the conference was a friend who was then Education Minister in Zanzibar. The UN chartered and paid for a plane and after a five and a half hour flight in a small plane from Nairobi we touched down in Mogadishu. With no meal on board, I was faint with airsickness and hunger but after some sustenance felt eager to engage with the conference. At the end of the Second World War Somalia had been made a trusteeship territory of the UN with the aim of independence within ten years. With all eyes on that outcome there were obvious parallels, and some notable contrasts, with the situation in Kenya, and politics inevitably entered our discussions. In fact we took the opportunity to deliver some very strong speeches against racialism in East Africa, and Kenya in particular, to impress upon people the negative effects of colonialism and how a majority of the population was exploited and humiliated by the British.

John Ennals was very happy with our forthright criticism and there was a lot of support from several members of Italy's Parliament and some well-placed Americans. We used the conference wherever we could as a platform to highlight the political challenges in East Africa, and met quite a few important Somali leaders in the Youth League, which would prove useful later, among them being Abdirashid Ali Shermarke who would one day become President of Somalia as well as a good friend.

After a most interesting week we flew back to Kenya where I resumed the daily routine at Madan and Shah, marking time towards the end of my pupillage. In the evenings I would meet Pio and the others at the Desai Memorial Library or Kiburi House and perhaps go on to the Blue Room, still one of the very few places we could have a meal, talk and relax. Elsewhere in Nairobi the colour bar was as rigid as ever, with the poor Africans confined to the most basic establishments, offering little more than ugali, a thin vegetable gruel scooped up with morsels of bread, and a scrap of meat as a very rare treat.

One evening, accompanied by my friends Abdul Bhaijee and Pio Pinto, I had gone to see someone off at the airport at Eastleigh. On the way back we felt very hungry and as all the Indian eating-places were by this hour closed, we entered an establishment on Government Road owned by an Italian called Bruno Fiori. A waiter came over immediately and told us he could not serve us. Though there were a lot of Europeans drinking in the bar, most of the tables were empty. 'Why?' we asked, gesturing to the tables. Because, came the expected reply, the restaurant was 'Europeans only'.

The owner Mr Fiori then came out and told us in no uncertain terms we must leave. As we tried to reason with him, there was a screech of brakes and three police cars pulled up outside. We realised he must have called them the minute he saw us come in. The officer in charge asked brusquely what we thought we were doing. We replied that we simply wanted something to eat, did not wish to cause trouble, and saw no reason to leave. He then said that he was arresting us.

Kingsway Police Station was only five minutes walk away. The officer informed us that he was taking us down to the cells for the night and would discuss things in the morning. As we were entering the rather full cell, I told him to think very carefully: if he held us in custody he would be paying half his salary in compensation to us for several years to come, because we would sue him personally for wrongful arrest. 'What, are you a lawyer?' he asked. 'Yes,' I replied, 'in fact I am a barrister.' He looked surprised. 'Oh – I didn't know there were any Indian barristers.' I told him, 'Yes, there are a few of us now, and we will fight you, and racialism all the way.' Reluctantly he released us. Later he would admit to me that he had already been sued after arresting some Jews when in Palestine, a mistake that had cost him dear.

Abdul, Pio and I headed straight back to the restaurant. 'You again!' exclaimed Mr Fiori, and promptly rang the police who once more arrived in several cars with the same officer in charge. Seeing us, he told Mr Fiori that we would have to be served. What happened next, either to make a point, to avoid upsetting the Europeans in the bar, or perhaps both, was that a table and chairs were placed outside, in the centre of the road, at which we were invited to sit. The only light was from nearby shops, and passing cars were screeching their brakes as they almost ran into the table. Unwilling to sit in the road when there were perfectly good empty tables inside, or risk being run over, we decided to call it a night and go home, but not before telling Mr Fiori we would be coming back the next day. He insisted he would not serve black people and would close his restaurant if necessary.

The next day we began to organise. A group of Asians and Africans, along with a handful of Europeans who had been involved in the East African Students Union in London, were assembled. Soon we were over 30 in all, and in the evening we met at Abdul's father's shop, F.M. Bhaijee Hardware. Seeing a few people had brought firearms with them, I requested that they leave these weapons in Mr Bhaijee's safe. But though not looking for trouble, we did need to look as though we meant business, so several of us had taken the precaution of arming ourselves with stout sticks. I myself had a 'rungu', a wooden club. We then proceeded to make our way to the restaurant.

Having sent a message in advance to the waiters that they should welcome us and if necessary support us in a fight, with as little violence as possible, they greeted us nervously. Mr Fiori glared. 'Yesterday,' I said, 'we were three, and you and your customers were 30, now there are 30 of us. We only want to eat, but if you want a fight, we are prepared. I have a big stick, and your head will be the first.'

Fiori was furious, not knowing what to do, but he could see we were determined, and after the previous night he knew the police were reluctant to intervene. At last he shouted, 'Very well, very well!' and waving his arms at his waiters ordered, 'Bring out the food, bring out the food.' With Fiori grimacing and muttering to himself in the background, we ate a good meal, drank only water and left a generous tip. As we got up to leave, the waiters cheered, 'Hooray for Mr. de Souza!'

Yet I could not have made this first chink in the hitherto impenetrable armour of the colour bar without the help of my brave companions. And we weren't giving up there. After that we went to two other restaurants and deployed the same strategy. After similar stiff opposition, hostile looks and some insulting remarks about 'bloody

Indians,' we were eventually served again. Some English people were very supportive, notably Peter Wright, a young teacher who campaigned proactively against the colour bar and would later be deported as a result, and Humphrey Claydon, manager of the East African Standard Bookshop in Nairobi. The English couple that ran the Halcyon restaurant gave us a positively warm welcome and expressed their approval of our campaign. We were determined it should remain peaceful. An Englishman called Miller came along to a meeting with a cry of 'Kill all the Europeans.' I knew the man slightly, enough to know he was the last person to do anyone physical harm. Had he suddenly gone mad? I then suspected he was a police informer or agent provocateur. It turned out to be true, and Miller was a member and office bearer of the European only Electors Union, which supported the racial divide.

The newspapers were not friendly towards us. Kenya's *Sunday Post* carried an alarmist story about 'a gang of Asian youths terrorising poor European restaurant owners, and the police... doing nothing about it.' Elsewhere, the real thugs were preparing to strike, and events in Kenya were about to take a dramatic turn. On the 3rd of October 1952, near to her home, a European woman was stabbed to death. The Mau Mau, the shadowy African organisation, membership of which had been declared illegal by the British since August 1950, was thought to be responsible. This time, however, they had claimed what was believed to be their first white victim. Six days later, Senior Chief Waruhiu, a loyal supporter of British colonial rule, was shot dead in his car in broad daylight.

The atmosphere in Nairobi was tense and no one knew what would happen next. We in the movement then received a message from the Indian Government saying they had heard from the High Commission in London that Kenyatta was about to be arrested. They said they would be willing to smuggle him to India if it could be arranged. The Emperor Haille Selassie of Ethiopia had also offered to send troops and bring him out discreetly. Forming a delegation, we went in haste to Lokitaung to warn Kenyatta, and asked if he might take up the offer of sanctuary from India. His reply was no, he wanted to be with his people, he was not going to run away. I thought this was very courageous, and a good stand.

The intelligence from India was not ill-founded. On the 20th of October, a few days after the killing of Chief Waruhiu, the newly appointed Governor Evelyn Baring ordered a state of emergency to be imposed throughout the country. On the streets of Nairobi troops and police were raiding houses and hauling people out. Hearing the commotion, I locked and bolted my door just before they passed by, banging on the wood so hard I thought it would splinter. Within 24 hours over 183 people had been rounded up. Among them were Bildad Kaggia, K'ungu Karumba, Fred Kubai, Paul Ngei, Achieng Oneko and the President of the Kenya African Union (KAU) Jomo Kenyatta. On the 17th and 18th of November all six were taken to Kapenguria and formally arrested and charged with membership and management of the Mau Mau.

After Kenyatta's arrest we simply didn't know what to do. I was surprised that having expected this, he hadn't nominated anyone to take over from him. There was the sense of being in a vacuum. Pio, who was not a member of KAU, called us together in the back room of the Garden Hotel. Although this was an Indian establishment, any gathering of more than four people was deemed by the authorities to be a political meeting, and, concerned that we were under surveillance and any one of us might be apprehended at any moment, we entered discreetly via a small alleyway. From a list of KAU members Pio proposed Walter Odede M.L.C. to be Chairman, Muinga Chokwe acting Secretary, W.W. Awori M.L.C. acting Treasurer, and a few other nominations. Fearing Chokwe would almost certainly be on the wanted list, we also advised him to go into hiding, but like Kenyatta, he refused.

Meanwhile, developments in Kenya had attracted international attention. Within weeks of the emergency being declared it was reported that senior British statesman Fenner Brockway, the eminent anti-colonialist, and Labour MP Leslie Hale were flying out to see for themselves what was going on. On the day the plane was due to land in Nairobi, Chokwe was eager to welcome the two Englishmen. Despite a warrant having now been issued for him, he joined the small crowd gathered at the airport, where he was spotted by the police and arrested.

At our next meeting, it was agreed that a new acting secretary for KAU must be someone not known to the authorities, but who? Then Pio said decisively, 'I have just the man for you my friends – Joseph Anthony Zuzarte.' This was the handsome and amiable young man I had met at the bus stop with Pio shortly after arriving back in Kenya, the 'honorary Goan' who worked for Morris Motors, and who had incidentally been very helpful in obtaining spares for my car. Joe stood up and said, 'I'm quite happy to help.' There was, however, a snag which someone quickly pointed out: 'How can you have an acting Secretary for the Kenyan African Union with the name Zuzarte?' This was not a criticism of Joe, but how he might be perceived as a plant to split the African and Asian support. Joe had an idea though, 'Look, don't worry – if it's a problem, my grandfather, my mother's father, was named after a place in the Maasai lands – Murumbi.' We agreed that using this name would help reassure the Africans they were being quite well represented, and so Joseph Zuzarte became Joseph Murumbi.

The most pressing concern now was to help Kenyatta and the others under arrest. I mentioned that in England I had got to know the left-wing QC Dennis Pritt very well and that we could contact him to come and assist. In the interim though, we urgently needed a defence lawyer on the ground. Although qualified as a barrister in England, I could not practise in Kenya until I had been back in the country a full year, but said that Chunilal Madan, of Madan and Shah, a Member of Parliament and a very good lawyer, would be the right person. This was readily approved and I agreed to make the approach, but said I would like someone to go with me. When asked who, I replied without hesitation, 'I'll take my friend Joe Murumbi!'

Joe and I made our way to the Macmillan Memorial Hall where the National Legislative Assembly was in session. The building was surrounded by a high barbed wire fence about 15 feet from the outer walls, and as we were not permitted inside, we asked an official to take a message to Madan. When he appeared I said, 'Mr Madan we have an important task for you, and we would be very happy if you would accept our request to be the lawyer for Kenyatta.'

Madan agreed, and shortly after we received word from Denis Pritt that he would come from England and lead the defence. To support him, a multiracial team comprising an Indian friend of Nehru called Chaman Lall, the Nigerian H.O. Davies, and for the Kenyans, Jaswant Singh, A.R. Kapila and myself, was put together. The trial was to take place not in Nairobi, but Kapenguria, a remote town in the Rift Valley clearly chosen for its inaccessibility and to make it difficult for us to attend there regularly.

Kapenguria was a banned area, requiring a special pass from the District Commissioner to enter. Of greater concern was a notice that had appeared in the official Gazette at the same time as the arrests, announcing the appointment of Ransley Samuel Thacker QC as Acting Resident Magistrate to the Northern Province, indicating that he had been chosen as the trial judge. Thacker was a very arrogant man and difficult to work with. In court he would shout and make racist remarks, which people could get away with in those days. These extreme attitudes were thought to be why the Colonial Office had never approved his appointment as Chief Justice. But now the Government's desire to secure a conviction against Kenyatta made him a favoured choice, giving him the chance of a brief but possibly momentous comeback. It was discovered later that before agreeing to take the job he had asked for considerable emoluments, money, a farm and other gratuities sufficient to make most judges happy, but not Thacker. But whatever the material incentive, we feared that his right-wing views alone would make him quite determined to put Kenyatta in prison. On the 24th of November Thacker arrived at Kapenguria, where the six pleaded not guilty before him and were held in jail. On the 28th of November, A.R. Kapila filed a motion to the Supreme Court for the trial to be held in Nairobi 'or some other convenient place in the Central Province,' charging also that Mr Thacker was prejudiced against Fred Kubai in particular. The motion was refused. The trial date meanwhile had been set for the 3rd of December.

There had been many articles in the press about the arrests, often accompanied by lurid accounts of the Mau Mau atrocities, and in cinemas in England Pathé News gave an impression of Kenyatta as a malevolent force, linking his name directly to the terrible acts of violence. Alongside an article about the case, my photograph had been printed in the Kenya *Sunday Post*. Highlighting the legal battle was good, but publicity could have unforeseen consequences, as I was about to find out. Returning from Kapenguria one evening, I had just parked my car by the Rebellos' house where I was now staying, when I heard someone call my name. Turning, I saw crouching in the back of a truck and beckoning to me furtively, my mother and my sister.

Kenyatta with fellow detainees Fred Kubai and Achieng Oneko

Chaman Lall, Denis Pritt, Achhroo Kapila and myself

Lawyers at the Kapenguria trial including the trial prosecutor, solicitor general, magistrate, H.O. Davies, Chaman Lall and myself

Chaman Lall, Denis Pritt and H.O. Davies at dinner

My father with H.O. Davies and me

Chapter Nine

The Trial of the Kapenguria Six and Operation Anvil

December 1952 to April 1954

Taking my mother and sister into the house, I was told what had happened. They had been in Magadi when my father had been summoned unexpectedly to the office of the General Manager of the Magadi Soda Company. There he was accused of being a traitor, and told that his son was a traitor: 'We have looked after him all these years studying in England,' the General Manager said, 'and see what he does, he goes and defends a murderer and a traitor.' They had seen my photograph in the paper with Kenyatta in Kapenguria. My father had done nothing illegal, nor had I, but he had been dismissed on the spot with no opportunity to explain, no right of appeal. In the eyes of his employers we had sided with the Mau Mau, 'bitten the hand that fed us' and betrayed those who had placed trust in us.

With my father's job, went the house in Magadi and the black box Chevrolet. My family had been forced to pack up their belongings, find someone to drive them and leave immediately. They were now in Nairobi looking around for somewhere to stay, remaining unobtrusive for fear of further reprisal. I was shocked by the turn of events and could imagine how my father must have felt to be thrown out of his job and house in such a shameful manner, given that he had been a Captain in the British Indian Army and proud of his status in the Indian Medical Service. He might have cause to be angry with me, but although I was distressed, I also felt he would understand and not blame me. When we met I was relieved to see that this was so and that his main concern now was finding another job and securing accommodation for the family. My landlord Mr Rebello was Chief of Security at the Nairobi branch of the National Bank of India, but being also involved in the nationalist movement in Goa, was very sympathetic. Mrs Rebello, seeing my concern, did not hesitate in offering to find extra beds for my parents and sister and also to cook for us as long as we wanted to stay.

We were very grateful for the Rebellos' hospitality, which would give my father time to find a medical practice in Nairobi. I hoped to start work myself soon, but it would be another few months before I was officially eligible to join the Nairobi Bar, 12 full months' residency being required. In the meantime, I was busy with the defence team for the arrested nationalists. Since the mass round-up of alleged Mau Mau sympathisers in October I had received letters from many of them asking me to be their lawyer, and was now representing 60 people in detention. I had to convince the police I was being paid for these cases or they would think I was either part of the syndicate or illegally touting for business, so I had forms printed, and at the prison asked the clients to sign my retainer so at least I could say they were giving me a hundred bob or whatever.

There were too many detainees to see all at once, held in different places within Kenya, but I would visit as often as I could, though the journey to Kajiado, the furthest at about 30 miles from Nairobi, was a strain on my old Morris. The camps were makeshift but secure, some constructed among thorny trees to make escape more difficult. Most of the clients I found to be courteous and peaceable, and I was keen to show my presence, letting the police know I had seen these people, lest they be spirited away at night, in other words secretly killed and all knowledge of them denied.

I would obviously have to talk at length with Jomo Kenyatta, and although I had been in his company often in the past, it had usually been in a fairly relaxed, convivial context, among other friends and acquaintances. Now for the first time I would have his undivided attention, and he mine, and I would begin to get to know this extraordinary, enigmatic man. Kenyatta had of course long been in my imagination. When I was still a student he was already a nationalist leader, a well-known figure in England as well as Kenya. Before ever meeting him, I had read something by a doctor that said Kenyatta had a very dominant personality, and, what struck him in particular, was that you could not look directly into his eyes. I thought this was a strange statement from a medical man. I had never experienced this myself with a person; that one looks in their eyes, becomes afraid and has to look down, though I recalled my father saying it about some of the Pashtuns in Afghanistan.

The first day I went to see Kenyatta in Kapenguria I was therefore fascinated, extremely curious, nervous and somewhat in awe as we met. But I looked at him very carefully and tried to look him in the eye, and I must say I was stunned! It was true, I could not do it, and as we sat and talked together my eyes had to either close or turn away for his eyes were the most powerful I had ever seen. It was as if he was seeing straight into you. It was not I think that he wanted to intimidate, but he did so automatically. You felt overwhelmed by the sheer strength and magnetism of his personality.

I also realised, considering the sociable side of him that I had already seen, that he could and did warm up to everybody. He was a fantastic actor. For example, if after making some criticism of someone they should happen to appear, he would be instantly jovial and affectionate towards them, 'Hello, hello, how are you!' and you would stare at him and think, good god is this the same man who said such nasty things about this person just a second ago? There is an assumption that all politicians are made this way, that they have two sides, and separate principles and ideas from personal feelings. A politician, it is said, can like someone enormously as an individual, but in the political arena, because of what that same person represents or the influence they wield, can equally hate them.

Sometimes there is no liking either for the person or their ideas, but there may be a crucial need to have them on one's side, to keep your friends close, and your enemies closer, as the saying goes. Kenyatta was a consummate actor in this respect. I don't think I ever met anyone who was so good at it. He could usually hide his feelings perfectly, except on the occasions he got really angry. Then you felt the immense power of the man. In Kapenguria you immediately sensed there was some distance between him and almost all the other accused, particularly Fred Kubai, Bildad Kaggia and Paul Ngei.

It became clear to us in the defence team that the government was using Kenyatta in an attempt to destroy the national movement. As part of this strategy, communication with detainees was closely controlled. Kapenguria remained a banned area and one day when we visited, Joe Murumbi was hauled out of the car while I was in seeing the clients. On the way back we saw a man sitting by himself in the bush. It was Joe. The police had taken him and left him there, miles from anywhere. It was only by chance that we saw him, or he would have been forced to walk 20 miles to the nearest town Kitale. Alone out here, there was also a real risk of being attacked by wild animals; hyenas, with their powerful jaws and limbs posing a particular danger.

Another time I had some letters that other members of the movement had asked me to take in to Kenyatta, Kaggia and Kubai. I wasn't supposed to do this, so I kept the letters out of sight in my pockets. As I entered, the Court Registrar, an Irishman called Quinn, stopped me. 'Mr de Souza,' he said, 'I am afraid I am going to search you. We have information you are passing notes.' I replied very angrily, 'Do not dare to touch me. If you do, I will walk out of this case now and tell the world that you are not a Registrar but a prisoner of the British Government.' He said quickly, 'No, no don't do that, it will look terrible in the international press, they will accuse the Government of harassment.' I said, 'Yes that is exactly what I intend, because it will be so.' He then let me through and when Kenyatta and I had gone outside into the yard and sat down by the cattle boma to talk I slipped him the letters and said quietly, 'Please for God's sake don't show these to anyone or they will want to know where you got them from.'

The Chief Prosecutor Mr Somerhough, a former fighter pilot, admitted to us privately that it was believed the actual leaders of the Mau Mau were Kubai and Kaggia. This surprised me, as Kaggia was one of the priestly types, with a church following. But why then, we asked, are you trying to prosecute Kenyatta? He replied that this was his instruction, since the whole Kenyan African movement was seen as directly or indirectly part of the terrorist organisation. I understood later how those on the outside, probably because of Kenyatta's effervescent personality and his long campaign for land reform, might have assumed this. People were certainly inspired by him, but if it went further and aroused them to violence, was that his responsibility? It is important here to remember the frightening nature of the Mau Mau, and how any connection to them, however tenuous, could utterly poison a person's reputation. The atrocities themselves were terrifying enough, but alongside the slaughter and intimidation of fellow Africans, the secret rituals, taking the oath while drinking the blood of a cow, a cat or even a human, however exaggerated in the public imagination, opened a deeper dimension, with haunting ideas of 'black magic', dehumanisation and a reversion to centuries-old barbarities.

Kenyatta would tell me many times, 'Fitz, I am not the leader of Mau Mau, I do not believe in violence. I believe you can achieve your goals without violence. But in any political party there are always some who believe you have to go further, you have to fight, and I know who they are – they are my friends, they are in this party, they are with us all the time. But I am not going to do the job for the British Government and expose them and fight against them.' When asked by the British to condemn those who practised violence, he would do so, but only in general terms, never naming names. 'The British would like us [Africans] to fight with each other and make this into a semi-civil war; they killing our supporters and we killing their supporters, and I am not going to allow that at all. I know what I want and they know what they want, our objectives are the same...'

It seemed then that the only disagreement between Kenyatta and those who supported the Mau Mau was the means to those objectives. 'They think I am too mild, and I think they are picking on something that is not necessary and creating too much pain and suffering.'

It was the 3rd of December and proceedings against the Kapenguria Six, as they would come to be known, were about to begin. Approaching the courthouse past armoured cars and roadblocks, as members of the public and journalists were searched for weapons, we entered and took our places. Across the room I saw Denis Pritt. The son of a scrap metal merchant and educated at Westminster School, Pritt had been expelled from the Labour Party in 1940 for his pro-Soviet views. When I once asked, quite politely, if he was a communist he had responded very angrily. Though not a very popular figure in Britain, he had frequently defended workers in compensation cases and was clearly a man of principle. Judge Thacker treated Pritt with a deliberate courtesy and respect in an attempt to convey impartiality. Pritt's line was that the charges against Kenyatta were unsubstantiated and that his client was being made a scapegoat for the recent outbreaks of violence in the country. He would describe the allegations as 'the most childishly weak case made against any man in any important trial in the history of the British Empire.'

As the charges were read out and the arguments and cross-examinations got under way, the atmosphere in the courtroom was often intense, but Kenyatta was not without a sense of humour; when Somerhough, impatient for an answer to a question remarked sardonically, 'We're hanging on your lips,' Kenyatta replied coolly, 'then you're in for a long fall,' which had everyone laughing. The key testimony for the prosecution was that of a young man called Rawson Macharia, who claimed to have taken a Mau Mau oath involving the drinking of human blood in March 1950 under Kenyatta's hands. Kenyatta consistently denied this, and that he had ever supported the Mau Mau, but at the same time he would not denounce others allegedly associated with the movement. The testimony of Macharia and other allegations could be challenged, but something Thacker's clerk confided to me one day during a break in court was worrying; Thacker, he said, was unconcerned about the possibility of a judgment against Kenyatta being overturned even on appeal, since a judge's opinion of a witness's demeanour would always override any deficiencies in the prosecution case, or any other defects, and be accepted even by the Supreme Court.

While the Kapenguria trial dragged on, on 2nd of April 1953 I was admitted to the Nairobi Bar. A clerk at the court had offered me a piece of advice: 'If you practise alone you will starve – Indians are very clannish, and a Patel will go to a Patel.' I understood completely. I was seen not as an Indian but a Goan lawyer, and with few Goan businessmen in Kenya I would struggle with a limited client base. My fellow pupil, Hirabai, also now qualified, actually was a Patel. It was his father who made the suggestion: 'Why don't you two go into partnership? He'll get the clients and you'll both get the fees.' This was a generous offer and Hirabai and I were both enthusiastic about the idea, but we needed premises. Finding a suitable office in a newly erected building called Progressive House above Bohra Road Post Office, we could not, however, find the full rent. I therefore made the landlord, Jamnadas, who was also a friend, an offer, that if he would reduce the rent I would perform, within reason, any legal work that he might require. We all shook hands happily, and thus began the firm of De Souza and Patel.

It was in fact not an Indian or an African, but Chief Justice Sir Hector Hearne, a white Jamaican, who rang up to offer me my first case. It was not a pleasant one. On the 23rd of January that year an incident had taken place in the Rift Valley that had shaken the whole country and stoked even greater fear of indigenous Africans. White farmer Roger Ruck and his pregnant wife Esme, a doctor, had just had dinner when he was summoned outside by one of his elderly African employees, with the report of an attempted theft. Ruck, forgetting the loaded gun he always kept beside him on the table, ran out urgently to investigate and was immediately set upon by a gang with machetes. His wife ran to his assistance only to suffer the same fate. Having dispatched them both, the raiders then entered the house, broke into the locked bedroom of the Rucks's eight-year-old son and killed him too. Some of the workers were also slain. Though not the first of such attacks, this particularly brutal murder of a family had sharply escalated the mood of fear and anger among Europeans. Some 1,500 people marched to see Governor Baring, demanding decisive action. Thirty suspects had been arrested, including the elderly farm employee, and I would be required to defend four of them.

The payment per day was not high by legal standards though more pro rata than my father's salary. Acting for the accused in this case was also likely to make one highly unpopular among most of the European community and moves were even made to bar me. However, even if I had wanted to refuse which I did not, the ethical requirements of my profession required me to accept or risk being struck off by the Law Society. I said I would need accommodation in Nakuru to which Sir Hector agreed and he said it would be paid for. When I made it clear I wanted a reasonable hotel, however, i.e. one normally reserved for Europeans, a Registrar made some disparaging remark along the lines of 'you Indians – thinking you can come here and order us around…" and I was refused. When the trial opened I didn't go in. Sir Hector wanted to know why. After I had explained, an acceptable room was quickly found.

On meeting the defendants, the first thing that hit me was their overpowering stench. The jail conditions were bad, but these men had also been living off the land, killing animals, eating the raw meat then rubbing salt into the skins, which they now wore tied about them. The old man who had worked for the family for several years pleaded he had been threatened into luring Mr Ruck from the house and told to keep a look out for other Mau Mau, police or soldiers; even if he were physically able to run, as the prosecution argued he should have, they could easily have followed him and killed him. 'What could I do against these young boys, Mr de Souza,' he implored me, shaking with fear, 'they call me a Mau Mau, but what could I do?' I understood completely, as any normal, compassionate person would. He told me he did not believe in killing innocent people and I could tell he was a very kind, peaceful person. I liked him very much. He was clearly distraught at what had happened to the Rucks, and considering his long employment with the family, must have felt for them as his own.

The trial took six weeks. Some of the accused were very rough men, and very frightening, especially when, to take instruction, I was put in a cell alone with them. I was aware of cases in which clients had threatened their lawyers if they were not acquitted. They might also think I was a police informer. I certainly felt they were capable of murder and might at any moment turn on me. With emotions running so high there was little that could be done, and all four of them, the elderly man included, were sentenced to death. This tragedy, my first case as a barrister, gave me many sleepless nights as I remembered him, and would continue to do so over the years.

Life was not all work. Kanta Kapila, the girl I had first met on the English ferry boat and then outside Lincoln's Inn, was back in Nairobi and we had been seeing each other. Her family were very welcoming, as were mine to her. Most days she would pick me up in her car at around five o'clock and take me either to her home for tea or we would drive somewhere and do what most courting couples did, smooch a little. There was no talk of marriage, but I suppose our relatives may have been assuming it was to follow at some point. My only reservation about Kanta's family concerned her barrister brother Achhroo, who had an unfortunate reputation that, as a case progressed, he would demand more money from his clients than originally agreed.

Kenyatta's trial had, in the meantime, reached a sudden and dramatic climax when on 8th of April 1953 all the defendants were found guilty of Mau Mau membership. Kenyatta asked if I would be able to make a speech of mitigation for him. After consulting with the judges I told him, yes, they would be quite interested. When the moment came, however, Kenyatta produced something he must have written earlier and began reading it out himself: 'May it please your honour, on behalf of my colleagues I wish to say that we are not guilty and we do not accept your findings... we do not feel that we have received the justice or hearing which we could have liked... we intend to appeal to a higher court... we believe that the Supreme Court of Kenya will give us justice. Thank you.' The faces of the prosecutors and Judge Thacker turned red with fury. The statement had challenged the Government, challenged the judiciary, the whole set-up. The other accused were then asked why sentence should not be passed on them, to which they replied in turn:

Fred Kubai: 'I have nothing to say. You can impose any sentence.'

Achieng Oneko: 'I have nothing to say at the moment. You can impose any sentence you are prepared to impose. I am only waiting to appeal to the Supreme Court of Kenya.'

Bildad Kaggia: 'I am in full agreement with what has been said by my colleagues, and have nothing to add.'

Paul Ngei: 'I strongly associate myself with what Kenyatta has said. You can impose any sentence you like.'

Kung'u Karumba: 'Just as you like.'

Judge Thacker was very, very angry with me: 'Mr de Souza you must have been in on this, you must have known he would make a statement like that and you have cheated me into thinking this would be a harmless speech for mitigation – it said nothing for mitigation, but was in fact against mitigation – how can you explain that?' Thacker had said of Asians that 'they bite the hand that feeds them,' so I should not have been surprised by the outburst. I replied only to say that my client was an independent person and was entitled to say what he wanted in mitigation. If he ignored my instructions and decided I should not represent him at this juncture, I could not stop him, and nor would I try to. Silence fell as the sentence was read out: all six men were to serve seven years' imprisonment with hard labour. Supporters of the national movement in Kenya and abroad were shocked and saddened by the outcome but determined to carry on the fight. A campaign for the release of the Kapenguria Six would be mounted immediately and it was agreed we would do all we could for them while continuing to work for freedom and equality throughout the country. On the 21st of April appeals for all six men were lodged with the Supreme Court of Kenya and a date for their hearing set for the 1st of July.

While we endeavoured to fight with words and the law, the Mau Mau descended further into barbarism and bloodshed. Superstition lay at the heart of much of it. When a witch doctor divined that all their remaining land would be taken away unless they captured a white man and buried him alive; they hesitated only long enough to find someone, a kindly priest whom they knew and who had done only good for the Africans. As his captors prepared his grave, he blessed each one of them in turn. Such acts prompted renewed response from the Government. In June 1953, Lieutenant-General Sir George Erskine was appointed Commander in Chief of security forces in Kenya. Reinforcements of three battalions of King's African Rifles and a British infantry brigade arrived, while the RAF dropped bombs in the forest areas, somewhat ineffectually, having little intelligence on Mau Mau movements.

On 1st of July in Kitale, the appeal for the Kapenguria Six opened. Denis Pritt had been put up in Kitale's top hotel, but the colour bar left Chaman Lall, H.O. Davies, Jaswant Singh, A.R. Kapila and myself without accommodation. It was only when the Chairman of Kitale's Indian Association, a local stationery shop owner, intervened, that we were offered a corrugated iron shack. It was a roof over our heads at least without the long drive to and from Nairobi each day. The appeal brought a surprise development. Due to a change in District administrative boundaries dating back to 1950 that the Government had overlooked, it emerged that when the Six were arrested Judge Thacker, as Acting Magistrate, had no jurisdiction for Kapenguria. On realising their oversight the Government had, on 23rd of June, swiftly posted a revised notice in the *Gazette* regarding Thacker's appointment, in an attempt to rectify the matter. Dennis Pritt, however, had now seized on this point and used it to attack the validity of the trial and the convictions, on the grounds that Thacker had at the time been assigned to the Northern Province and could not lawfully try the case in the Rift Valley Province, i.e. Kapenguria. This question of jurisdiction probably explained why lately a number of Africans had been apprehended by the police then taken off to another part of the country before being formally arrested. After several days of debate, a retrial was called for. A further hearing was then set for 17th of August, to take place at the Nairobi Law Courts.

The Nairobi hearing lasted five days, at the end of which the President of the Court of Appeal for Eastern Africa, Sir Barclay Nihill, ruled that the 'order of the Supreme Court directing a retrial is set aside and the convictions entered against and the sentences imposed upon the six respondents by the resident magistrate are restored.' Pritt announced his intention to appeal to the Privy Council in England.

Speaking to journalists afterwards, Denis Pritt 'lived up to his reputation for charm and wit' with his bodyguard reportedly commenting, 'I can't agree with anything the bloke says but he certainly is pleasant.' Pritt told the press that Kapila would probably go to England for the Privy Council appeal which if granted would take place in March the following year. He also added that Kenyatta and the others were 'in good health and good spirits' but that he couldn't talk about the situation in Kenya 'because the Kenya Government won't let me open my mouth.'

In the New Year of 1954, came a joyful occasion; our good friend Pio Pinto, journalist, political leader and tireless and inspirational campaigner for the national movement, was getting married. His bride was an intelligent and lovely young lady called Emma Dias, who had arrived from India just a few months earlier, her father employed by a Parsi family that owned bars, and whose twin sister Joyce was already in Nairobi, married to Tomé Mendonca. Apparently, when Emma first heard rumours that Pio was a communist and asked him about it he replied that he was not, but was a socialist with strong Gandhian principles. At the couple's wedding on the 9th of January in the Catholic Church in Nairobi, to which their many friends were invited, they were wished all the happiness in the world and a wonderful future together.

The decision on the Kapenguria Six appeal was issued on 15th of January 1954. Judge J. Rudd's response to the defence's 183 grounds for appeal was long and detailed, with the 60-page treatise concluding that 'As far as Kenyatta is concerned, both the charges have, in our opinion, been clearly established against him... His appeal fails.' Of the remaining five, only Achieng's appeal was allowed, though he too was destined to remain in detention.

The confirmation of the sentences of imprisonment with hard labour sent a strong message backed by a public condemnation from the court, where Judge Thacker had already expressed his own judgment on Kenyatta: 'You have successfully plunged many Africans back to a state which shows little humanity... persuaded them in secret to murder, burn and commit atrocities which will take many years to forget.' He added that the defendant had: 'let loose upon this land a flood of misery and unhappiness affecting the daily lives of the races in it, including your own people,' and ended with a statement of resolve: 'Make no mistake about it, Mau Mau will be defeated.'

The military were equally determined. On the same day that the appeals against all but one of the Kapenguria Six were rejected, the Mau Mau leader Waruhiu Itote, known as General China, was captured, and at his subsequent trial, represented by A.R. Kapila, sentenced to death. On the suggestion of Police Chief Ian Henderson, however, a deal was struck; in exchange for his life, the General would provide information on the Mau Mau. Erskine began to coordinate the army and police resources and attempted to win over the populace by providing medical services. To secure the villages and prevent Mau Mau attacks or recruitment, a Kikuyu Home Guard was set up, numbering 25,000. Some of these men were over-zealous in their duties, resorting to brutality against those whom they were supposed to protect. Knowing that an army marches on its stomach, village women were ordered at gunpoint to stand guard with sharpened pangas in the forest approaches challenging any man who came in search of food.

Through such means, and with the Home Guard and British troops controlling villages, the Mau Mau fighters now fled to the forests in the Aberdares and around Mount Kenya. The RAF bombing raids also became more effective and no wonder: a police officer later recounted to me how he had been leader of the 'pseudo Mau Mau', young European men who would black their hands and faces and, speaking perfect Kikuyu, lure large crowds of Africans to supposed meetings at a certain compass point in the forest, then melt away as they sent word to the waiting planes. Among the newly arrived British security personnel was

Frank Kitson, alleged by some to have endorsed torture, and who would later be awarded a Military Medal.

Every African had to wear a metal identity plate around their neck, and carrying ID papers at all times was compulsory for Asians. The night curfew applied everywhere, and in areas declared prohibited any unauthorised non-European without a special pass could be shot on sight, day or night. Even abiding by these rules though you could fear for your life. One night at the Rebellos' house in Nairobi with Pio and other friends, Karunga Koinange, panting for breath, came hammering on our door. He said that some soldiers had taken him to the forest and told him to run. He felt they could not possibly shoot him, as they were his friends. Nevertheless he had run backwards as far and as fast as he could. As soon as he had turned his back, sure enough came the order to fire. Zig-zagging through the trees, by a miracle he had avoided the shots, escaped into the forest and found his way back to Nairobi. The brother of Peter Koinange, a Rhodes Scholar who would one day serve in the Kenyan Parliament, Karunga had I believe been managing a petrol station, but the police had for some reason beaten him up and he was quite disturbed. We immediately contacted Dingle Foot QC who rang the Colonial Secretary who I assume had the matter straightened out.

Not everyone could count on friends in high places, and we made it our job wherever possible to keep an eye and ear out for those who had been arrested. One day my clerk Viram Sisodiya received a phone call about a man being held by the police in the Kiambu area. I said if his wife and family wished me to act for him, they should wait at the main road and look out for my car – I gave them the registration – I would then ask them to sign a note confirming they had engaged me. This was essential to avoid any accusation of illegal touting for clients. Drawing up, I saw three women, one of whom approached my car, 'Mr de Souza? Thank goodness! I was worried they would kill my husband.' I assured her I would do all I could and since she could not write asked her to put her thumbprint on my paper.

When I arrived at the police station, however, the officers said they had no such man under arrest and no idea what I was talking about. Then as I was driving away I heard a voice calling from the bushes, 'Mr de Souza...' Stopping my car I found a man tied to a tree. It seemed I had found my client. In a poor state, he told me he had been there for two days without food and had felt like killing himself. At that moment a policeman drove up demanding to know what I was doing. I said I intended to obtain a writ of habeas corpus ordering them to deliver my client to court to establish whether they had any legal right to detain him. The officer's response was to threaten me with prosecution for entering prohibited land without a permit.

At this point I was a little fearful. The rule of law in Kenya was fragile and being 'spirited away' by the powers that be could happen to anyone. If I had been married with a dependent family I might have been inclined to leave and say no more about the matter. But seeing such gross ill-treatment I thought I only have my own freedom and safety to worry about and I persisted. The police, equally stubborn, repeated their threat. Cleverly though, they made it clear they were not arresting me or taking me through the open courts and a magistrate, which would attract unwelcome publicity for them, but would bring me before a Law Society disciplinary tribunal. By this means they hoped to discredit me.

I went to see Kanta's brother Achhroo Kapila, one of my colleagues on the Kapenguria defence team, and asked if he would take up my case. After saying he was willing, that evening his father Seligram rang to say he was sorry but Achhroo could not take the case as he had too much trouble with the Government already. My clerk then advised me to go and see a Mr O'Brian Kelly. Mr O'Brian Kelly came to the door in his dressing gown. After listening to my story he said not to worry; when Europeans wanted to steal someone's land they would often bring a trumped-up charge against them in the expectation of being bought off.

The tribunal met in the Chief Secretary's office in Government House. My client's wife was there. Attorney General John Wyatt was the Chairman of the tribunal, and there was another Indian lawyer who never uttered a word the whole time. From the outset the Attorney General was rude and aggressive towards Kelly, warning him, 'Do you know what trouble you could be in?' I called the client's wife as a witness and said I had her thumbprint as proof she had engaged me and had not therefore touted. And I had only gone to the tree, on so-called prohibited land, after hearing my client's desperate call for help.

As Kelly was verbally attacked and called a 'black stooge,' I was worried that if this went on, they would imprison the client's wife and myself on spurious charges. The wife was cross-examined: 'How much money did you give Mr de Souza – and do you know you have sworn an affidavit that you had never met Mr de Souza?' It turned out to be true, she had sworn this – but only when subjected to extreme pressure while under arrest, the police frightening her so much that she had wet herself. I whispered to Kelly to insist they drop the case or I would go to the newspapers and tell them the whole story. This appeared to work, and the proceedings were brought to a close.

It was O'Brian Kelly who had told me how when he refused to draw up invented land deeds in Kenya for his upper-class English employer he had been sacked on some ridiculous pretext. I was reminded again of the description of the worst of Kenya's European rulers – particularly some of the white South Africans or Afrikaans – that they were not uneducated, but dis-educated – people with all the privileges of good schooling who chose to come out to Africa and be the ruffians.

The nationalist movement was under increasing pressure since the introduction of the Emergency. With the Kenya League banned, the Government was now forming a federation with Nyasaland and Northern and Southern

Rhodesia (now Malawi, Zambia and Zimbabwe respectively). This multinational alliance being under white leadership, we feared racial equality and democracy would become ten times harder and had responded by starting an Anti-Federation League. Pio again had largely been the mentor of this organisation, but it too was soon banned.

International cooperation was something I supported provided all the participants promoted democracy and racial equality. Inspired by the United Nations conference in Mogadishu in 1952, I had started enrolling members for a Kenyan UN Association, but faced a lot of resistance from many in the white community who thought it would be under the influence of the Indians, which of course was true. I did though organise a lot of meetings under the auspices of the United Nations, most of them quite successful, though the American Government's representative in Kenya declined an invitation. I spent almost two hours trying to persuade him, arguing that a country so interested in democracy should have the courage to come and speak on the aims and objectives of the United Nations, but he flatly refused.

While studying in England I had also joined an organisation for world government, and believed strongly this would eventually replace the nation state and the United Nations. When it came to resolving disputes, the United Nations was so often hamstrung by the sovereignty of states, a concept with which I totally disagreed, having been devised by human beings from basically selfish motives to keep yourself as an island of power, allowing you to do whatever you liked within your borders, even attack your neighbour without being sued. A country's foreign and or internal affairs could therefore be despicable, and its government embark on imperialist missions, with the people who were being dominated, murdered, pillaged and robbed having no supranational authority to which they could appeal. The League of Nations, formed by the victors of the First World War was a start but had proved a failure, and the United Nations too, in my opinion had not come very far and never would unless it had teeth and a coercive army and did not remain a talk shop.

Meanwhile, in Kenya the Kapenguria Six remained incarcerated. Kenyatta's name was still firmly equated with terrorism and despite the continued efforts of Fenner Brockway, Leslie Hale and many others the authorities seemed determined he should serve the full seven years of his sentence. Anyone associated with the movement was also under suspicion, and one day it came to my attention that the Portuguese Consul, Dr Jules De' Mello, had put on record that 'Fitz de Souza is a Mau Mau leader, and had taken the Oath in the house of a prostitute.' Worse, the person making the allegation was a friend of mine, or so I had thought. There was a hidden agenda at work, however, relating to my involvement along with Pio in the campaign for Goan independence from Portugal. Luckily a third party who had some authority came to my defence with the assurance that 'Mr de Souza is a person who would never approve of such things' and made a note on the relevant Government file to this effect. Nevertheless one still had to be careful, and with political meetings banned, these had to be held covertly. Even if we were not raided or arrested, when larger numbers attended we could never be sure whether or not police informers had slipped in amongst the crowd to find out what we were planning and see who was there. Pio was helping the relatives of Mau Mau members, including the families of some who had been killed, and it was also believed he was running arms to the forest fighters, both activities that could carry a death sentence. Our names and addresses were very well known to the police force, which under the powers of the Emergency could apprehend anyone for little or no reason.

Meanwhile, I was still visiting numerous clients who were in detention, driving sometimes hundreds of miles a week to do so and often working late into the evening. One particular journey did not turn out as planned. I was on my way to see a client who was being held a long distance from Nairobi and I was keen to arrive before it got dark. I was a little way out from the city and making good time when I saw what looked like a sea of water or a small river flowing over the road ahead of me. Instinctively I put my foot on the brake but the car skidded and flipped over. I was conscious but very confused and disorientated. As the dust settled I managed to get out of the car, feeling very shaken and aware of pain in various parts of my body, most intensely in my back. I had to accept I would not reach my client by nightfall now. I could not even get home on my own for I was barely able to stand and even if my car was drivable I was in no fit state to get behind the wheel. I would just have to wait for assistance, which on this lonely stretch of road might take some time. Judging by the pain, I was also going to need some kind of medical treatment. Fortunately, within a few minutes a passing motorist noticed me. The car pulled up and an Indian man came over: 'Do you need help?' 'Thank you, yes.' As he got me into his vehicle I could see now that what I had thought was water was a large patch of glistening oil stretching halfway across the road. We discovered later that a tanker had overturned and been towed away leaving its spilt cargo behind.

The man kindly took me to the nearest police station where they phoned a message through to a friend of mine who arrived a little while later accompanied by his girlfriend. My friend had a box estate car, and putting the seats down he laid a mattress out in the back for me. The girlfriend produced a piece of cloth that she cut and tied into a makeshift bandage around my torso. After I was laid down on the mattress, my friend started his car and set off in the direction of Nairobi Hospital. He drove slowly and as carefully as possible but avoiding every pothole in the road was impossible and whenever the car jumped I would scream out in agony from my injuries. 'Sorry Doc' apologised my friend. They all called me Doc, either because I was doing a PhD or because they knew my father.

Arriving at the hospital, my friend and his girlfriend helped me from the car, and leaning on their arms I hobbled slowly into the building. The hospital was mainly for

Europeans but I believe there were also sections set aside for Asians and Africans. A member of staff looked up and seeing me her expression did not appear to be very welcoming. A nursing sister came out, and it seemed there was some problem about taking me, perhaps because the non-European sections were unavailable, I wasn't sure. After some prevarication she said that they would agree to admit me but I must agree not to say anything about it. Although I was still in considerable pain and would be grateful to receive treatment I did not like the idea of having to keep quiet about the fact that the Nairobi Hospital had decided to give me a bed as if it were some special concession and I said so. The sister then said they had a doctor who did emergency operations and summoned him.

While we were waiting for the doctor someone else mentioned that he did private work at a hospital in Uganda where he used a separate entrance for Asians and Africans. I said that in that case I didn't want him to treat me. At that point the doctor appeared. I said to him, 'Can you call Dr Anderson?' Anderson and Hopkirk were two of the medical team at Magadi. Hopkirk was basically a pathologist who also did x-rays and I believe Anderson's father had been a co-founder of the *East African Standard*. When I mentioned Anderson, the doctor I was speaking to said, 'You mean that old fogey?' I said, 'I don't know about old fogey or not,' to which he replied, 'If he comes in, I walk out.' Hearing this I told him to walk out anyway. 'You mean you can do without me?' he said. 'Yes,' I told him plainly, 'I don't need you.' When it was clear we were leaving, I was helped back out to my friend's car and laid down again, his girlfriend tightening the piece of cloth around my middle. They were worried about a possible spine injury, and complications.

Thanks to my friends I was delivered home safely. When my father spoke to me he was shocked that I had not agreed to be admitted to the hospital: did I want to die? He was also probably remembering a patient at Magadi who had cycled over an unseen iron bar in the road, come off his bicycle and been permanently paralysed. It was at this point that I cried. X-rays were later arranged, confirming spinal damage, and my father booked me in for an operation at a medical practice in Hamilton Road. I remained in bed and in plaster for six weeks, at the end of which I was stiff but seemed to have made a full recovery. On leaving I was warned to take more care on the road in future.

By the spring of 1954 plans for Operation Anvil, a mass round-up of Mau Mau suspects, had been drawn up and the net was about to be cast in our direction. It was in April, just five months after his wedding, that Pio was arrested at the Desai Memorial Library and a warrant issued for me. As soon as I heard I got in my car and headed for my friend Abdul Bhaijee's father's shop, explained the situation and asked if I could possibly borrow some money as I needed to get out of the country urgently. At that moment the shop's phone rang. It was my parents. My mother said the police had come looking for me. She was very anxious and upset and urged me to make peace with the Government. I said I was not at war, and told them not to worry and that everything would be all right. My mother had spoken in Portuguese, a prearranged signal to warn me the police were listening. I was also aware that they knew the registration of my car. Reassuring her again, I told her I was going to Mombasa, said goodbye and replaced the receiver. Abdul took out the cash till and handed the contents to me. It was too much, I protested, but he insisted almost in tears that I take the lot. Thanking him profusely, I got quickly into my car and sped off. I did not take the road for Mombasa, however, but instead headed in the opposite direction, towards Uganda.

Chapter Ten

Behind the Iron Curtain and Other Excursions

1953 to 1957

My reasoning was that I would be no good to anyone if taken and held in detention where I could be denied phone calls or outside communications. Once in Uganda they could not, I hoped, arrest me. My plan was to check into a hotel and, from there, contact the Indian High Commission in London to ask them to intervene on Pio's behalf. It was about ten hours drive to the Ugandan border and I did not stop. I learned later that roadblocks had been set up on the Mombasa road to intercept me.

    During the last few miles, people began appearing on the roadside offering help to ensure my safe passage out of the country but at a price. I said I was not willing to pay them anything. Arriving at the border I pulled up and the Ugandan police came over and looked me up and down. Did I have an agent, they wanted to know, someone to vouch for me and say I wasn't a crook? I replied that I had no one. I showed my passport and was asked for 100 shillings. When I handed this over I was asked for another 100, then another – for this man, that man, a whole cluster of officials now hovering round my car. After parting with 500 I said firmly, 'No more,' and was waved on.

    By the evening I had reached Kampala. In the lobby of the Imperial Hotel a large crowd of people was waiting to check in. When I finally reached the desk the receptionist asked if I had a reservation and when I shook my head I was turned away. What now? Then I heard a voice call out, 'Mr de Souza?' Looking round I saw it was a fellow economics student I had met at the LSE. He was one of the Ismaili family that owned the hotel. When I told him why I was there, with great kindness he immediately offered me a discounted room. Furthermore, he said if I should run short of money while there, to let him know and he would return whatever I had paid. Next day I put a call through to the Indian High Commission in London. I was told they would request Pio's release and advised that he should then go to London, have a chat and sort things out.

After a few days the Kenya Government contacted me at the hotel and issued an apology for the attempted arrest. When I returned to Nairobi, Pio was as promised duly released, and shortly afterwards flew to England to meet with the Indian High Commission. The situation in Kenya remained extremely fraught, however, and a few days later when Pio returned from London he was promptly rearrested. I took his wife Emma to see him in the jail, where Pio, being Pio, was buoyant and full of ideas. As for my own position, I had so far taken everything in my stride, and though being a lawyer had helped keep me out of jail, I was quite prepared to be arrested if necessary, for my conscience was perfectly clear. But these were dangerous times, and after the dash to Uganda and then Pio's rearrest, I realised I was skating on thin ice. Now, driving my car I was always on the lookout for a roadblock or sitting at home would be listening for a knock on the door.

One day I felt a pain in my stomach. When it wouldn't go away I realised something must be wrong. A medical examination revealed that I had developed stomach ulcers. In those days people did not talk about stress, but I suppose that's what had caused them. Along with some prescriptions and a spell in hospital where I was given opium internally to try to cure the ulcers, I was advised to avoid worrying, take things easier and perhaps have a change of routine. There seemed too much to do though and so many probably innocent people in detention. One of my clients, a teacher called Johnstone Muthuria, I had managed to save from a death sentence, though he had subsequently been rearrested on a lesser charge. The Government could do almost anything it seemed.

In January 1955, 'Safe Conduct' leaflets were dropped in and around the forest pledging 'fair treatment, food and medical attention' to Mau Mau fighters, who would be detained but not prosecuted for non-serious offences committed prior to 18th of January 1955. Talking to Mau Mau suspects and those on the fringes about this was no easy task, for none of us wanted to coax a man in, only for him to be wrongly imprisoned. Prior to his arrest, Pio had been approached to act as a go-between, but at a meeting in Nairobi in a large room filled with 30 or more frightening-looking Africans no one could guarantee that if they did give themselves up they would receive justice, or be safe from their own side. The Surrender Passes would bring in some 300 men but many more who were caught carrying them by other Mau Mau were slain.

In recent months there had been less time for Kanta and I to see each other, though I would still go for tea at her home. I was surprised her parents didn't object by now, since we had no plans to get married, nor declared any such intention to anyone. Neither had we had sex, which simply did not happen before wedlock in those days. Kanta was not short of suitors but seemed in no hurry, and one fellow who was very keen on her, she had put off by feigning a limp. Then I got a shock; she had received an invitation from a doctor in Uganda to discuss marriage and was considering it. Perhaps, I thought, I had been fonder of her than I had realised.

As the weeks went on my stomach ulcers persisted and I seemed generally low. I had also been stopped a couple of times by the police. Be careful, my father cautioned. I thought again about some kind of change. With the national movement in Kenya stalled, maybe this was an opportunity to improve my qualifications and extend my understanding of politics and economics. Talking it over with my father, I said perhaps I could return to education, if possible at the LSE to continue my postgraduate research which I had left off in 1952 on hearing of his illness. It would mean going to London again of course, and cost money. There I could still do something for the nationalists, at least talk to English people about what was really happening in Kenya. My parents were both very supportive and said they would pay for as long as I wanted to study. My father was, however, concerned that this time there was an even greater risk I would meet and marry an English girl. He had nothing against English girls but feared loneliness would lead me to act in haste and he might never see me again. As before, I assured him it would not happen and I would be back.

England in 1955 seemed much as I remembered from three years before – the winters cold, the people mostly warm and welcoming. There was a new monarch, Elizabeth the Second, who had been on holiday at the Treetops Lodge in Kenya when her father George VI had died in early 1952. Treetops had since been burned down by the Mau Mau. There was political change under way. Churchill, the wartime leader, and Attlee, architect of the welfare state, both stepping down, the Conservatives returned under Anthony Eden in the May election.

Among my fellow postgraduates at the LSE was a 31-year-old assistant lecturer in Political Science called Ralph Miliband. A Belgian émigré whose parents were Polish Jews, Miliband had fled the Nazis in 1940, served in the Royal Navy during the war and was now completing his doctorate on 'Popular Thought in the French Revolution'. Almost six decades later, his two sons David and Ed would famously compete for leadership of the Labour Party.

I found a boarding house opposite Manor House Tube Station. There were about ten fellow occupants sleeping two or three to a room, but to have privacy to study I made sure I could get a room to myself. Within a mile as the crow flies from the Arsenal football stadium, that first summer sitting over my textbooks, my feet stretched out on the open windowsill on a Saturday afternoon, I could hear the home crowd roar when the Gunners scored, and the far more muted response if the away team put one in, and without ever seeing the match, always knew the result.

If there was a difference this time in England it was in me. Three years older, I was more confident and outgoing, and even drank the odd glass of wine on occasion. The LSE was very sociable, with students from many parts of the world, dances, talks and outings. As before, I was struck by the kindness and courtesy of the British, and their modern attitudes. When a girl asked me to tea at her home one day, I arrived to find her parents just walking off. 'Our daughter said she had a boy coming round,' they smiled, 'and we've been told to stay out of the way!' Socialising had also been made easier with a letter of introduction from one of my father's bosses, a Mr Billington, a manager at the Magadi Soda Company, to his sister, who was a Professor at the St Martin's School of Fine Arts in London. I was invited to her home and introduced to her daughter, who took me to dinner. 'Do you drink beer?' she asked. I replied, 'Of course not, don't be ridiculous.' Then she led me for a walk along the Thames until we reached a place amid some trees where several couples were kissing and more. 'Do you want to lie down?' she asked. 'No thank you,' I replied.

Things never went further than tea or dancing and explaining how I had promised my father not to get serious with any girl earned me the nickname 'Daddy's Boy' among some of my friends. If a girl asked, 'Do you love me?' I might answer, 'What is love?' or sometimes rashly 'Yes,' prompting the next question: 'So why won't you marry me?' I had no proper answer. Romance or not, life was very pleasant, with tea parties, tennis, relaxation and quiet study, balanced by some lively dances. Within a couple of months my ulcers had gone.

Meanwhile, my fellow students and I were learning about the world not only in the lecture halls. Trips to Europe, including Vienna, skiing in the Alps and a visit to Madrid where I attended a bullfight, were unforgettable experiences. A British Council coach tour took a party of us to the pit communities of Wales to see how the miners lived and worked. Staying overnight, my roommate was Julius, who was about seven older than me and taking a Masters in Economics at Edinburgh, while also developing an interest in Fabian socialism. In 1962, Julius Nyerere would become the first President of Tanganyika, later the independent Republic of Tanzania.

The following year all the talk was of the Suez crisis, the seizure by Gamel Abdel Nasser of the strategically vital canal and Eden's rush to military action. The events had global significance, with superpowers America and Russia, and the UN getting involved. Krushchev quipped that Eden had a 'blockage in his canal', the uncharacteristic attempt at humour perhaps part of the 'Thaw', which since Stalin's death in 1953 had seen millions of political prisoners released from the gulags, censorship relaxed and foreign visitors encouraged. 1957 marked the 6th World Festival of Youth and Students, an annual event organised by the World Federation of Democratic Youth and the International Union of Students. For the first time the Festival was being held in Russia, attracting an estimated 34,000 people from all over the world, of whom I was to be one.

Travelling across Europe by train, I had been told to say I was only going as far as Berlin and that I wouldn't need a visa. By the time we reached the border, however, I had fallen asleep, and when a guard shook me and asked my destination, I replied drowsily, 'The festival... Russia.' The next minute armed police were escorting me off the train and into a car. As we sped through the streets I felt like a top criminal. Several hours later we pulled up at a police station in Holland. It seemed I had needed a visa after all.

The nearest place to get one was the Government offices at The Hague, but I hadn't enough money left for either a tram there or to get me back to Berlin. A friendly stranger directed me to the offices of the *Daily Worker*, where the staff literally passed the hat round. With my passport stamped I took a train back to Berlin. The police inspector recognised me and offered his congratulations, saying another young Indian had recently been arrested for not having a visa. Most people were desperate to go the other way, from East to West; 3.5 million before 1961 and the building of the Berlin Wall. The train shunted steam, and under the watchful eyes of the border guards rolled through the Iron Curtain and into Eastern Europe.

In Warsaw I watched horse-drawn carts laden with rubble from bombed out houses, whole streets still in ruins 12 years after the war. Pushing further east the countryside opened out, giving way to the vast emptiness of the steppe, devoid of trees and habitation, a place I remember thinking, in which it would be very hard to survive. Someone had told me to take some Western clothes to sell, and coffee powder and a thermos. During the long train journey, whenever we stopped I would walk up to the engine and ask the driver for some hot water from the boiler. The Russians loved any type of coffee, and my tin of Nescafé and I soon became popular, providing cheap warming drinks for my fellow passengers.

Leningrad was huge and dramatic, the sheer width of the Neva and the magnificence of the Winter Palace a breathtaking sight. On to Moscow and Red Square, where the forbidding walls of the Kremlin loomed over crowds of cheerful Russians and tourists. There was dancing and singing on the street corners, and arts events wherever you looked. In the foyer of the Bolshoi Theatre, I was reading a poster for *Prince Igor*, when a man smiled and handed me a complimentary ticket, a generous gesture to an obvious foreigner. I was led into the auditorium where the orchestra was warming up. Someone said, 'How do you know the conductor?' I replied, 'Who is the conductor?' before realising he meant my benefactor. Gazing later at a statue of Stalin I saw the opposite spirit, the dictator's cruel features even in stone casting a sense of fear over the onlooker. I had been taking photographs, which prior to the 'Thaw' would probably not have been allowed. Later that day though, my camera went missing. Had I left it carelessly on a bench or wall, or had it been stolen? 'Don't worry,' a friendly Russian told me, 'It will turn up.' Sure enough, back at the accommodation my Box Brownie was waiting, complete with the film.

Back in London a friend told me he had recently bought a house. Tired of living in rooms, I asked how much for. Four thousand pounds, he replied. It seemed a great deal of money. But thinking I might at least rent somewhere larger, I went to see my friend's estate agent and asked if he knew of a small flat. When I told him I had about a thousand pounds, he said I could buy a house for that. He had one right now in Hornsey for £3,500. Remembering some advice about property negotiating I said, 'How about half?' The agent shook his head. The vendors had just refused an offer of £3,000. '£2,000... £2,400?' Nothing doing. It was back to my books and my small room.

Three months later the agent telephoned. The Hornsey house was still on the market – was my offer of £2,400 still on? I told him yes, but I would need a loan. Of course, how much was I talking about? 'Ninety percent.' Ah, then I would need a reference – did I know anyone of standing in London? I gave him Fenner Brockway's name. Two days later he rang again: 'Congratulations, the house is yours.' From a card in a shop window I found a small firm of lawyers who worked in an attic to handle the contract, and within a few weeks moved into my very own house.

My first visitor was Pio's cousin Oscar, who was living in London. Pio was still in detention on Manda Island, segregated from all the other inmates. In a later letter he would tell me that the hundreds of Africans on the other side of the fence had been given one football between them while he had a ball all to himself. Knowing Pio was very athletic and could outrun even the Maasai, I wrote back saying it must be hard having to play alone. Not at all, he replied, all day long he could kick the ball high in the air and run to catch it.

Seeing Pio's cousin was a sharp reminder that the struggle in Kenya was still going on. Working on my doctorate had also refreshed my knowledge of the origins of that struggle, how the rich pastures that became known as Kenya's 'White Highlands' had by express statute continued to be denied to Asians and indigenous Africans, as settlers from Britain, Australia, Germany and South Africa descended on the country. It was in the early 1900s that Colonel Ewart Scott Grogan first arrived in Kenya and began acquiring large swathes of land. When I met Grogan he had seemed an amiable old gentleman and it was hard to attribute to him some of the deeds he had committed, as well as the outrageous words attributed to him, such as, 'A sound system of compulsory labour would do more to raise the n***** in five years than all the millions that have been spent in missionary efforts.'

Arrested for flogging an African rickshaw driver to death, Grogan was cleared of murder by an all-white court which reduced the charge to one of common assault, with a sentence of two months hard labour, believed to have been not that hard in reality. Grogan was a resolute colonialist and emphatic that, 'We Europeans have to go on ruling this country and rule it with iron discipline.' As for the Europeans' attitude towards Asians, the following comments of the then Governor show a wariness as well as disrespect: 'The average Englishman tolerates an African but he cannot tolerate dark colour combined with an intelligence in any way equal with his own.'

I had also re-read of how in 1914 the East African Indian National Congress was formed. Both the membership and the interests of the EAINC were largely concentrated in Kenya, where it passed a resolution calling for equality, including the right to farm in the White Highlands. The Europeans would have none of it, but as the Asian population within Kenya grew, their economic strength afforded greater bargaining power. In 1920 they were offered two seats on the Legislative Council, which were rejected as insufficient for the size of their community.

When the right to five seats was won in 1927, however, both the Asians and Europeans blocked African representation.

Meanwhile, the Indians would have their own difficulties, including the railway workers who were plunged into economic insecurity in the 1930s when their jobs were made temporary. In an attempt to improve the situation, in 1935 a young Indian called Makhan Singh set up the Labour Trade Union of Kenya, and in 1949, together with Fred Kubai, established the first East African Trade Union Congress. Singh's father had travelled from the Punjab in 1920 to work as an artisan on the railways, and at the age of 14 Makhan and his mother and sister had followed. Being very good at mathematics, on leaving school in Kenya, the young Singh wanted to go to England to continue his education. However, his father, who had now left the railways and started a part-time printing business, insisted that his son should remain and work for him. Developing a strong interest in the trade union movement, Makhan had declined the pugree due to him from his father on reaching maturity, and allowed this money to go instead to his brother. Among the first strikes Singh led was against employers in the printing industry. It was thought to be his organising of a strike of 6,000 African workers in Mombasa, that brought him to the close attention of the British, and in 1939, to avoid being arrested, he travelled to India, ostensibly to attend a family wedding. Whilst there he donned a disguise and spoke at a mass meeting of textile workers who were striking for better wages. Shortly afterwards he was arrested by the colonial authorities and spent the next five years in prison.

Following his release in 1944, Makhan Singh became involved in the Indian nationalist movement, editing a weekly paper in Lahore called *Jange Azadi* ('Struggle for Independence'). On 15th of August 1947, as Nehru was raising the Indian national flag at the Lahori Gate of the Red Fort in Delhi to signal that independence had been won at last, Makhan was on a ship returning to

Kenya to continue the struggle there. In January of that year there had been another strike in Mombasa, led by the African Workers' Union, in which for 12 days about three-quarters of the city's employees, including 4,000 dockers, together with servants, railwaymen and hotel staff, had stopped work. Mombasa being a vital port for the colonies of both Kenya and Uganda, this industrial action had been debated in the British Parliament. The strike ended with the key issues of low pay and unequal treatment still unresolved. When Makhan Singh arrived back in Kenya that year, the British tried to deport him straight back to India as a 'prohibited immigrant'. Since India was now independent, however, its government was not obliged to comply.

Integral to Makhan Singh's aims was the attempt to unite the Indians with the large numbers of African workers who were by then living in Nairobi, but had been historically less organised in terms of union representation. This was allied to the broader objective, one that Pio together with myself and others also strove for later, of convincing Kenya's Indians to support the nationalist movement and the fight for independence. On May Day 1950, Singh expressed this ultimate goal in a speech made at Kaloleni Social Hall, railing against the British occupation of Kenyan land and calling for 'Uhuru Sasa' – Freedom Now. A fortnight later he and Fred Kubai were arrested. Kubai was released, but when he was rearrested two years later under the Emergency and taken with the other Kapenguria defendants to Lokitaung, they apparently found Singh there. Singh was held at various locations, and on one occasion, when he asked to be allowed visits from relatives, his captors instead offered him freedom if he would agree to take his family and leave East Africa for good. Singh declined and remained incarcerated.

A few people with progressive views were, however, one way or another still holding out in Kenya. For the sake of Pio, Makhan Singh and all who were being held unjustly in captivity, it was important that we try to connect, and with this thought in mind it was not long before I was packing my trunk again.

On a tour of coal mines in Wales

The group that toured the coal mines. Julius Nyerere fourth from the left

Skiing in the 1950s, myself on the left

Jomo Kenyatta, Fenner Brockway and me

Chapter Eleven

Kenya: The Promise of a New Dawn

1958 to 1962

Things had not stood still during my absence. In October 1956, Dedan Kimathi, a key figure in the Mau Mau had been captured in Nyeri and four months later hanged. With a reputation for violence, Kimathi had forced the Mau Mau oath on many fellow Africans. His sentence, delivered by an all-black jury under Chief Justice O'Connor almost four years from the start of the uprising, was a significant turning point. It would signal the end of the war in the forest.

Subsequent developments, however, would have a quite different impact on the Government's credibility. In the spring of 1958 Rawson Macharia, key witness against the Kapenguria Six, contacted the Nairobi Press claiming that he had been paid to lie and that he and six others had perjured themselves at the trial. The prosecution witnesses he claimed had been coached, some rewarded with plots of land at the coast, while he had been offered a degree course in public administration at Exeter University, protection for his family and a Government job on his return to Kenya. In November he signed an affidavit to this effect. A beer shop that he had been later helped to set up had apparently failed, and now, through conscience, resentment or possibly both, he wanted to come clean. The Government, maintaining they had paid him only to testify, not lie, rather than prosecuting him for the perjury, promptly put him on trial for what they said was a false affidavit. Dennis Pritt, who had sought to undermine his initial evidence, now returned to defend him.

With the Mau Mau threat subdued and the Government compromised by Rawson Macharia's allegations, there seemed at last a glimmer of hope for all those still being held in detention. In April 1958, Pio had been moved from Manda Island to Kabarnet, a remote spot in northern Kenya where, although still under restriction, he was allowed to have Emma come and stay with him. Eighteen months later, in October 1959 he was set free. Four years at Manda had left him even leaner than before. Despite the harsh conditions and a campaign to confuse the inmates with disinformation, Pio had striven all the while to communicate with the other prisoners, and the resulting strength of morale had surprised the authorities. Following their reunion, he and Emma had also been blessed with a child, Linda. Her proud father had returned to work with gusto, writing, organising and planning the creation of a newspaper called Sauti Ya KANU. A general election was coming and Pio was determined that KANU – the Kenya African National Union which had now replaced the KAU – should win.

Pio's release had coincided with the near completion of my doctoral thesis. Back in London again, I met with my LSE supervisor Lucy Mair, reader in Colonial Administration and Applied Anthropology. We had talked a lot about colonialism, with me reminding her of all its injustices. She in turn reminded me one day how people's attitudes are formed: 'You have got to be generous with us Fitz, we were taught as children that we were a special race, a super race, made by God to rule the world, and like McCauley and Kipling, to believe in the greatness of the British Empire.' Somewhat incredulous I had then said, 'You mean you were taught this at home, even though your mother and father were both professors at the London School of Economics?' Lucy said it was so, and that as far as they were concerned they were the greatest race, and that she had grown up thinking Indians were coolies, meaning porters, and she had assumed all Indians were coolies. She hadn't even known it was a derogatory word and would have called me a coolie if she hadn't known me otherwise. It was very sad she said, but they had even put to her the question if God had not chosen the British, then how did they come to rule the world.

Having written approximately 90,000 words on my chosen subject, I had to compile an index. No, no, said Lucy, it would not be required. A few days after handing in the thesis a senior professor came back to me, all very positive but wanting to know where the index was. What should I say? I went back to Lucy. Through a closed door I heard a heated argument ensue between her and the Professor. At the end of it she emerged and said, 'Well Doctor de Souza, I'm pleased to say the matter has been resolved'

The final page of my thesis carried these words:

> *"The future of East Africa is certainly not a dark one, and after many years of strife, the possibilities of a political settlement are in sight. East Africa, where races and civilizations from three continents meet, provides a challenge to its people: the evolution of a new way of life based on liberty, tolerance and equality of opportunity for the individual, far from the frustration and bitterness of racial intolerance and domination. In a world where East and West continually meet, East Africa can provide a beacon light to the people of the world who have yet to learn to live peacefully and to adapt their different ways of life in a new and fast contracting world."*

Many would share such a vision, but who could make it a reality? The Kikuyu were looking to Jomo Kenyatta, the 'Burning Spear', to lead them to a better future. On the 12th of January 1960 the Emergency was lifted, and at a meeting on the 28th of February in Nairobi,

25,000 people called for Kenyatta's release, followed in April by a petition of one million signatures, and in May, his election in absentia as President of KANU.

People were also beginning to talk more about a free Kenya, towards which end certain recent shifts in the world order could prove favourable. Since Indian independence, Kenya's value as a staging post for Britain's interests in the former Raj was less significant, and behind the scenes, neighbouring Tanganyika was on the verge of breaking away. But to the south, Mozambique remained firmly within Portugal's empire, and the existence of British Kenya had long been a reassuring block on its expansion. The most stubborn resistance was likely to come from Kenya's aristocratic white settler community, and mindful of the patrician attitudes and vested interests at stake, I believe that some kind of committee had been set up under Harold McMillan to break the news to them gently that independence was coming. The first public step was taken with a conference of African, Asian and European delegates at London's Lancaster House under Colonial Secretary Iain Macleod. It was here that Michael Blundell's New Kenya Party began to get some agreement on a way forward. Many white settlers remained unhappy, however, and when discussions ended inconclusively and McCleod issued what was called an 'Interim Constitution', it was clear the road ahead would be neither easy nor straight.

One day I was called for a cup of tea by two very good friends, one of whom was Kanji Mangaldas, whose father had come from India as a hawker selling saris from a little cart and become one of the richest men in Kenya. My other host was a commercial manager of Air India, Surya Patel, whose father had died young. His mother had settled in East Africa and worked hard to give her sons a good education. Surya and his two brothers were all good cricket players, which was very important for Indians. As we drank our tea, Kanji and Surya brought up the subject of politics and asked me if I had thought about standing for Kenya's Legislative Council, or 'Legco' (pronounced Ledgeco) as it was referred to. 'No,' I replied, 'for a start I don't have the money for a deposit, or to run a campaign, and I don't have sponsors.' With the advent of 'national members' for Legco, on the grounds of racial parity, the Europeans, even though far fewer in number in Kenya, had insisted on being equally represented among those sponsoring members, who now had to have two Asians, two Africans and two Europeans backing them. Kanji and Surya immediately said they would provide the necessary funds and be my two Asian sponsors. I thanked them, and agreed to stand on the Indian Congress ticket.

Now I needed four other sponsors. First I went to see people in KADU, which was led by Masinde Muliro and Ronald Ngala. Muliro said he was very impressed by my speeches and would be happy to support me. For the Europeans I decided to approach Michael Blundell of the New Kenya Party. The son of a QC who had wanted his son to follow him into the law, Blundell had instead come to Kenya and ridden bullock carts around to learn about running a farm. From what I had heard of his party, I believed him to be progressive and a man interested in justice. Hearing my request, Blundell said he was too busy at present and that I should come back in a few days. I did so, and was given the same story. I must have gone to Parliament five or six times to see him, until the deadline for nominations had almost expired. By now I had assumed he wasn't interested and was just putting me off.

Then two days before the deadline, at a function where Blundell was present, as I went into the toilet, he, a man called Havelock and another English colleague of his, followed me in and stood in uncomfortably close formation around me as I used the facilities. Blundell, who had a rather arrogant way of speaking, addressed me: 'de Souza – we and the Goanese get along very well,' he said, 'stay around and do what we tell you and you'll get a few goodies.' I was furious. 'How dare you speak to me like that,' I said, 'I am Mr de Souza to you. And what are these "goodies" – are you trying to bribe me?' No more was said.

Sadly, many Indians in the Kenyan Parliament became mired in corruption from the day they began and retired as moneyed men. The country's largesse was all in the hands of the Europeans, who had acquired the land and farms almost for free and could therefore call the tune to those that would dance. Blundell was not a bad man, but I was very hot about anything like that in those days and I realised he had kept me hanging as long as possible before showing his hand, in the hope it would be too late for me to find anyone else to support me.

Still I decided to try and early next morning called on Howard Williams, who had an ambitious scheme to irrigate land from Lake Victoria, about which he often wrote in the *Kenya Weekly and Settlers' News*. I told him it was a good idea and one that I would support, and he agreed to be one of my European sponsors. The other was Cleasby, an English lawyer from Mombasa. I was just in time. If successful, I would represent not a particular region but the country as a whole, which suited me better; Kenya's ethnic and religious groups were clustered in discrete areas, and being politically non-denominational I could neither support nor rely on any one demographic group. When the elections took place my friend Saif Karim Anjarwalla, son of a very big Mombasa importer of Indian saris and dress fabrics, came out of Parliament and gave me the thumbs-up. I was in, as a Member of the East African Indian National Congress.

Saif Anjarwalla

Getting the message across remained very important and with the British Press still largely endorsing the status quo of colonial rule, we were grateful for the efforts of people in various walks of life that continued to support the independence movement. Sarjit Heyer was one such person. Born in 1935, Sarjit had completed his first degree in Birmingham, England, and subsequently during his postgraduate study he and I had been together at the LSE. By profession an economist and statistician in the East African Statistics Department, seconded to the Ministry of Agriculture in Kenya, Sarjit was a progressive, politically on the left, and if he had any regrets they were the fact that he was too young, and the wrong colour, to do more. He did all he could though, devoting his time, energy and considerable skills to research and planning for the independence movement, and in writing briefings and speeches for both Pio and myself. Sarjit played a key role in the early days of independence. He married the economist Judith Cripps, granddaughter of the distinguished Labour statesman Sir Stafford Cripps. She would later be elected a Fellow of Somerville College Oxford.

The commitment of people like Sarjit, and Pio's efforts on behalf of KANU, were about to bear fruit. In the February elections of 1961, KANU won 67.5% of the overall votes, giving them victory. The following month, nationalist leaders including Daniel arap Moi visited Kenyatta in the remote district of Lodwar where he was now being held. On 16th of April, with his daughter Margaret, he was moved to Maralal, where he met with the world's press.

Sarjit Heyer and me with our eldest daughters

On the 14th of August came the momentous day: after nine years in detention, Jomo Kenyatta was a free man. Around the globe, all eyes were on him as never before, waiting for him to make some decisive move. One of the first things we arranged was a delegation to London with James Gichuru, Tom Mboya and a few others. Also with us was the white South African Bruce McKenzie. Bruce was something of an enigma, but, as we were to discover, he would prove very useful to Kenyatta. An RAF pilot during the Second World War, he had been shot down twice, the second time over the Mediterranean where he had drifted for two days with most of his face blown away.

Awarded the DFC bar, and with his jaw rebuilt, he had come to Kenya in 1946 and set up as a farmer. By now in his early forties, about ten years older than me, we had first met in Parliament as national members, he for the Europeans. Then suddenly, I discovered he was in KANU and anti-European, saying emphatically we had to fight them. It didn't make sense to me – why had this man suddenly changed sides? I remembered in one of our first KANU meetings, as Bruce was shouting against the whites, Jackson Angaine, an African who was sitting behind me, muttered, 'This bastard, he was a torturer in the camps, he dislocated my thigh trying to get a confession.'

Although a good farmer, Bruce always seemed short of cash. Once when he was staying in a flat in Nairobi West, he asked me to lend him 300 shillings for the rent, which I did for three months. On another occasion quite out of the blue he asked, 'Fitz, do you like chicken?' I nodded, attaching no significance to the question. A couple of days later my mother told me that a 'Mzungu' had come in a pickup truck and delivered 70-odd chickens, plucked and cut up. Having no fridges then, I told my mother she had best give the meat away to her friends. Then one day, Bruce said to me, 'You know Kenyatta, can you introduce me?' Sure, I told him, and sent a request to Kenyatta, who invited us over to his farm at Gatundu at 5.30 in the morning. I was surprised to find him already dressed and down in the valley inspecting his crop. He shook hands with Bruce and they talked about farming. Kenyatta seemed to take to him straightaway. Bruce then said, 'You know Mzee, I don't think this maize you've planted is the best variety, it's the hybrid stuff you want. It'll yield three or four times what you're getting now.' Kenyatta said he'd look into it. The next thing we knew, Bruce was replanting all his maize for him.

The real intrigue though began when we got to London. We realised Kenyatta had no money and that we'd have to pay for him. The Cumberland Hotel at Marble Arch was £3 a night, a week's wages for many. Kenyatta also liked to eat well, especially after his time in prison, often putting away three or four steaks for dinner. When we asked for the bill, however, the manager informed us that it had already been taken care of. 'By whom?' I asked. 'Mr Mackenzie.' Surprised, I told Bruce he was very kind, but knowing he was hard up, he must at least let me pay my share. It was then that he put me in the picture; Izzi Sommen, Consul at the Israeli Embassy, had arranged with Joe Lyons, who owned the hotel, to cover all our expenses. Lyons ran the large chain of 'Corner Houses', where in my student days in London I had enjoyed many a cheap meal. He was also Jewish. Apparently the Israelis, mindful of their interests in a future independent Kenya, were anxious to forge a relationship with Kenyatta. Bruce it seemed had, behind the scenes, been the intermediary. It would not be the only time he played such a part. Previously, Kenyatta had always been broke, and I remember when he came out of prison and found his house demolished by the British Government, he asked us if we could find some money to help him build just a simple garage to live in. We had previously raised small amounts from donations, but things were always tight. After meeting Bruce, however, Kenyatta was mysteriously never short of cash.

London was also the backdrop for a more startling piece of drama. Kenyatta was addressing a public meeting in the hotel, when suddenly something flew through the air towards him. It turned out to be the entrails of a chicken. There was a gasp as we saw Kenyatta take up his walking stick, and drawing from it a gleaming blade, spring into the audience. I ran forward to restrain him, which was not easy, he was so strong, his anger immense. Grasping both his hands in mine, as he continued to shake with rage I said, 'Jomo, think please, I cannot defend you against a charge of murder.' After a few seconds he began to calm down and put away his swordstick. The man that had thrown the entrails, presumably a right-wing thug trying to paint Kenyatta as some kind of primitive savage, had already fled.

Back home, fellow Africans were vying for his approval. KANU, comprising Kikuyu, Luo and Kamba, and whose natural figurehead was Kenyatta, was the largest political group. A year earlier, however, the other main tribes, Kalenjin, Maasai, Turkana and Samburu, had formed their own party, KADU, the Kenya African Democratic Union. Both had invited Kenyatta to lead them, and although KANU had elected him while still in detention, he was in no hurry to accept the offer, or decide either way, or gave that impression at least.

In my view Kenyatta was playing the perfect politician. He discussed the issues with those around him, particularly Pio and myself, as he knew we had no personal interest in leadership. Tom Mboya was also used as a sounding board in these private discussions. Kenyatta's criteria for choice of party were simple: the tribal structure of each, and which was most likely to win an election, and he told KADU quite frankly that theirs was a minority party and his intention was to lead the majority. Reluctantly, I saw his point. It would be foolish to try to take control of KADU, whose members were tribal opponents of his natural supporters throughout the country. Kenyatta was a very strong nationalist but also a tribalist who believed in the greatness of his own people, the Kikuyu. My greatest sadness in Kenya, which I discovered at this time, was that tribalism played a very important part in politics, and this truth would be borne out by events.

Kenyatta had recognised the very strong loyalties that lay beneath the surface of Kenyan politics a long time ago, and in his view the country had to be ruled by a coalition of tribes, under whatever collective party name. He felt that through this process the Kikuyu would dominate, and would say as much in political meetings, his rhetoric along the lines that if you have fought for the independence of Kenya, you have planted a tree and watered it with your blood, so who should receive the fruits of that tree? As expected, the answer would come: 'He who fought for them.' And if you slaughtered a cow for a feast, which person should have the best parts? 'He who slaughtered the cow.'

Very many people agreed. Having worked so hard for freedom, been imprisoned for nine years and given decades of his life to his nation's struggle, Kenyatta felt it was his right to have the best. Few could question his industry and commitment, and without him it was unlikely the national movement would have taken off. So many Africans had emerged from detention with nothing, having lost businesses, property, social position and support. It was only to be expected that they would endorse Kenyatta and seek something for themselves now.

Kenyatta's fellow detainees in Kapenguria – Karumba, Kaggia, Kubai, Oneko and Ngei – had also waited a long time for freedom and were expected to play their part in the new challenges and huge opportunities about to burst forth in Kenya. How would they align themselves? It would be a mistake to assume because these men had stood trial and been locked up for a common cause, that they now, or had ever, shared a completely common agenda. Karumba, whom we had hardly ever met, did not speak English and seemed something of a law unto himself. Kaggia and Kubai, both very strong personalities, were, or so I had originally thought, quite close. This impression was swiftly revised when one day in Kapenguria we broke the news to Kaggia that a close friend and ally of his had been hacked to death outside Nairobi. Without saying a word, Kaggia looked furiously at Kubai, who just smiled slyly as if to say, 'I've got one over on you now.'

Achieng Oneko was a very mild, affectionate and gentle person, and though committed to the national movement, it was known that he had never been involved with the Mau Mau. A journalist, I think his basic concern was to fight for equal land rights for Africans. In the early days of the movement this was what most people wanted, with few talking of independence. Although acquitted at the appeal, the British had kept him in detention, and fearing a Kikuyu–Luo alliance, separated him from Kenyatta. He had, I discovered later, been asked by fellow Luo Oginga Odinga to be his representative in KAU.

Paul Ngei was a show-off, a charming fellow who laughed a lot and treated everything as if it were a big joke. It was said though, that in Lodwar detention camp he had intervened to stop Kenyatta being beaten, wresting the whip from the guard and asking that it be used on him instead. When I realised he was the son of a senior chief of the Akamba tribe, it explained a lot. Life, now he was a free man again, became one happy-go-lucky affair for Ngei, and from the way he talked it seemed he was always having a lot of fun. Though a strong nationalist, I got the impression he hadn't been a serious Mau Mau leader, and had attended meetings to show solidarity rather than take any part in killing or physical fighting.

A second Lancaster House Conference was announced for the beginning of 1962 and the leading figures in Kenya's national movement would be attending. I too had been invited. Flying into London on a cold February day, I took rooms in the south west of the capital, from which to travel up by train each day to Green Park. From the Tube station, Lancaster House, a large imposing mansion dating back to 1825 and situated in the St James's district, was just a five-minute walk. On the first day, the press were waiting eagerly as the delegates arrived.

Kenyatta, wearing a heavy greatcoat, circular African hat and carrying a briefcase and walking stick, waved his familiar flywhisk and smiled for the cameras. The hat was a Luo design, signalling to the tribe that he represented them too.

Once all were seated in the grand hall, Colonial Secretary Reginald Maudling commenced his opening address: 'Gentlemen, on this conference depends the whole future of Kenya.' Sat to my right facing out from our side of the long table was the lawyer Argwings Kodhek, and to his right Maasai politician John Keen. On my left was Kenyatta, then Tom Mboya. Kenyatta had insisted I sit beside him during the debates. I was a barrister and had a PhD, he reminded me, and with my knowledge and expertise I should be at his side. There was another reason for the request though, and the fact that Oginga Odinga, a leading figure, was seated behind me, which I will come to in a moment.

Tom Mboya and Oginga Odinga were two totally different personalities. Odinga, a 50-year-old Luo chief, was warm-hearted and affectionate, and more of a humorist than a socialist I would say. He loved people, helped them in whatever way he could, and had nothing against money, seeing the creation of wealth as a way forward. He had started a bus service from Kisumu and given it to an Indian to run, and also set up a Luo thrift society. I think he was keen on everyone having a better life all round. As leaders do, he liked to show himself off, but didn't seem vain, preferring traditional African dress rather than, like some, the most expensive modern suits and shoes. Odinga's only real flaw I would say was a tendency to lose his head occasionally, and speak too strongly and emotionally.

Tom Mboya, also a Luo, was already a seasoned trade unionist and prominent figure, and at the time of Lancaster House, still only 31 years old. From humble beginnings he had already achieved great things in Kenya's trade union movement, lobbying, addressing meetings and campaigning for fairer conditions for workers. I had got to know him early on, before he had any formal higher education, then later, when he went to study for a while at Ruskin College he would often come to see me in London when I was completing my PhD at the LSE. During these visits I was amazed at the transformation, and what a brilliant man he had become academically; in those few months he must have read more books than I had in five years.

Tom was also a born speaker, very eloquent. I have still never met anyone like him, able to get his point across and answer questions as clearly in English as in Swahili, whatever the audience's anxieties or grievances, whether to KANU, KADU, the British Government or the European settlers. At the same time he roused people's emotions, moved and inspired them. He had become famous for the student 'airlifts', when he had gone to see Jack Kennedy, who then made a personal cash donation of $150,000 for Africans to study at American universities. Kennedy also aimed to benefit from the airlifts, by winning the black vote, so Tom was useful to him. Eighty-one students went from Kenya, followed by over 700 more from various African countries. Tom took an active part in the programme, and one time, having a couple of last-minute seats on a flight, asked me if I knew of anyone who might go. My mother suggested a Goan family of several children in Zanzibar, who were very poor. One of the sisters said yes, she could be ready the next day, and so off she went to study in America. Another 'airlift' student, who had left Kenya in 1959 for the University of Honolulu was Barack Obama Senior, father of the future US President.

As well as being a remarkable organiser, Tom was also the most brilliant orator I have ever heard, his speeches absolutely full of logic. Kenyatta would laugh and joke when addressing meetings, and was also very eloquent, but you often came away asking yourself if the audience's questions had been properly answered. Tom's answers were always delivered clearly and backed up by a set of reasons – one, two, three, etc., which made sense and stayed in people's minds. Odinga, aware of the younger Luo man's ability and charisma, appointed Tom secretary of his African Independent Members Organisation. It was Odinga saying, 'Look, Mboya is my secretary – mwandishi wangu – he takes the minutes and writes the notes – why would he try to compete with me?' Tom thought himself the more competent leader though, and being sharper and more organised, he was right. The only thing against him was his youth, which for Odinga was also a threat.

Kenyatta, now around 70 years old, was also well aware of young Tom Mboya's appeal and potential as a leadership contender. At Lancaster House, knowing Tom's gift for oratory, he urged me not to let him take the stage but to answer every question myself and not worry that people might think I was talking too much. That wouldn't have been a problem for me, as once I start talking I just can't stop, but because of the seating layout, if I sat next to Kenyatta, Odinga would have to sit behind us. I told Kenyatta this wouldn't be fair to Mr Odinga, who was Vice-President of KANU, while I was nowhere in the party. Odinga though seemed unconcerned and told me not to worry: 'Fitz, I know you're a good man and you're not going to take my job. I'll sit behind you, and if there's a photo opportunity I'll just put my head out in front.' I assured him there was no need to do that; whenever any pictures were being taken he must take his rightful place and have my seat. He appreciated this and was a humble man in that sense, willing to step back from his official position and let someone else speak.

And speak I did! Anyone looking back over the minutes of the Lancaster House Conferences of 1962 and 1963 will probably find I talked more than anyone else. There were more technical discussions than anything else, trying to find compromise between the numerous communities – Indians, Muslims, Hindus, KANU, KADU, the two European parties, the Mau Mau party, which wanted independence at the coast, and the Kenya Freedom Party, supporting KANU and the Congress Party. The sharpest division was between the two large power blocs: KADU, which wanted Kenya to have a localised system of administration or 'majimbo', Swahili for regions, and KANU, which under Kenyatta wanted a centralised, national authority to govern the whole country.

Trying to bring the two sides together was a tricky business and there was stubborn resistance, as well as disagreement and rivalry within each group. KANU was led in effect by Michael Blundell and Wilfred Havelock. Tom Mboya hardly made any speeches, and his relations with Odinga were all right, but only just. Kenyatta I think liked Odinga more, but used Tom more. I believe he saw Tom as the better organiser, with a lot of energy, both useful attributes. Unfortunately in this world, particularly in politics, people use others even if they don't like them, and Kenyatta always had this quiet feeling about Tom, that though this young man is clever, he is not going to take my job. At the same time, Kenyatta also leaned on Pio, another great organiser, to counter-balance Tom's methods. Pio, it should be pointed out, being Indian, had no support or money from his community, but managed to run things very well nonetheless.

Representing KADU were Chairman Daniel arap Moi, Ronald Ngala and Masinde Muliro. Ngala was quiet and dignified and made few enemies, and in that sense was a very good leader. Moi was considered, I'm afraid, like a 'little mtoto' in the old days, brought in because he was the only Kalenjin in the area. He in turn brought Jean Marie Seroney, and he and Muliro were the only two who spoke in KADU as far as the Africans were concerned. Seroney was a very competent man, an able lawyer who worked hard and was happy to be KADU President. Muliro was a fighter, who got very worked up when making a speech, foaming at the mouth metaphorically. Strongly expressive in his views, he had enormous spirit and determination and was to my mind the most meaningful and effective leader. I noticed though, that he too was a little wary of both Mboya and Odinga.

When official meetings were finished, we talked over the day's events, or socialised a little. Kenyatta, avoiding Tom Mboya and Njoroge Mungai, his personal physician, spent most evenings drinking on the veranda of his hotel room with Odinga. Kenyatta drank only VAT 69. He joked it was the Pope's phone number. They would sit and chat for hours, and being both older, I think felt they understood one another. It would transpire that Kenyatta wanted Odinga as his number two, as Finance Minister in the new Government. When the British overruled this, however, he accepted their wishes, and it shocked us all that he gave in just like that. We realised Kenyatta was very fond of Odinga in a way, while at the same time he wanted to make sure he was the right man, who would implement and support his own policies. There was only one other person close to Kenyatta during the Lancaster House conferences; anyone wishing to see the Kikuyu leader at his hotel had first to get past Achieng Oneko, who slept in the next room, barring the door with his bed. With the continued death threats against Kenyatta, it was the mild-mannered Oneko who was, literally, putting his life on the line for him.

As the discussions at Lancaster House wore on, it was clear that a major remaining stumbling block was the European settler community. The British Government told us plainly: the only way they could give us independence was if we could promise the farmers that we would pay them for their land, buy them out in other words. They had calculated a value of £36 million. That sounds like nothing today but was a fortune in 1962. I said, but we don't have the money. No, they said, we'll give you the money. Good God, I said, we could never afford to pay it back. They said, who's asking for it back? We don't want it back, we want to give it to you, and every year we'll write a bit off, until the whole lot is written off. We don't want the British here to say we called you Mau Mau, and now we're giving you money! You must buy the land from the European farmers on a 'willing buyer and willing seller' basis. So when they are willing to sell, you buy. Thus would come into being the Land Settlement Board, under Chairman Norman Feather of the Standard Bank, with the British Consular General and Moi, appointed to the post by Kenyatta, as committee members.

Among the wide media coverage of the 1962 conference, *Time* magazine in February published the following report:

> *In London's splendid Lancaster House,* where constitutional conferences compete with a baroque painting of Venus and the Graces, sat three graces from Africa, attired in tribal costumes of lion and monkey skins. Together with 62 other delegates from Kenya and ten British officials, the chiefs were attending what was already billed as "the last-chance" conference. Its aim: to prepare the way for Kenya's independence.*
>
> *Of more than a dozen countries on three continents that have won independence from Britain since World War II, none has seemed so ill-prepared for nationhood as Kenya. Yet British officials fear a bloody resurgence of Mau Mau savagery if Kenya does not get its freedom from British rule in the near future — possibly by the end of this year. Thus, once again, Africa's remote and bizarre tribal politics were thrust at puzzled European officials who were trying to give a colonial country freedom without chaos.*
>
> *Land for Everyone. Kenya's bitterly divided leaders have their own proposals for a constitution after independence; their plans seem irreconcilable, yet each faction warns that, unless its ideas are accepted, the rival tribes will revert to spear and poisoned arrow in Congo-style civil war. The*

conflict involves Kenya's two major parties and their bosses: KANU's grey-bearded, rheumy-eyed Jomo Kenyatta, 71, and restrained Ronald Ngala, 39, president of KADU and Kenya's leader of government business. After eight years' detention for his ringleader's role in the Mau Mau uprisings, Kenyatta is still a hero to millions of Africans; he insists on a strong centralized government with a one-house legislature and an elected head of state. KADU urges a Swiss-style federation of six largely autonomous regional constituencies, divided along tribal lines, with a two-house federal parliament and a coalition cabinet.

Each plan reflects the fears of either party. KANU's strength comes overwhelmingly from Kenya's three most powerful tribes: the Kikuyu (Kenyatta's kin), Luo and Kamba, who represent nearly half of Kenya's entire African population.

KANU also commands the allegiance of most detribalized urban Africans, who devoutly believe Kenyatta's pledge that there will be work or land for everyone when his party has won independence on its own terms. KADU, on the other hand, draws most of its support from the Maasai, Baluhya and other smaller tribes who, though a minority, occupy a far bigger area than the land-starved peoples represented by KANU. KADU's majimbo (regionalism) plan is thus aimed at protecting minority rights of the smaller, often nomadic tribes against political and territorial domination by the big tribes.

Hope for Moderation. Though KANU has countered with reassuring proposals for a strong bill of rights and an independent judiciary. KADU leaders remain deeply apprehensive: impartial administration of justice, they argue, will be hampered for years by Kenya's almost total lack of trained native lawyers and the reluctance of white officials to stay on. Last year alone, 3,000 whites— 5% of the white population—left the colony, where they are outnumbered 100 to 1.

Urging his followers to sharpen their spears, KADU's fiery William Murgor warned ominously last fortnight: "If it's clear that KANU has succeeded in bamboozling the British against our plans for a future Kenya, I'll blow a whistle from London and you will know there must be war." Opening the conference, Britain's Colonial Secretary Reginald Maudling insisted that Britain will not free the colony "unless we can be sure that we shall be handing over authority in Kenya to a stable regime, free from oppression, free from violence, free from racial discrimination." If Britain can stick to its pledge, despite a $50 million annual bill to keep Kenya's ailing economy from total collapse, the most hopeful prospect for the future is that a moderate third party will emerge to break the deadlock and agree on a constitution acceptable to big and small tribes alike. Already touted as its leader is KANU's astute, ambitious Secretary Tom Mboya, 31, who has already impressed responsible Africans as offering the most promising alternative to Kenyatta's erratic leadership. Meanwhile, as one African put it: "The melon is split wide open. We can only try to cover it with gauze."

As the second Lancaster House Conference drew to a close, after a great deal of talking, endless minutes, figures, legal details, questions and amendments raised and batted back and forth, there was still a great deal to settle. But if the melon was still split, the protective gauze had been strong enough at least to produce some decisive action, and an historic moment for Kenya: a commitment to the creation of a multi-racial Coalition Government. On Wednesday 2nd of May 1962, its newly appointed members assembled for official photos in the grounds of Government House Nairobi. The line-up was as follows:

Mr D.T. arap Moi, Minister for Local Government; Mr A. Jamidar, Minister for Tourism, Forests and Wildlife; Mr B. Mate, Minister for Social Services; Mr M. Muliro, Minister for Commerce and Industry; Sir Anthony Swann, Minister for Defence; Mr B.R. McKenzie, Minister for Land Settlement and Water Development; Mr T. Towett, Minister for Lands, Surveys, and Town Planning; Mr Ronald G. Ngala, Minister of State for Constitutional Affairs and Administration; the Acting Governor, Mr E.N. Griffith-Jones; Mr Jomo Kenyatta, Minister of State for Constitutional Affairs and Economic Planning; Mr L. Sagini, Minister for Education; Mr T.J. Mboya, Minister for Labour; Sir Michael Blundell, Acting Minister of Agriculture; Mr T. Chokwe, Minister for Works and Communications; Mr J.S. Gichuru, Minister for Finance; Mr A.M.F. Webb, Minister for Legal Affairs. Mr F. Mati, Minister for Health and Housing was not present.

One of the three Lancaster House Conferences (Kenya) (1960, 1962, 1963) at which Kenya's constitutional framework and independence were negotiated.

Lancaster House Conference

Kenya's first Coalition Government
Source: The National Archives, Kew

Jomo Kenyatta, Mama Ngina and myself

James Gichuru, K.P. Shah, Jomo Kenyatta, George Nthenge, Ronald Ngala, Peter Okondo and others

Paul Ngei, Jomo Kenyatta, Oginga Odinga and Jeremiah Nyagah

A larger group of politicians around that time including Timothy Muinga Chokwe, Fred Mati, Tom Mboya, Derek Erskine, Ronald Ngala, Jomo Kenyatta, Masinde Muliro, George Nthenge and Peter Okondo

Chapter Twelve

Majimbo v. Harambee: The War of Ideas, Plots and Manoeuvres

Events from 1963

In early 1963 we were back in London. This, the third Lancaster House Conference, would be an attempt to agree the final steps to an independent Kenya. After long debates about what should be the shape of the new country's constitution, Kenyatta's KANU were still holding out for centralised government, while Ngala's KADU argued for majimbo, a patchwork of more autonomous geographical and tribal regions. It was stalemate, and no one seemed to know how to end it.

      Then one day Kenyatta called us to a private meeting. He said it was time to move forward and that we should accept, more or less, whatever terms were being proposed for the constitution. When there were murmurs of disapproval, Kenyatta said not to worry about majimbo or anything else, because later on, once he was in power, he would change it all. 'But Jomo,' I said, 'that is not right, we are negotiating in good faith, and we want to keep to whatever we agree on here.' He replied, 'Fitz, you don't know what you are talking about. A leader is a leader only as long as he has people behind him. If not, for whatever reason, he is no longer a leader. I have got to keep these people behind me. Even now Kikuyu are saying we should go back to the forest and fight. I don't want them to do that, and I don't want to fight with them either. I support democracy, I fully support equality, but we've got to make sure we don't lose our heads.' I couldn't understand what Kenyatta was saying. Later on I would, and much more.

The Land Settlement Board under Moi would be one scheme that got used not quite as some people had intended when they had drawn it up. As each farm of say a thousand acres came up for sale, the Board decided who should buy it. In one case, after about 500 Kalenjin agricultural workers had formed a co-op, collected money and applied for a large acreage, the Consular General told me quite frankly that you could guess who got the land, the Kikuyu. One British fellow did remark that it was a bit unfair, but if the Government wanted to give the farm to the Kikuyu, the Europeans had no objection and what's more it was 'their man' Moi's decision as to who got what. Moi of course was Kalenjin but wanted Kikuyu support for his political career. My friend Jean Marie Seroney would get very irate, saying, 'this man Moi is mad, giving all our Kalenjin land to Kikuyu, and one day there is going to be trouble.'

In African politics outward impressions were considered very important. When the two main parties were competing for Kenyatta's favour, Ronald Ngala had given him a Standard Vanguard car. It was then that Njoroge Mungai had arrived on the scene and, announcing himself as Kenyatta's cousin, presented us with a brand new Mercedes Benz for KANU. I thought this was fantastic, as previously I used to drive out to Gatundu in my 1938 Morris 8 to pick up Kenyatta, or he would wait for a bus or matatu into town and then walk everywhere. On hearing about the gift, however, Kenyatta demanded to know who was this man who was telling everyone he was his cousin. It turned out that Mungai had only paid a deposit on the Mercedes and it had to be sent back. Then the British community clubbed together and bought Kenyatta a Land Rover, while their American counterparts presented him with a Plymouth convertible, which he loved being driven around in.

I suggested that now having four vehicles at his disposal, he donate at least one of them to the party. 'Why?'

he asked. I replied, 'Jomo, the members need transport to attend meetings. Most of them don't even own a bicycle. I do my bit with my little Morris but I can only make so many trips.' 'No, no,' he said, 'You are thinking like the Wahindis, that only Indians can drive around in big, big cars. These cars have been given to me and I think I must keep them. In any case, you know, I want you to realise one thing. The Africans only respect a man with a lot of mali [wealth]. If he is a poor man they will think he is useless. You have to have a lot of hangers-on and your youth wingers going with you, and a lot of cows, houses, etc., then they'll think, "Ah, he is a great leader".'

I was a bit shocked by this, but then realised it was true. Some time later, talking to a Luo gardener of mine, I mentioned that I believed Odinga was not well off. 'No, no,' he replied, 'Odinga is very, very rich, richer than Kenyatta, he has a lot of money.' I remember thinking that in other communities this would be a minus point. I then met other Luos who tried to tell me how rich Odinga was. I suddenly understood why Tom Mboya had bought a Mercedes Benz and went around hooting and showing it to everyone, and each year he would buy a new one. Odinga's money was coming from the Chinese and Soviets, Mboya's from the Americans.

As the move towards independence gathered pace, anxiety among the European community grew. The white settlers had long been Kenyatta's sworn enemies, and thousands would like to have killed him if they could. Up until now the British Government had protected them, but if the troops went and Kenyatta took over the country, they feared reprisals. Kenyatta though had the ability to look forward, not back. His strategy was to disarm the Europeans morally, assuring them they were quite safe and that there could be a shared future for them in Kenya. Though this wasn't what a lot of Africans wanted, Kenyatta stuck to it, making his slogan the word chanted for generations by his African brothers as they toiled and sweated on the land – 'Harambee!' – 'Let's Pull Together!'

Kenyatta had put this philosophy into practice in his own life. When he came out of prison he pointed out to me his house and land at Gatundu, which the Government had taken and given to his younger brother James Muigai. He remembered carrying James in his hands when he was a baby. On being released, he could have used his authority to demand the property back, but he knew that this was what the Government wanted, to turn brothers, and Africans, against one another. Instead he bought the land and house back from his brother, and it is important to stress that he used his own money to do this and there was no question of him grabbing anything. Kenyatta had taken a similar approach to the Mau Mau; Peter Koinange put it right when he said, look, if you see your brother stealing from someone you don't like, would you rush to the police and report him? No, you try to convince him not to do it but you don't want to put him in prison, and you don't want to fight with him.

A good influence and a useful go-between in the transition to independence was Malcolm MacDonald who had just come in as Governor General. An Oxford graduate and experienced diplomat, MacDonald was pro-British naturally, but along with a shrewd intelligence was also very warm and personable. Though dressing in full regalia for formal ceremonies, in England and in Kenya he frequently dropped in on people, myself included, just to say hello, and it wouldn't have surprised me if he had done so in his pyjamas, such was his style. Kenyatta liked him very much. His wife was also very charming and considerate. When, during a dinner at her house, noticing I was not eating, she asked me what was wrong. When I explained I had a seafood allergy, she immediately offered me an omelette and went to the kitchen herself to make it.

In May 1963, Kenya was scheduled to hold its first ever general election. I was standing for Nairobi North West, which included Parklands, and I was having a hard time. The Putelkadias, or stonebreakers, were very anti-me, and supporting their Gujarati fellow, Jamindar. Hearing of my problem, Tom Mboya offered to accompany me to the constituents' temple in Grogan Road and speak to them on my behalf. 'How will you do that?' I said, 'you won't understand their language, I've already tried.' Undeterred, Tom said he would go with me anyway. So one morning we set out early, arriving before 4.30am and the start of their prayers. Tom was asked to cover his head like the other Indians, and doing so with his handkerchief, sat down cross-legged with them. I spoke first for five minutes then introduced Tom.

Speaking in Swahili, without trying to mimic or tease them, but in an accent they could understand, he explained point by point the message I wanted to get across. I could see them taking it in, and how he was touching their hearts. He spoke for a good half hour, at the end of which they all cheered and got up to embrace him. All the Indian shopkeepers now thought Tom would be the saviour of Kenya, and while not expecting him to support their particular interest, felt he would not terrorise them. They weren't so sure of Kenyatta, fearing that if the Mau Mau, with whom they identified him, took over Kenya, it would be a big blow to them.

On Election Day on the 27th of May, when the voting had reached 58 seats in the House of Representatives for KANU against 28 for KADU, it was already being called a certain win for Kenyatta. The only white candidate, Edward Hawkins, lost his deposit. That evening the BBC reported that: 'Thousands of Kenyans ran through the rain-drenched streets of Nairobi, cheering at news of the results. The following day Malcolm Macdonald summoned Kenyatta to form a Government. In his speech, he affirmed his commitment to reconciliation, 'We are not to look to the past – racial bitterness, the denial of fundamental rights, the suppression of our culture – let there be forgiveness.' He also called for unity under the principles of 'democratic African socialism'.

Kenyatta was sworn in as Prime Minister, and on the 12th of December 1963 Kenya was declared independent. Standing in an open-topped jeep, accompanied by Mboya,

Odinga and Gichuru, and flanked by a motorcycle escort and waving to the crowds, Kenyatta led a proud procession through the streets of Nairobi. On the snow-covered Mount Kenya, the black, red and green flag, replacing the Union Jack, was hoisted. Newly printed postage stamps bearing Kenyatta's image showed the mountain in the background, along with the word Uhuru – Freedom.

Not all Africans were jubilant. Moi, who through the Land Settlement Board had given Kalenjin land to the Kikuyu, was furious when he found out they had not voted for him as he expected, and could not forgive them. Kenyatta also equated loyalty with land, and as early as the Lancaster House talks, had told me that when independence came I should have some as a reward and to be patriotic. Without land, he argued, a person had no stake in the country and was not a true Kenyan. He offered me not one farm but several. I told him that the land was for the Africans, I was just one of the Wahindi, a rather dismissive term for Asians. He tried very hard to persuade me. In the end I just said, 'Jomo, I'm a city person, I don't know one end of a cow from the other,' at which everyone laughed, and we left it at that.

Meanwhile, Kenyatta rolled out his first independent cabinet: Odinga was in charge of Home Affairs; Tom Mboya, Justice Minister; Gichuru, Finance; Oneko, Information, Broadcasting and Tourism; Bruce Mackenzie, Agriculture; and my friend Joe Murumbi given the title of Minister of State in the Prime Minister's Office, equivalent to Minister of Foreign Affairs. I realised why he had chosen Joe and Bruce. I could see quite clearly how it worked. Almost everyone, Tom, Odinga, etc., had their group, their supporters, but Kenyatta had very few apart from myself, though I wasn't anyone's supporter in that sense. He wanted to be able to say, 'Look, this is my group,' people who, when an issue arose in Parliament, because he had put them in would back him.

Joe, though half Maasai, had no constituency in that community as yet, though it would come later. He was a very nice man, amiable and sociable, but not a politician. Pio had taken him into politics, got round him, saying come and help us. Joe was very good to me; after approaching the Maasai Council for somewhere to build a house, he said, 'Look Fitz, I'm going to get eight acres in Ngong, I'm half Maasai and half Goan, do you want some?' At that time millions of acres were available and they would have given him much more, which he would have well deserved in my opinion. 'Let's go and have a look,' he said. We jumped in my little Morris 8 and drove out to Ngong, stopping to push the car up the steep hill.

And so Joe gave me two acres of his land. He was generous in other ways. In his capacity as Minister of Foreign Affairs, he one day invited me to be his number two on a delegation to the United Nations in New York. I said it was very nice of him but I didn't feel I could go. He was insistent. 'Come on,' he urged, 'we'll have a good time together.' We did, though we both worked very hard. It was the first time I had been to America, and New York was a dazzling place, but this wasn't a jolly and we had a lot to do. At night I was shocked that while Inderjit Singh Boy and myself sat down to draft speeches for the next day, all the other delegates seemed to be off on dates. I said, 'What type of people are you? We've come all the way here, to the UN General Assembly, and you don't want to work?' Tomorrow, they would say, we'll work tomorrow. Several were civil servants, all very nice people, but I couldn't understand why they weren't making the most of such an opportunity. Inderjit and myself, working until gone 2am, then had to call up the chauffeur and escort the female typists home, New York being too dangerous for them to walk at night. By the time we'd dropped three or four of the girls in different parts of the city, the sun was almost up over Manhattan.

Joe treated everyone with kindness and courtesy, and spoke very well in debates. By this time he had a pretty firm grasp of foreign policy. Working as a clerk with the Somali Movement had brought him into contact with a number of people destined for prominence, and it was through Joe that I was introduced to, among others, Abdirashid Ali Shermarke, who in 1967 would become President of Somalia. I thought Kenyatta had made a very good choice in Joe. He was very much a member of our group with Pio, which I wouldn't call Odinga's group, but more of a 'left' group, though I don't know how left we were! But put it like this, we were not yet a group that wanted to make a lot of money, nor could we be bought, none of us.

While Kenyatta hoped Joe would do a good job as Minister of Foreign Affairs, his early appointment of Tom Mboya as Minister for Labour in the 1962 Coalition Government, had had a different agenda. The trade unions were Tom's baby, for whom he was use to fighting the Government; changing sides would be difficult, and Kenyatta, expecting him to fail, was out to embarrass him. Most of us thought this would be the end of his career, but to many people's surprise he had done quite a good job. When Kenyatta then made him Minister for Justice and Constitutional Affairs, Tom was equally determined to do his best. He would be in his office at 5am dictating letters, and, not being a lawyer, was not afraid to ask questions – how does this work, what would be the legal framework of such and such a policy, etc. He would often come and sit with me for hours, then go away and read up on the subject. I was surprised by the number of books in his home, many very good editions on law and on constitutional politics. Turning the pages and seeing copious underlining and notes in Tom's handwriting, it was clear that he did not, as some people do, buy books for decoration.

Thorough and industrious in everything he took on, we were lucky to have a man like Tom in those days. I disagreed with him on many issues, but when Kenyatta and Pio had been in jail, it was Tom who, in a subtle way, by supporting workers, had kept the struggle for land reform, social equality and African dignity alive. In helping his members, while not over-alarming the British – who would have banned the unions as they had every other political organisation – he had performed a skilful balancing act. The student airlifts to America had also raised his international profile, and since 1960, when he became the first Kenyan to appear on the cover of *Time* magazine, there was an image around the world of Tom Mboya as a charming, dynamic and progressive young statesman, destined for great things.

He was certainly ambitious. Anyone entering politics at that level, given the intelligence, would want the top job, and though he never said so, it seemed to me that everyone was aware of his desire to take over from Kenyatta at the first opportunity. He knew he would need a lot of Kikuyu support though, and he had virtually none. One man who did back him was James Gichuru, to whom he would often give drinks. Gichuru owned a bar on Campos Ribeiro Avenue and one night he invited Tom to meet him there. Also present was Charles Njonjo. I had known Charles in England, where, referred to as 'the senior chief's son', which he was, he was regarded as a kind of monarch in waiting, a 'Prince of Kenya' who would one day be King. Those who held this impression knew little about Kenya. Charles had an upper-class air and spoke like an English aristocrat, with tremendous charm and self-assurance – "Lord Charles of Kabeteshire" as the young Africans called him.

In London in 1948, when we started the East African Students Association with me as Literary Secretary, we had only one African and were taken in by Charles's charisma. The British members appointed him President, but he never took part in debates or our visits to the House of Commons, except on one occasion when he told off a Conservative MP quite strongly. Studying law, he went from cocktail party to cocktail party, and if he did sit exams, never seemed to pass them. He had still not finished his Bar exams when I returned to the LSE in the 1950s.

When the Kapenguria Six were released, I remember saying to Charles that we – Kapila, the other lawyers and myself who had defended the Africans – had done all we could and it was now his turn to take over. His reply was that he was not getting involved in that sort of rubbish, but intended to work for the British Government. He took a job in the Registrar General's Office as little more than a clerk, most of whom were Goans. I was surprised that he was totally uninterested in helping the people of Kenya.

What Tom saw in Charles Njonjo was an opportunity. Like Bruce, he realised that Charles's bearing, outward intelligence and ability to express himself could be used for political gain. He also assumed that Charles had no ambitions. When Charles called me to have tea with him one day at the Queen's Hotel, I arrived to find Tom there also. 'Fitz I have something very serious to say to you,' announced Charles. 'Tell your friend not to back that old man as President of Kenya.' By 'my friend' I knew he meant Pio, and the 'old man' was Kenyatta.

'Why?' I asked.

'Because,' replied Charles in his lordly tone, 'he is totally incompetent, he's senile.'

'But who could you put in his place?'

'He's sitting right here, Tom is the man.'

Exactly who had first latched onto whom was hard to say, but both men had now shown their hand, to me at least. Charles clearly saw Tom as likely to be the next leader of the country, and perhaps a place for himself in a future Government.

Charles's use of the word 'President' was not accidental. Kenyatta had spoken to me of how he saw leadership. He believed strongly that just as you could not have two chiefs in one household, a country could not have two leaders. On 1st of June 1964 he amended the constitution, and on the 12th of December, one year after independence, Kenya was declared a republic, with the office of Prime Minister replaced by that of President, a position Kenyatta automatically assumed, making him Head of State, Head of the Government and Commander-in-Chief of the armed forces. Odinga was appointed Vice-President.

One of the senior figures in the rival KADU party, Moi, whose fellow Kalenjins occupied much of the prime Rift Valley land, was promoted to Minister for Home Affairs. At the same time KADU was dissolved and merged with KANU. There was now no clear official opposition.

Kenyatta seemed keen that I should have a position in the new Kenya, and as well as offering me farms, asked if I would like to be a minister, or Attorney General. I declined. As Deputy Speaker and a lawyer, I had plenty of work, but more importantly, I wanted to keep my independence. Tom, as Minister for Justice and Constitutional Affairs, in due course asked that Charles Njonjo be made Attorney General. Kenyatta, who only knew Njonjo distantly as the son of a chief, was not very keen. Tom told me he also had a fight to persuade the 'inner group' including Odinga, who probably had someone in the Asian community such as Kapila in mind for the job. Though Charles and I had never really agreed, he did get on well with Kapila and a few others in the Asian legal community. Among the few African lawyers in Kenya at that time, Argwings Kodhek and Jean Marie Seroney were both very competent, but Charles was perhaps unique in that he moved almost exclusively in European circles where he had many friends, and Kenyatta, once he got to know him, found his English mannerisms not at all offensive, but rather charming and a good bridge to the Europeans who all liked him.

Thus, at Tom's request and with Kenyatta's assent, Charles Njonjo, the man who had seemed so uninterested in advancement, was handed one of the most powerful positions in Kenya. He would even in a sense come to exercise more control than the President himself. Kenyatta did not attend to the day-to-day business of running the country. Njonjo was quite happy to do so. Why? Because he was ambitious and with it, very clever. Not only did he move in Parliament to bring police investigations under his authority, but he also acted in such a way that all the CID officers now looked on him as their boss and kow-towed to him. The prosecution also came under his authority, and as side prosecutor he would appoint his own people in the department, and though allowing them a degree of independence, they had basically to follow his preferences, which they always somehow knew and understood. The judges, who had previously had a separate board and budget, were now subsumed within the Attorney General's board. In a relatively short space of time, through force of personality and the widespread belief that he was close to Kenyatta, the whole judiciary was effectively being run by Njonjo.

With such power he could arrest anybody at any time. I remember the case of an Englishman, a sailor on holiday who, strolling along the seashore and happening to pass what was then the Provincial Commissioner's house, was apprehended and locked up. When someone applied for bail for him, Chief Justice Wicks announced, 'I haven't been able to ring my friend Njonjo yet to see whether the man should be released or not.' A friend of mine was in court at the time, 'I'm sorry,' he objected, 'but you are a judge and are supposed to be in charge, you cannot approach the Attorney General.' Wicks replied simply, 'But I always ask him.' I was very surprised when I heard that, and thought if the Chief Justice is taking instructions from the Attorney General, we don't have a judiciary.

While some were bent on consolidating their power base, the ambitions of other players on the stage of the newly independent Kenya were focused through constructive politics of one kind or another. Tom Mboya's Sessional Paper 10 was an appealing mission statement, emphasising the Government's belief in private enterprise combined with social and cultural programmes, what they called African Socialism. While this paper bore Tom's name, it is my belief that it was written largely by the civil servants in his department. It was due to be delivered in Parliament on the 29th of April 1965.

Practising what you preach takes effort and one finds very few people in this world who are dedicated to an ideal and prepared to work for it. Bildad Kaggia of the Kapenguria Six was one of them. A very sincere, modest person, in the 1963 elections he had won a seat in the Kandara constituency and looked set to stick by his vision of bringing justice to Kenya, by which I mean fairness for everyone. He didn't want anyone to enrich himself for the sake of it, nor use his authority to make money for himself or his family. Without ranking him alongside Mahatma Gandhi, he was, like Pio, willing to sacrifice personal gain for what he believed in. Here lay the seeds of a clash with Kenyatta, a leader who saw the fruits of independence as belonging not only to the country and the party, but also to himself and those close to him. He also knew how determined both Kaggia and Fred Kubai were in the pursuit of social equality, and was a little afraid of them.

Though Kaggia was known to associate with Odinga, in what one might call the left-wing group, they had never become great friends. Friendship with Pio was all they really had in common.

Pio was different. Although from the beginning the main political organiser, he had remained a man behind the scenes. He would write literally hundreds of letters, make endless telephone calls, issuing instructions to do this, go there, post that, and people did it, myself included. I didn't always agree with him, and we discussed our differences openly, but I knew his intentions were good. What he didn't want was to be an MP.

Perhaps the reluctance was because Pio's commitments were wider than just one country, having previously helped to liberate Goa from the Portuguese. I recalled how he had mentioned to me that we in East Africa should do more to assist. Since we had been so focused on the situation in Kenya at the time, I had been a little surprised. I remember saying that while I was sympathetic to such an aim, and indeed to the idea of liberating countries and people from economic and political oppression throughout the world, I felt that we might be in danger of dissipating our energies, and of our own loyalties being misunderstood by our supporters, and even by our friends.

Pio had then told me more about his active involvement in Goan liberation as a student, when he had helped to form the Goa National Congress. The authorities had clamped down and a warrant was issued for his arrest and deportation from Goa to Cape Verde, a distant archipelago off the west coast of Africa, still under Portuguese control. Pio described to me how he had managed to evade the police and escape to Kenya. He had since travelled to Delhi, where he met Nehru and officials of the Indian Government to talk about Goa, and while there took the opportunity to ask Nehru for assistance to start a nationalist paper in Kenya. Nehru duly provided funds, with which Pio began the Pan African Press, publishing *Sauti ya Mwafrika*, *Pan Africa* and the *Nyanza Times*. Most people in Kenya believed that the financial backing for these newspapers came from China. Naturally, India had to keep quiet about its support at the time, but as I said after Kenya's independence: now that we are a free country we can tell the truth to the world.

Pio had said he thought Portuguese colonialism was as bad as any other and that even if we no longer regarded ourselves primarily as Goans, as socialists it was our duty to lend what assistance we could to all liberation fronts. Our Goan heritage, even if only by virtue of our surnames, was an asset which could provide much-needed moral support, signalling to those in Goa that Goans in other parts of the world felt strongly that they should be an independent country.

Pio and Fitz holding "Anti-Imperialist Demonstrations" placards

Getting such a message out was important, since Portugal's Government was actively involved in propaganda, using the Goan Organisation in East Africa to convey the idea that Goans overseas, even the educated ones, supported the regime and were happy with the Portuguese. To offer a counter-argument, raising awareness of the injustices of colonial rule and stating the case for independence, Pio saw the need for a Goan vernacular paper and had launched *The Uzwod* in Nairobi. An alternative to the Goan Organisation was also needed, and the name proposed was the East African Goan National Association (EAGNA), but unfortunately, before we had time to form this organisation, in April 1954, Operation Anvil had been sprung and Pio was arrested. Others went ahead nonetheless, and J.M. Nazareth had been selected as president, myself one of the vice-presidents. Our activities had some effect, but the Portuguese acted swiftly, getting together with their fellow colonialists in Kenya to have the organisation banned. Despite this, the work continued, and we had been pleasantly surprised by the amount of support we had throughout East Africa, particularly from educated Goans. I believe that by this time even if we had wanted to cease functioning with the EAGNA, it would have proved impossible. Contacts that had been established with similar organisations and individuals in Bombay and Goa flourished. Of necessity, the work had to remain secret as the Portuguese Consulate and its stooges were vigilant and constantly sending dossiers on all of us to the British Special Branch. As usual, they labelled the lot of us 'Communists' as that seemed the easiest way to get us suppressed.

In 1960, only a few months after his release, Pio had formed a new organisation, the East African Goan League. As before, the Portuguese Government asked their colonial counterparts in Nairobi to issue a ban, but by this time things had moved on in Kenya, the nationalists were much stronger, and the request was unsuccessful. Pio then led a delegation from the League to visit Mzee Kenyatta at Maralal. The British had consistently refused Pio permission to see Kenyatta, but when the East African Goan League applied for a visit, no one asked for the individual names. Everyone at Maralal was quite shocked when the delegation arrived with Pio as the leader! In May 1961, a delegation from a Goan Ashram led by Prof Lucio Rodrigues and Dr Laura D'Souza had arrived in Kenya. Largely under the pretext of singing Goan songs and reciting Goan literature, they instilled some form of self-respect and dignity into East African Goans, many of whom had hitherto been loyal and servile servants of the British Crown. The Ashram delegates were amazingly successful in their aim. Tom Mboya, General Secretary of KANU and Muinga Chokwe, the party's Coast Region Chairman, accepted an invitation to attend a Conference on Goa in Delhi at the Ashram.

Some Goan nationalists later told me that Tom was extremely eloquent at the conference: he delivered a forthright speech, telling India and its Government that they hardly had a right to attempt to liberate Africa while at the same time afraid to liquidate Portuguese colonies within their own country. I believe these words made a deep impression on Pandit Nehru and influenced his decision to free Goa in 1961. After hearing the speech he organised an International Seminar on Portuguese Colonies. Perhaps his mind was already made up about Goa and he was testing reaction to the idea among friends. Among those in attendance were Kenneth Kaunda from Zambia (Northern Rhodesia), Nsilo Swai from Tanzania (then Tanganyika) and Pio. All the delegates urged military intervention to liberate Goa, with Pio particularly active in canvassing support for the action as a means of cracking the bastion of Portuguese imperialism in Mozambique, Angola and throughout the world. Pio was also aware that the use of force was likely to attract considerable adverse reaction from Western countries, and had told me that he thought a few rousing and impassioned speeches would convince Nehru to risk such criticism.

A few months later Mrs Lakshmi Menon arrived in Kenya, and it was obvious that the liberation of Goa was very much in the offing. Pio and Mr Chokwe even offered to organise an international volunteer brigade to assist, but this was not necessary. The Indian Army was deployed and the cowardly Portuguese fled. There was hardly a shot fired up until when two Indian officers went to accept the surrender of Aguada Fort after the Portuguese had raised a white flag and were killed at almost point blank range. Pio, his brother Rosario, Peter Carvalho and I were invited to Goa to take part in the victory celebrations. Pio met many old veterans of the campaign, people he had not seen since he had left India in 1947. Most of them begged him to stay. They wanted him to be their leader and it was obvious that he had lots of friends and a good deal of support wherever he went. But he declined. He said he was born in Kenya and Kenya was his home, and while he still had a soft spot for Goa and India, Kenya would be the home where he would work and die.

Back in Kenya, he worked on the launching of movements for the liberation of Angola and Mozambique, and in 1962, together with Chokwe, formed the Mozambique African National Union, based in Mombasa. Many of the delegates to the inaugural meeting had travelled hundreds of miles to be present. But the British Government was able to ban the organisation and it faded away. Nevertheless, Pio had formed valuable contacts with Mozambique nationalists, and 1962 saw the founding under Eduardo Mondlane of FRELIMO – the Frente de Libertacao de Mocambique – with whom Pio later worked very closely, as well as the Committee of Nine of the OAU. With Mozambique controlled by the police and nationalist activity forbidden, President Nyerere of Tanzania being sympathetic to the Mozambique nationalists, FRELIMO set up an HQ in Dar es Salaam where Pio would often visit to assist them.

While everyone understood Pio's continuing commitment to the cause of Mozambique, we still kept trying to persuade him to take a seat in the Kenyan Parliament, where we felt he would be of great value. He was always telling everyone to do this and do that, why didn't he get on board and do it himself as it were? We almost had to force him into it, but in 1963 he became a Member of the Central Legislative Assembly and in July 1964 a Specially Elected Member of the House of Representatives.

Kenya was not alone in undergoing dramatic change in the region during this time. The British Protectorate in Zanzibar had also ended in December 1963, leaving the islands to the Sultan as constitutional monarch. A lot of ill-feeling, however, had been quietly simmering between the Arabs and Africans. Zanzibar's militia had been trained and employed by the British but their loyalty was to whoever paid them. Like many African armies they had been given skills but no ideology. Knowing that the Sultan's power rested on military support, a fellow from Uganda called Okello, who was a house painter, seeing the conditions of his fellow Africans in Zanzibar, decided he was going to stage a revolution there, and on the 12th of January 1964 after mounting an armed raid on the police station, he forced the Sultan to flee into exile. Hearing of these developments and the reports of widespread bloodshed, our family was very worried about our many friends in Zanzibar.

But fools rush in where wise men fear to tread, and in my view this was what Okello had done. The British approached Murumbi to ask Kenyatta about going in and reinstating the Sultan. Kenyatta, concerned that if the uprising were allowed to succeed, it could spark similar events across the region, agreed to British intervention. He also felt it fair to inform Julius Nyerere, the leader of neighbouring Tanganyika. Nyerere took this as an opportunity. Calling the Sultan, he said look, the British are going to invade, but then they'll take over Zanzibar again, unless you sign a treaty and become part of Tanganyika. And this is exactly what the Sultan did.

Another more protracted crisis had been unfolding in the Congo. On the Nairobi streets, cars with Belgian number plates had appeared in increasing numbers as people sought to escape the mayhem in the former Belgian colony. In 1961, the first democratically elected leader of the independent state of Congo, Patrice Lumumba, had been executed by firing squad and the country remained unstable. At around the same time, a few people in the Kenya national movement had bought a piece of land in Nairobi, about eight acres, from an Indian called Dev Gidoomal. Dev had let us have it very cheap and we thought it might come in handy one day. Then after Lumumba's death, Pio had the idea of setting up a college in Nairobi in his memory. The land would be ideal. The new members of KANU, the 'youth cadre' could be educated and receive training as party activists, in minute-taking, accounts and other administrative skills, rather like the original concept of the LSE. We realised it was very important for any political party, even with a strong presence in the centre of the country, to have workers in every town and village, drumming up and maintaining support to win elections. The college would be called the Lumumba Institute, and Pio decided that Odinga should be its chairman. I drew up the legal documentation and soon the building was under way. I had no idea that this well-intentioned project would quickly become the focus of an intense political drama.

Still not fully understanding how powerful the tribal factor was in Kenya, my impression was that we were moving towards a bipartisan left/right split within politics. A commonly held view was of Tom Mboya on the right, Odinga on the left and Kenyatta somewhere in the middle. This was simplistic; Kenyatta pretended to be on the left when it suited him, and on the right when it suited him. I think his ideology was basically that of himself as ruling patriot, if that makes sense, and he had an absolute determination to remain in power. In his early years of political campaigning, as a young man in the 1920s, he had given up his job and walked overnight many miles to Laikipia and other places, in constant danger from wild animals, staying in labourers huts or hiding out on settlers' farms. Capture would have meant imprisonment or worse, and the only person who went with him was Jessie Kariuki, who later became KANU Director of Organisation. After all this sacrifice, toil and commitment and the long, brutal years in detention, who could doubt his vision of leading his nation for the rest of his life?

Either side of Kenyatta, there were now two unofficial groups: the left-wing people around Odinga and Pio, and what was called the Corner House group with Tom Mboya, who used to meet in a local bar. Tom had begun to tell me of the concerns among his group about Odinga making a bid for the Presidency. They did not think, however, that he could succeed alone. Instead they saw the 'hub of the wheel' on the left as Pio. This view, fear as it turned out, only confirmed Pio's reputation as a brilliant organiser, as a lynchpin, and his power behind the scenes to make things happen. In 1959, when the African American civil rights leader Malcolm X had visited Kenya, he and Pio were reported to find much in common. More recently, in May of 1964, it had not gone unnoticed that he had taken Odinga and Joe Murumbi to Peking to meet with the Chinese communist leader Zhou En-Lai, who was on record as saying that 'the revolutionary prospects in Africa are excellent.'

As for myself, since joining Legco prior to independence, and now as MP for Parklands West, parliamentary life had brought me into contact with a wide variety of people. One person of whom I had been very suspicious was the Speaker, the Old Etonian Sir Humphrey Slade. He had been part of the extreme European group towards the end of the Mau Mau period. I thought: this is the swine who said that for any African found on the street, 70 should be arrested, 30 of them publicly hanged and the rest left to tell everyone who was boss in Kenya. However, I had now been invited by a number of friends, including Surya Patel from Air India and Mangaldas Kanji, whose father was one of the biggest landlords in Kenya, to stand for election as Deputy Speaker of the Kenya Legco, standing in for Sir Humphrey Slade when he had to leave the chamber for a call of nature, or could not attend for some reason. So I wrote to Sir Humphrey and asked him what he thought. He replied that he considered it a good idea. There were two other nominations and I was elected on the first ballot.

On meeting Sir Humphrey I could not believe it was the same man I had heard and read about. He was so gentle, with a very good sense of humour. As we got talking, I asked him about his life and how he had come to Kenya. He told me he was from a quite well to do, but really very ordinary middle-class family in the West of England. Qualifying early as a lawyer, people thought he was too young and not too intelligent, and no one would give him briefs. In 1938, he had heard that a lawyer called Hamilton was looking for an assistant in Kenya. Knowing nothing about the place, not even where it was, he had decided to take a chance and seek a new life, and found the country very much to his liking.

I wondered again: was this really the fellow who had belonged to that dreadful right-wing group and talked about hanging people in the streets? 'I'm afraid to say yes,' admitted Sir Humphrey. 'But I'll tell you this much, if you are part of a European community, and have never met any Africans or Indians, and you're a member of Parliament for a constituency in Mount Kenya, and one of your best friends and his wife and child are brutally murdered, other people whom you knew well suddenly turn on you, accusing you, saying, "What are you doing, why are you not protecting us, why aren't you raising the issue in Parliament? You should have martial law, call for more troops from Britain".' The incident he had referred to was the Rucks murders, my first case, acting pro bono for the defence. Sir Humphrey confessed to me that because of all the pressure at that time, he had run out of steam, been too overcome with emotion and said things he didn't mean. He understood why he had done so, but regretted it now and felt ashamed. I understood too.

Outside of Parliament, legal work was keeping me busy and I now had a couple of interned clerks working at the office. As the practice grew, I realised I also needed a secretary who could sit downstairs to answer the phone and make appointments, rather than have people come up and interrupt me. One day I had a call from a woman called Maria de Savros. She was desperate for a job in order to feed her family and had heard I was looking for help. Not long after I had taken her on, she reported one day that a woman had just called in asking for me, but did not have an appointment. 'I told her,' said Maria, 'that Mr de Souza is a very important man, and doesn't see anyone without an appointment.' As she said this I happened to be coming out of my office to find a file, and looking outside I realised whom the visitor was. A long time ago on the golden shores of Zanzibar, she had sat reading at her window while I played cricket with her brothers on the sand. She was a lovely young woman now.

Calling her back I said, 'Romola, what are you doing here?'

We began talking, and I learned that she had studied medicine in Gwalior in India, followed by three years postgraduate for her M.R.C.O.G. in the UK. She had been about to travel back to East Africa when her father had contacted her, warning her not to go to Zanzibar, which was still unsafe because of the revolution, but to go instead to Nairobi, see Fitz de Souza and ask him to find her a job. It later transpired that she had stopped in Nairobi, but wanted to do things by herself and not rely on anyone else, and so had gone instead straight to the City Council to ask if they had a vacancy for a gynaecologist/obstetrician. The Council had said they could not offer her very much as a salary and advised her to try elsewhere. Romola said she did not mind this and really wanted to work for them. They said they really needed an obstetrician and offered her a position at Pumwani Hospital at 4,500 Kenya shillings, which she had accepted. When she had phoned her father with this news, he had told her, 'Now go and see Fitz and give him my regards.' She said, 'Do I have to?' to which he replied, 'Yes.' It was obvious that her father had wanted her to make contact with me and thought it would be nice if we hit it off.

Romola was impressed that I had recognised her straightaway. I had not seen her since she was 12 years old. She had made an impression on me too. She was now living in doctors' quarters at Pumwani Hospital. Over the next few days I asked her out to dinner a couple of times, after which she invited me to her place and said she would cook. I arrived at the small accommodation and Romola made me comfortable in the living area, while she got busy in the kitchen, which was behind a low semi-partition, allowing us to talk as she prepared dinner. After a few minutes I smelt smoke, and looking across the partition saw flames coming from the stove. I asked if everything was OK and she replied, 'Yes.' This went on for some time, and eventually I said, 'Romola let me help you,' and went into the kitchen. In the bin I saw about 12 burnt sausages and more about to go the same way. Romola then admitted that she did not know how to cook and had never before had the opportunity.

Some days later it was Good Friday, and I went out to have a meal with my good friends Sarjit and Judith. I ordered prawn curry and rice for the three of us, and we ate very well. Returning to my home in Bingley Road, Lavington, I felt slight indigestion, but went to bed. Later I woke up and began vomiting like hell. I phoned various medical people I knew but was unable to get hold of any of them as it was now the Easter weekend. Feeling increasingly sick, I rang Romola and asked her if there was some remedy she could advise. She replied that she would come to my house right away. I said no, no, I didn't want her to come over, as by now it was the middle of the night and it would be difficult for her to find the way as she was not even familiar with Nairobi. She said it was no trouble, and before I could say any more she put the phone down. Half an hour later I heard a car pull up outside. It was Romola, in the little blue Mini Minor she had bought in the UK, thinking it would be ideal for the narrow streets of Zanzibar. She came in, gave me some medication and stayed in the living room, coming in to my room throughout the night to minister to me. In the morning I was OK.

We continued to see one another for a few months, until it was time for my trip with Joe Murumbi to the UN conference in New York. I was at the airport waiting to board the flight when I suddenly realised I had forgotten to tell Romola I was going. Finding a phone I called her up and said I was going to be away for a bit, and asked her not to do anything silly. She asked what I meant by 'anything silly', not go out with other boys? I said, 'Yes.' In New York I went shopping and bought Romola a bangle. Soon after my return I proposed to her. She accepted, but made two conditions: number one, she didn't want any gold or diamonds, nothing like that, and two: she wanted 12 children. This I took to be a joke. All right then she said, make it six. Why? She loved children. She had grown up as one of five and their home was very happy. Very soon our wedding was being arranged.

Romola

Romola

Joe Murumbi and me at the United Nations conference in New York

Chapter Thirteen

Assassination of an Idealist

1965 to 1966

Romola and I were to be married the following summer of 1965. The news soon got round, and one day as I was coming out of my house I saw Achhroo Kapila, Kanta's brother. All he said to me was, 'You f****** b******!' Kanta had not married the doctor from Uganda, which I believe had been her decision, having found the fellow too flash. Achhroo was clearly offended that I had now chosen someone other than his sister.

Everyone else was looking forward to the event, and family and friends were all invited, including of course Pio and his wife Emma, who now had three lovely young daughters. Emma worked as secretary to Oneko in the Information Broadcasting and Tourism Ministry, but the family had very little money and I had raised some funds to buy them a small house in Lower Kabete Road, Westlands. Pio was as busy as ever with politics and welcomed anyone who showed an interest. One such person though was not what he appeared. A pleasant well-spoken gentleman, his official role was that of Labour Officer at the American Embassy. Noticing that he was meeting with Pio regularly, I said, 'You know this man is CIA, what the hell are you doing?' Pio brushed it off, 'No, no, he is a very good man and he is supporting us completely.' Walking into Pio's house at all times of day, he must have known everything he was doing. The American influence in the country was very strong, CIA people were everywhere and the US Government had, behind the scenes, taken Kenya over.

Pio was increasingly vexed about the land bought from the Europeans as part of the independence deal. A chosen few, mainly the Kikuyu, now seemed to be getting lots of it, while so many other Africans remained poor and unemployed. Several of the farms had also been sold on to other Europeans for large profits. For all his hard work, Pio did not expect to earn any money for himself, nor did he want land for himself. Kenyatta certainly wanted particular people to have land, and driving out to Laikipia with me one day, he raised the subject again, 'Fitz, where is your farm?' As before I told him I wasn't a farmer. He repeated that I must have farms, preferably three, four, five of them. I said I would think about it, expecting the matter to end there.

The next day, the Commissioner of Lands, an Irishman called O'Loughlan, arrived at my office with a briefcase full of maps and documents. He had been instructed, he said, to ask which farms I had decided to buy. I said, 'I haven't decided to buy any.' He replied, 'President Kenyatta says you have to have a farm. For a thousand pounds you can get a hundred acres and a gigantic European style house with 10 or 15 rooms and a ballroom with chandeliers.' I thought, these Europeans must have had a fantastic life before independence! I shook my head. 'But this is almost for free,' he said. 'No thank you,' I replied. If I had taken up the offer my attitude would have changed.

I was surprised that in the political groupings Pio had got so close to Odinga, but the land issue must have had a lot to do with it. Pio had a certain amount of respect for Kenyatta, and it wasn't that he had given up on him, but he had become a little disillusioned. What was the good, he would say of the thousands of acres in the Highlands, of replacing the white Lord Delamere with a black Lord Delamere. In Pio's opinion, the top people should lead by example and not grab things for themselves. He wasn't exactly keeping quiet about his views either. Together with

Odinga and others, he was preparing a reply to Tom Mboya's Sessional Paper 10, amendments that would argue for their own version of African Socialism to be enacted. The plan was to present this alternative paper in Parliament on the same day as Tom's.

One night Tom took me aside and mentioned again the concern on his side, and how Pio was increasingly seen as trouble, a left-wing firebrand out to oust Kenyatta. 'Once certain people realise that the possibility of Odinga succeeding Kenyatta is due to this one man,' he said, 'and that when the time comes, he can provide the necessary organisation to pull it off, then those same people will want to get rid of him. Take Pinto out, and the whole thing collapses like a pack of cards.' I wondered what exactly he meant by 'take out.' I said, 'Tom, Pinto is a good organiser yes, but it really wouldn't be as easy as that.' I asked, 'If it came to it, would you take any part in getting rid of him, whatever that means?' Tom said no, but there were people who would. He then told me earnestly to speak to Pio and to warn him that his life was in danger.

It was Odinga who later picked Pio up and drove him out of Nairobi. He took him overnight to Mombasa, to a small beach property in Kurwito we had bought for 18,000 Kenya shillings. It was the only house on that stretch of coast that was not European-owned and my friends and I often stayed there. After dropping Pio, Odinga headed back to Nairobi. A few days later Pio received a visitor at the beach house. It was Joe Murumbi, who had just returned from England and decided to look in. He was surprised to find Pio and asked what he was doing there. Pio replied that he had been asked to stay because it was believed he was in danger. Joe said that was ridiculous and asked Pio to come back to Nairobi, saying he would talk to Kenyatta and sort it all out. Pio took Joe's advice and returned to Nairobi on the train.

Pio arrived back home in Nairobi in the morning. That evening, J.D. Kali's driver, a Kikuyu called Ndegwa, stopped by the house. Ndegwa was also with the Special

Branch, and drove Kenyatta too. He asked if Pio had returned. Someone told him yes, and he drove off. Also in the house at the time was a very close friend of Pio, an African called Cheche, who had been with him in detention. Cheche acted as Pio's bodyguard, and it was said would die for him. When Pio was told about the caller, he said he knew whom Ndegwa was and that he was trying to organise to kill him.

Perhaps the visit was a warning. If so, it did not deter Pio and he was soon busily compiling a list of farms and land which in his view had been stolen from the African people by the Government. The list would form a key part of his group's opposition to Tom's Sessional Paper 10. The expectation was for there to be an explosive result: a vote of no confidence against Kenyatta. I reminded Pio of Kenyatta's strength, of the sacrifices and struggles he had made and his firm belief that the fruits of independence should be his. I said, 'Pio, I think you have a lot of good things to say, but however much you say them, Kenyatta is not going to give up power or go away. He is a very courageous man and would fight to the death to stay leader if he had to. So don't try to attack him morally and not expect to get on his bad side, you are just wasting your time, it is not possible to remove him.'

It was on an afternoon in February, as I was taking a break for tea outside the Parliament building, that I heard someone calling my name. 'Mr de Souza, come quickly please!' Turning around I saw that a few tables away an altercation had broken out between Pio and Kenyatta. Both men were gesticulating and swearing, and as their voices rose, everyone on the veranda could hear. Tom was standing nearby, now joined by several onlookers. Pio, his face contorted with anger was shouting, 'I'll fix you!' Kenyatta, equally incensed, was shouting back at him. I knew immediately what they were arguing about: the English farms, which Pio claimed Kenyatta was grabbing. Running up behind Pio, I put both my arms around him, trying to restrain him and calm him down.

When Kenyatta had gone we sat down. I warned him not to shout at Kenyatta again, as Kikuyus rarely forgive someone who becomes their enemy. 'In the eyes of most Africans,' I said, 'you are just a Muhindi, you are perfectly dispensable, but he is not.' I reminded him how at almost every meeting Kenyatta would ask the same rhetorical question: if a man plants a tree, who has the right to claim the fruit of that tree when it has grown? Ask any African, I told him, and they will say that Kenyatta has been very little compensated for the sacrifices and hardship he has endured in the struggle for independence. 'If it comes to the push,' I said, 'there'll be two shots fired at you and no one will remember you in a year's time.' Pio shook his head, 'No, no, there would be a bloodbath.' I said, 'Pio, you are overestimating your position; maybe if you were a Kikuyu or a Luo, then yes, there would be a backlash, but you've nobody to support you; like me you've no support in the Indian community, and none outside it.'

On the 25th of February I was in court in the middle of a case when one of my articled clerks came in looking for me. 'What are you doing here?' I asked him. 'Mr de Souza,' he whispered, 'I am very sorry to tell you that your friend is dead.' I knew immediately that he meant Pio. The English judge, a good friend, looked across the courtroom at me. I stood up and cleared my throat, 'I am very sorry, but due to an unfortunate occurrence I have to leave. The judge said, 'I can see you are shocked. Is this about your friend Pio Pinto?' I nodded. He said, 'This court is adjourned.' I went straight to Pio's house. Two police officers were there, the gate was closed and the car was in the driveway. Pio was inside, his body leaning to one side as if asleep at the wheel. Looking at him I suddenly thought, he's all right after all, and reaching in, touched his shoulder, saying, 'Pio, Pio.' Then I saw the bullet hole. It was true; Pio was dead.

That night I cried and cried. I felt really shattered. Pio had been just 38 years old, but had done so much for the country, spent seven years on Manda Island, not even allowed to see his dying father. All he had ever wanted was justice and fairness for all. He did not deserve this fate. Pio's bodyguard Cheche came to see me later, crying, 'Our friend is dead, our friend is dead.'

Through my day-to-day legal work, I had got to know one of the Nairobi CID officers, an Englishman. It wasn't long before he and I had a lead. A taxi driver described some men with guns being taken recently in specially hired Fiat cars to South C where, it was said, they were to 'fix' some trade union people. Could they also have been sent to fix Pio? The taxi driver took the CID officer and me around the streets and within a short time had identified a young African man in a red shirt. After being placed under arrest, the 22 year old, Kisilu Mutua, admitted to shooting Pio.

My mind was full of questions. On the day Pio was killed the end of Lower Kabete Road had been blocked off and the traffic stopped. And why, when he was found in the car, obviously preparing to leave as usual that morning was the gate to his drive closed? Pio was a good runner, faster than the Maasai even, at one time predicted to run for Kenya in the Olympics. If he had got out of the car, no one would have caught him. The roadblock and the closed gate had been no coincidence. I began asking around and challenging people to find the person or persons responsible. My father was worried. 'Fitz you must be careful,' he urged me, 'they might want to shoot you too.' I said, 'Look I've known Kenyatta for years, been his lawyer and helped him.' My father replied, 'People can forget things.' I could not in any case believe that Kenyatta would have wanted Pio dead.

About two weeks had gone by when walking on the street past the Standard Bank in Nairobi one day, I heard someone behind me. I looked around and saw Bruce McKenzie hurrying to catch up with me. His manner was friendly, chatting about general things, but I sensed something more, something he wanted to say. Bruce was a big man, with a strong handshake that overpowered you, and I felt that strength in him now. 'Fitz,' he said, 'I like you very much, you're a good friend.' I said, 'Bruce, have you been sent to talk to me about Pio.' He nodded. I said, 'To warn me, that if I carry on asking questions, the same is going happen to me?' Bruce said yes, this was the message he had been asked to give me.

Then Mungai came to see me. He was a mysterious figure, some hinted he had been a Mau Mau leader, others a Government spy. Telling me that I was now on a 'wanted list', he reached in his pocket and took out a pistol, complete with licence, advising me to keep it for protection. I had been under threat before, when Pio had been arrested and I had driven across the border to Uganda. The concern then was possible imprisonment. This was different. Pio was gone, and Bruce had come to tell me, on whose authority I did not know, that I could be next. Mungai had confirmed it. I had seen Pio's limp body carried from his car, the small hole in his body where the bullet had entered, witnessed Emma's shock and grief. As the reality of the danger I was in hit me, I became very nervous. I took some Valium, and not knowing what else to do booked into the Hilton Hotel. Nowhere in Nairobi was completely safe, but here at least there were people around, I could stay behind a locked door. How long for though? I would have to come out sometime.

I thought carefully. I was getting married in a few months. Now there were not just my parents, my brother and sister and myself to think of, but also my future wife Romola – our future lives together and in time, probably a family of our own. After a few days I let it be known that I was no longer pursuing my inquiries, checked out of the hotel and went home. I hid Mungai's pistol in a strongbox behind a loose brick in the wall and kept the key in my pocket. Still anxious and in shock, I decided to go to England and from there, seeking a complete change of scene, take a trip to Scandinavia. At that time permission was needed to take money out of the country, so I rang Kenyatta to ask if it could be arranged. Yes, yes, he said, and gave me the name of someone who could help. Talking to Kenyatta, he was clearly very distressed and crying over the phone. When I broached the question of who might be responsible he said, 'Do you think I could possibly have murdered my own friend?' and said he had been equally shocked by what had happened.

A couple of weeks later I returned for Pio's funeral. The mourners were mostly Africans and church people. Kenyatta, who was not expected to attend, sent an ivory carving in tribute. Joe Murumbi was full of remorse, blaming himself for persuading Pio to leave the beach house at Mombasa and come back to Nairobi that day. While Pio's alleged killer languished behind bars, sentenced to 30 years' imprisonment, there were whispered rumours that the 'powers that be' had organised the assassination, or the Kiambu Mafia, CIA or foreign governments, and the riddle remained unanswered.

I remember how shabbily dressed and almost penniless Pio and I were the first time we met in 1952. Perhaps it helped to put us at ease with one another, but mainly it was that our ideas about independence and socialism were similar. We must have talked for three or four hours that day, until it got to lunchtime and Pio invited me to join him at the most expensive and luxurious restaurant that non-Europeans were allowed to eat in, where our meal cost us about 3 shillings each. When we returned to his office after lunch to continue our discussions, I remember reading through the speeches of past presidents of the Indian Congress and those of Kenyatta, who was president of the Kenya African Union at the time. I was very impressed with Pio, and that was how we began working closely together. His role in Kenyan politics has been described by other friends, and I know that history will record he had a hand in the preparation of most of the memoranda and statements issued by the K.A.U. in those days. Many were the nights he would sit up until 5am in the Congress Office, drafting political papers in the nationalist cause. For all this he never expected payment. His reward was in the contribution he made to the struggle. He never looked for personal credit.

Pio Pinto visiting Mzee Kenyatta when he was in detention at Lodwar

A couple of years later when he was the editor of the *Daily Chronicle*, the Royal Commission on Land asked for evidence regarding ownership and there was no one to put forward the African case as all the leaders were by now in detention. Pio promptly resigned his job and for three months read the voluminous Carter Commission Report and other documents on the land issue, and took statements from Kikuyu elders and others. He then wrote out, typed and cyclostyled, always working into the early hours of the morning, the 200-page Kikuyu Tribe's Memorandum, as well as memoranda for Mbari clans in the Central Province. Again, Pio never told anybody about this work, only those around him observed the time and effort he was putting into such matters. When I sent a copy of the memorandum Pio had compiled to the President at Lodwar, he was so impressed that he suggested we publish it, but for lack of funds the work was never done.

I have described Pio Pinto's commitment to the cause of Mozambique, and a few weeks before he was assassinated he told me that his ambition was to resign his seat in Parliament and retire to Lindi or Mtwara on the Mozambique border, and from there lend his active support to the freedom fighters. His friends would not let him go, arguing that he was needed in Kenya. He might not have lived to join the struggle on the ground in Mozambique, or see the country set free, which would take ten more gruelling years, but his commitment to the birth of the movement is unquestionable, and it is without doubt that in Kenya he died with his boots on.

For a long time Pio's contribution to Kenyan independence was not officially recognised. The house in Lower Kabete Road, Westlands, where he and his family lived at the time of his assassination has been demolished, but now a permanent memorial, Pio Gama Pinto Road, running beside the Sarit Centre, marks his place in history for all to see. In addition, in recent years many articles and books have appeared, paying tribute to Pio's generosity of spirit and his tireless commitment to humanity and justice. The work and example that he and so many others began will not be forgotten, and must not be abandoned.

Pio Gama Pinto

Pio Pinto with a group of politicians including Bruce Mackenzie, Tom Mboya, K.P. Shah, Rosaria Pinto, Muinga Chokwe and myself

Pio Pinto in the background

Pio Pinto with friends

Our wedding was to take place on the 31st of July 1965 at the St Francis Xavier Catholic Church in Nairobi. My mother and father would be there of course, and Rix was my best man, though being prone to stutter, he would not be making a speech. I intended to say a few words myself off the cuff. I had also left it to the last minute to collect my suit, bought off the peg from a Sindhi tailor who spoke no English. It fitted fine though, and everything went smoothly until it was time to make my speech. As I stood up, and everyone went quiet and looked at me expectantly, I could not for the life of me think what to say and promptly sat down again. It must be the only time in my life I was lost for words. Afterwards someone asked, 'Is anything wrong, don't you like her?' I assured them I was very happy.

For our marital home, I looked at a house in Parklands from where I might build up my constituency. The price was 120,000 Kenya shillings and in those days I didn't have 120 cents! Tom Mboya said he could arrange a

100% loan with repayments of 10,000 shillings a year. This seemed like a bribe, which were commonplace. Romola was very principled and said we should not accept it. I had my parliamentary salary and some other income, but it would be insufficient to buy the house. Romola, however, now held a full time position at the Pumwani Maternity Hospital, the largest in Nairobi, and with this extra salary we would be able to go ahead with the purchase. I was unhappy about Romola going every day to Pumwani, as it was an unsafe area. The hospital was always short of staff and supplies, and the African mothers were treated unfairly, with babies being born in the corridors and even outside the building. For Romola these problems were all the more reason to work there. Whenever she was on a night shift I would wait for her outside in the car, accompanied by my dog.

Meanwhile, that summer there had been uproar in Parliament when a group of students from the Lumumba Institute were alleged to have attempted a party coup at KANU headquarters on Mfang'ano Street. The Institute was immediately suspected of being some secret society run by Vice-President Odinga to take over the Government. It was a case of people reading too much into something very simple; it had been the same with Pio, whose intentions I think were harmless, but for those who wanted to see something criminal or conspiratorial in everything a person did, even their choice of girlfriend would be looked on as suspicious, perhaps seen as a means of spying on others. With the Lumumba Institute people asked: why did Odinga buy a farm in Kamiti, did he want to attack the nearby prison? I think at this time there was a fear complex around politics, everyone was suspicious that someone else might be plotting to betray them or take over, or bring in a foreign government, and as a result the Institute was closed down. Lumumba poor fellow had died and it was in his memory, not meant for any communist or counter-revolution, but for the training of young people to form and run a party. It was really a harmless idea, but they didn't give it a chance.

With the Lumumba Institute discredited and Pio no longer there to help behind the scenes, Odinga found it harder to operate politically. He did, however, have the invaluable advice and support of Pranlal Sheth, a lawyer and former editor of the *Daily Chronicle*, who had been a strong campaigner for the national movement. Following the press clampdown during the Emergency, Pranlal, who was four years my senior, had gone as I had done earlier, to Lincoln's Inn to train as a lawyer and been Called to the Bar in 1962. Now residing in Kisumu, he continued to play an important role as organiser and guiding hand to the sometimes headstrong and over-emotional Odinga. Pranlal was also a generous host, and whenever I had to drive out to Kisumu or was en-route to Uganda, he would offer me the guest room of his house for an overnight stay.

In an attempt to restore faith in the wake of Pio's death, Tom Mboya moved a vote of confidence in the Government and in Kenyatta personally. Tom made a good speech. I was in the Chair at the time. But when he asked for support, Odinga like an absolute fool, opposed the motion on the grounds that as Vice-President he should have been the one to bring it. Oneko and the rest of Odinga's group followed suit, and I thought to myself, with great respect, do they think they can rouse the whole country to say they are anti-Kenyatta? Voting against him only lost them further support.

There were to be other setbacks for Odinga, not of his own making. One morning, pages purporting to be copied from a Greek Communist Party article appeared in all the MPs' pigeonholes. The article suggested that Pio was killed not because of his anger about the farms being given away, but because the Chinese and Russian 'Mafias' had been fighting one another, each wanting him on their side, and that Odinga was involved in an alliance with foreign communist governments to bring down Kenyatta and take over as President. I thought it very strange that the article was written in English, and when the Greek Communist Party denied even having such a paper, it looked like the whole thing was fabricated, a piece of disinformation intended to demonise the left-leaning Odinga, distancing him still further in people's minds from Kenyatta and drawing a veil over the land issue. Some said the CIA was behind it, but it was anyone's guess. If Kenyatta was not furious, which I think he must have been, the public certainly got incensed; they didn't want Odinga siding with some outside communist power to change the Government. If this had been true – and many people believed it – even I would have resisted it. I was against communism, had never agreed with those who favoured it, and thought it wrong for anyone to have a communist regime support him.

The Government was still taking no chances with Odinga, and one day we heard that his organiser Pranlal Sheth had been issued with a deportation order. Then I received a phone call from his wife, Indu. Knowing that I might seek to intervene on Pranlal's behalf she urged me not to. Pranlal she said, was seriously concerned that if he resisted the order and stayed in Kenya he might be killed. It was better that he go to England, where she hoped that she and their children might join him in due course.

There was almost a disintegration of Vice-President Odinga's activities, a change that Hilary Ngweno, then editor of the *Daily Nation* would tell me he noticed clearly. In March 1966, a conference was held at Limuru which the *Daily Nation* would much later describe thus: 'When KANU decided to clip the wings of the national and party Vice-President, Jaramogi Oginga Odinga, a special delegates conference – the infamous Limuru Conference – adopted a master plan hatched by Mr Tom Mboya: to create provincial party vice-presidents. With a stroke of the pen, Mr Odinga found that he was no longer the KANU vice-president, not even one of the eight KANU vice-presidents alongside figures representing each of the seven provinces and Nairobi. An angry Odinga reacted by quitting in a huff his positions in both the Government and the ruling party to found the ill-fated Kenya People's Union. The rest, as they say, is history.'

Odinga issued a public statement in Parliament, addressed to Kenyatta. I was in the Speaker's Chair at the time, and Odinga's words surprised me: 'You have not given me any consideration as your number two in state matters... I earn public money but with no job to do... [and] lest the future generation question my sincerity... I hereby tender my resignation.' Whether Odinga had anticipated the moves that were made against him, I do not know. I had not attended the Limuru Conference. I had really lost all interest, feeling that as we seemed to be just fighting and killing each other now, there was little point in having a conference.

Odinga did not give up though. To oppose KANU, he formed his new socialist party, the Kenya People's Union, with Oneko and Kaggia among its members. In June 1966 a series of by-elections were held. KANU won more seats, but the KPU took more votes overall. Bildad Kaggia, who had been elected by the people of Murang'a, was ousted in a re-election the following day. The whole thing was stage-managed. There was no way anyone else could win. Tom Mboya, always a brilliant organiser, did everything, and behind him were the Americans and their money. I remember Tom once asking me to fetch something from the boot of his car and making a point of telling me not to disturb anything else there. Curiosity getting the better of me, I looked in a suitcase and found it packed with several thousand dollars. A key election held at Tigoni was a blatant fraud, paid for by the American Embassy. They had people in the Mayfair Hotel, a white man handing out cash notes to all the delegates, giving them free rooms and paying for everything.

It was not only the Americans that provided foreign money, nor were Kenyatta's group the only ones to receive it. William Attwood, the American Ambassador whom I met at cocktail parties now and again, was too high up to be involved personally, but in 1967 he would write about the political events of the time in *The Reds and the Blacks*. To most Africans Kenyatta was a god, and Attwood's book would make Attwood the most hated man in Kenya, based largely on a damning review in the *Daily Nation*. In fact, as the title was swiftly banned it is believed most Africans never read it, which though betraying confidences, was not uncomplimentary to Kenyatta. It claimed that the source of Odinga's funds, about which my Luo gardener had earlier surprised me, was China's Communist Government, Njonjo alleging that the Chinese Embassy in Dar es Salaam sent him well over $100,000, exchanged in Mombasa for Kenya shillings, to buy votes in Limuru.

I too was approached by foreign powers. First was the Chinese Ambassador who rang up wanting me to be his legal representative in Kenya. I invited him to my office. No, no he said, come to dinner with me, as people in China do. I replied that this was not really the custom here and that the client came to the lawyer. He seemed very reluctant. I said that if he didn't like it, he could get another lawyer. Soon, however, I was the lawyer for the Chinese, Soviet and Polish Ambassadors. All I had to do was attend parties with them, for which I was paid a retainer. When they began to flatter me though, telling me what a nice fellow I was, I realised that they expected more than legal representation and wanted me to be a mouthpiece for their interests in Kenya. I was also concerned that they would ask me to report conversations and pass information. To avoid being suspected of corruption or espionage, at the end of each month I would return any amounts I could not account for legitimately in fees and expenses. Aware of the attempts to coax me in, eventually I stopped attending the parties, especially with the Chinese who seemed rather crazy; when they moved their Embassy's HQ behind ridiculously high brick-built defences, Kenyatta remarked that the Great Wall of China had come to Nairobi.

Kenyatta, meanwhile, had offered Odinga's former position of Vice-President, to Joe Murumbi. People asked why, given the circumstances of Pio's death, Joe accepted.

One might as well ask why is power so sweet, why is fame so sweet? Many thought Joe was idealistically inclined, more left than right, but I don't think he had any strong ideology to support it. In Joe's case though, I think he couldn't say no to Kenyatta. He knew he was being used, and why, which was to attract Kalenjin support – Joe was half Maasai, who up to a point were considered Kalenjin – and to split the left. But who, even today, when people are supposedly much more enlightened and educated, would refuse the Vice-President's job? Joe believed he could make a difference. Later he would write, 'I didn't know what I was letting myself in for.' In August 1966, after just four months in the job, he told Kenyatta he wanted to resign. Kenyatta persuaded him to stay on until the end of the year, when the resignation was made public.

Joe still blamed himself for Pio's death, and thought he could have stopped it. I never heard anyone cry like Joe, and whenever anyone mentioned Pio he could not talk, only weep bitterly. I was sorry about his resignation. I think he said it was because of his job with a cigarette company, but I can't believe this was the real reason. The corruption in Kenya had outrun him and he could not put his foot on the brakes. Honest, fair and just to everyone, Joe Murumbi was not a politician but a true democrat. He had worked harder than anyone for independence for Kenya and freedom for Kenyatta and been the mouthpiece for Kenya for a decade.

In 1966 came an event I would never forget. It began with plans to take some friends on a trip to Mount Kilimanjaro. For some reason though, my father begged me not to go. It was soon apparent why. Fifteen years had passed since the onset of his diabetes, during which time it was thought at one point that he had contracted TB. We had all been greatly relieved when this turned out to be a false alarm, and it had prompted my father to quit his long-term smoking habit of several packs a day, and he had continued to lead a busy life as a doctor.

Only a few days after I had been due to leave for Kilimanjaro, he suffered a heart attack. Rushed to hospital, he was in urgent need of oxygen, and finding no cylinders to hand, the medical staff attempted to get him to the upper floor where there were further supplies. Getting the stretcher upstairs, however, proved problematic. By the time the oxygen had been made available, my father had died.

It was suggested that we sue the hospital. Compensation would have felt like blood money. This was not what we wanted. My mother, Rix, Iva and I were all in shock. It had been so sudden. For several days our black Labrador dog, missing his master, walked round and round the outside of the house. My father had been 78 and had had a good life, loving and caring for his family and unfailingly conscientious towards the thousands of people who must have come to him for treatment over the years. I recalled all the adventures we had when I was still growing up, driving his black box Chevrolet miles into the bush to find and tend to someone, watching and admiring his skill and reassurance in helping the sick and injured. A dedicated man of medicine and a much-loved husband and father, he would be with me always.

My family in Nairobi before my father passed away

Chapter Fourteen

Dangerous Times

1967 to 1969

It was now over two years since Pio's death. Emma, understandably, had found it hard going. Along with the grief, she was haunted by her surroundings. 'I want to get out of that house Fitz, every time I go near the gate I shiver.' Pio had often said, 'If anything happens to me, please look after my family.' Pio had always given any money he had to others and Emma had been shocked to find that his bank account was empty. What she needed now was a fresh start, away from bad memories, somewhere for her children to grow up safe and happy. Canada was agreed upon, and after contacting their Embassy to arrange the emigration procedure, and for Emma's mother to go with them, I set about gathering donations from friends and well-wishers for the airfares and accommodation.

Joe Murumbi's swift departure as Vice-President had left an unexpected vacuum, which in 1967 Kenyatta filled with the appointment of Daniel arap Moi. With Odinga out on a limb, Tom Mboya, who in 1966 had organised the Limuru Conference so skilfully to achieve just that, was now seen more than ever to have his eye on the Presidency. He had married Pamela Odede, one of the young Kenyans sent to study in America, daughter of Professor Walter Odede, a politician and renowned veterinary surgeon, and they now had three lovely daughters. Well known to the international media as a bright, engaging, articulate young family man, Tom Mboya would seem to the outside world a natural successor to lead Kenya.

Close observers agreed this was indeed Tom's ambition, and a key part of his strategy was to make himself indispensable to Kenyatta, which could already be seen working. But at some point after 1966 two things began to go wrong for Tom. One was that he started to lose his supporters in Parliament. It was happening for a simple reason that, sad to say, stemmed from an aspect of his personality. As a clever man, he couldn't suffer fools lightly. In debate, at which he was so strong, he would always flatten the other fellow completely.

One day he came to see me and took me for a drive. He was a big Minister and I was a nobody, but he wanted to talk. We went to the airport bar. When we had sat down with a drink, Tom leaned over and said, 'Tell me something Fitz, why do people hate me?' I said, 'Tom, you are so intelligent that when you attack a man in debate, you make him feel absolutely stupid, and a fool in other people's eyes. It is much better to refute the other fellow's arguments, while at the same time telling him he has a very good case; if he asks a question of you as Minister, don't make him think he is idiotic; thank him for raising the point so perceptively, then answer it objectively. By complimenting him in the process, you make him your friend, not your enemy.'

I had learned this lesson from a very shrewd man, Sir Humphrey Slade, who told me one day, 'Fitz, don't be too hard on people, try to praise them a little.' I realised it was very good advice, which I would follow throughout my life, and in the law courts. As a result there were several cases in which fellows, Indians mostly, whom I had proved to be liars, came to me afterwards and said, 'Mr de Souza, would you be my lawyer now?'

Tom and I were very good friends and had known each other from our youth when he used to come to our house, talking, organising dances and parties, having a lot of fun together. I felt I could be honest with him. I told him again, 'Try to be reasonable, realise other people have an ego, dignity, when you make them feel like children they could hate you for the rest of their lives.' He frowned, 'That's difficult you know.'

Tom's vanity was a problem. Kenyatta would imitate him, saying, 'The man walks like this.' We all knew whom he meant. It was like George W. Bush walked as he approached the podium for a press conference, a sight that annoyed me, showing off his power to the press and to the camera crews, to the world. Tom had that arrogance. As his star had risen, others, jealous of his youth and appeal, saw the power he was wielding within the Government and feared that Kenyatta had become too dependent on him. Kenyatta I think never really liked Tom, but as always it was a question of who was using whom, and how far Kenyatta would allow it to go. While Tom might be losing friends in Parliament, he was still a force to be reckoned with, aligned with Kenyatta and very much at the centre of Government. He was, however, a Luo, and here lay his second problem, tribalism; the more he pushed himself forward, the more determined were the Kikuyu that he should not take over. The question now was would he give up trying or would he have to be stopped somehow?

The other prominent Luo, Odinga, was now out of office and in the political wilderness, but hanging on. Any Kikuyu saying publicly that he accepted rule by Luos, risked being hounded out of his constituency, but with money from the Chinese, and the Soviets too probably, Odinga could buy wider support. Kenyatta, aware of the risk that he might yet stage a successful comeback with the KPU, set about countering it. At a meeting in Nakuru, he attacked Odinga personally, telling the people they could not support the 'black necks', meaning the Luos. Next, intermediaries who passed or smuggled money into the country for Odinga were arrested. With his funds being cut off and Kenyatta denouncing him, Odinga would quickly lose his support with all the other tribes, and even people like Oduya Oprong and Zephania Anyieni, who before had backed him very staunchly, turned away. Oduya, who I think had once said Kenyatta should resign because 'he has let us down', suddenly became very pro-Kenyatta.

Among those who did not were fellow Kapenguria inmates Achieng Oneko and Bildad Kaggia. Kenyatta was very upset with them both. Oneko had resigned as Broadcasting Minister in 1966 and joined Odinga's KPU. Kenyatta told me himself that he had treated Oneko like a son and felt bitterly that he had now betrayed him. Kaggia, who had quit his ministerial post as early as 1964 in protest at the Government's failure to return confiscated land to its rightful owners, had stuck to his belief in equality and helping the poorest people in Kenyan society. He was a Kikuyu leader willing to support the left-wing group, who were very keen he should be president of KPU, but the elders said no, Odinga is the more senior person. Kaggia's response was: I don't mind, let him be leader; that sort of thing doesn't worry me; power doesn't worry me. I think maybe this was the mistake.

Kaggia was taunted by Kenyatta, who said: look this man has fought for freedom, but has nothing to show for it. Kaggia's stance was alien to Kenyatta's philosophy. I must have attended ten or more meetings, during which he repeated his allegory of the one who slaughters the cow being expected to feast on the choicest meat, leaving the lesser cuts to his guests, and the fat to drop from the spit and feed the fire. This was the African way. Kaggia claimed to have turned down bribes of land. Like Kenyatta, he had played his part in slaughtering the cow, but unlike him, refused to feast. In African terms it must have seemed incomprehensible, a form of rebuke even. In this humble, principled man, lay another threat to the ruling elite.

In 1968 Kaggia, having organised a public gathering at Kisii, was arrested. The charge was holding a meeting of more than 50 people, which without a licence was illegal. A fellow gave evidence there had been 51 present, but Kaggia maintained there had been less than 25, which given the tiny room seemed very likely. The magistrate, however, was directed to impose a one-year prison sentence. The Acting Chief Justice, Arthur Farrell, took an appeal. Not yet aware of Kaggia's arrest, I happened to meet Farrell at a party at the Panafric Hotel and ventured to say that he looked very worried. He nodded, 'Yes Mr de Souza, I am. I have to decide whether to follow my conscience and lose my job, or ignore it and go on to be very successful.' I said, 'Follow your conscience, you don't have to worry, nothing in this world can go wrong if you do what you think is the right thing.'

A few days later I knew the reason for his dilemma, and his decision. He kept Kaggia in prison but on a reduced sentence of six months. The compromise did not satisfy Kenyatta, and Farrell was packed off immediately. Kaggia was not only imprisoned, but humiliated, brought to his own area of Kandara and made to cut grass. I was quite amazed to see him. He told me this was the worst part, as if he had done something really shameful. In Kapenguria he had been regarded as a great leader, now people saw him cutting grass and thought: look at him he is not only poor, he is a powerless, useless politician.

Everyone then seemed to think it would be a brilliant idea to replace Farrell with Charles Njonjo. But Charles didn't want to be Chief Justice as it carried less power than his current position of Attorney General. He was already the grease behind Kenyatta, reading him the paper, becoming friends and getting close to him. Charles liked the idea of putting another person from his office into the job, someone who was a thorn in his flesh, and closer to the left-wing group than himself: the current Solicitor General Kitili Mwendwa. The idea had in fact come from the left-wingers who saw Mwendwa as a means of keeping Njonjo, who had a great love of all things British, hob-nobbing with aristocrats and singing God Save the Queen with great gusto at any opportunity, in tow a little.

Poor Kitili Mwendwa was in Machakos when he was summoned unexpectedly to State House. He didn't have a clue what was going on, and thinking he was going to be asked for a donation, he reached for his chequebook and said to Kenyatta, 'Mzee, I have a present for you.' He was surprised, not to say shocked, at being suddenly made Chief Justice at the age of 39, the first African in the job, joining 11 judges in the High Court, including Arthur Farrell, Sir James Wicks, Chunilal Madan, Chanan Singh, Cecil Miller and Alfred Simpson.

Tom Mboya's escalation of power and influence had by now for his political enemies become too much, and it was decided he must be reined in. As with Odinga they began damning up his source of money, writing to the US Government, issuing statements in the American Press and bringing US business consultants to State House to be lectured by Kenyatta himself about how illegal and immoral it was to support other parties in Kenya. Everyone knew to whom he was referring. Tom seemed undeterred though. He was getting very unpopular with Kenyatta, Odinga and the African leadership generally, and to try to get him out of the way they offered him a job in the United Nations as Kenya's Permanent Representative with the chance to go to New York and live in a sumptuous house. After accepting, Tom quickly realised the job was a way of excluding him and changed his mind. I don't think he even got as far as leaving the country.

Tom realised he couldn't fight the Kikuyu, but he was very resilient and resourceful, and using his own youth wingers fought back brilliantly, retaining his position as Minister of Economic Affairs. However, although he had a few friends, like Oduya, Odero, Jowi and Sam Ayodo, his enemies were the more prominent. Mungai and Moi in particular hated him. Just after Joe had resigned as Vice-President, Moi had picked a fight with Tom in the parliamentary dining room, accusing him of wanting to take his job. Tom was a brilliant man, no doubt about it, but he couldn't stand anybody coming on his wrong side. At one point he even brought a no confidence vote against me and announced it in the House. One day I was in the chair when he appeared. Watching him walk very arrogantly across the chamber, the idea just flashed into my mind, by Jove this man is going to be dead in a few weeks, and I thought, what a shame.

The New Year did not begin well. On the 29th of January, Argwings Kodhek, Kenya's Foreign Affairs Minister, was killed in a car crash. As Kenya's first black lawyer, Kodhek had defended many of the Mau Mau suspects, and challenged the prejudices of the settlers by marrying his sweetheart Mavis Tate, a white girl. After winning a debate in court one day with a Chief Justice who still thought blacks could not practise English law, he declared, 'Woe and wilt upon Britannia, that she chooses to export the most stupid and vile of her sons to civilise Africa.' The crash had been declared an accident, and with no available evidence to the contrary any other possibilities remained conjecture.

It was Tom Mboya who had warned me Pio was in danger. If, given the concerted efforts to sideline him, he thought he might now be the one at risk, he did not show it. Perhaps under the surface he was very afraid, but there was no sign of him bowing out of politics. If anything he seemed more audacious than ever, as witnessed during a party held at State House. The guests included a glittering array of international VIPs, among them Nehru. On arrival, Tom, whom I got the impression had been drinking, and already knew many of the visiting dignitaries, proceeded to take Kenyatta's arm and lead him around the room, introducing him to everyone in a grandiose manner, as if he himself were the President and Kenyatta the underling. Kenyatta was obliged to grit his teeth and endure the humiliation. The following day, I found Kenyatta in a foul temper, calling Tom Mboya all the names under the sun, saying how he wanted to crush him, and to emphasise the point, grinding his foot into the floor. A moment later the door opened and Tom walked in. Kenyatta immediately smiled, greeting him warmly and heartily like a long-lost friend. Once again I thought, what a fantastic actor.

It was now 1969, and Tom, increasingly short of funds was begging and borrowing. He would ring me quite often to ask for a loan, but I had nothing to spare. On the morning of the 5th of July I parked my car in Government Road as usual and was walking towards my office when, passing the ground floor pharmacy, I saw a figure standing close against the wall, his arm outstretched. I carried on and went up to my office. A while later I heard shots. A man had been hit twice as he came out of the pharmacy. While crowds quickly gathered at the scene, an ambulance rushed the patient to Nairobi hospital. But it was no good. Tom Mboya was dead.

KANU youth winger Nahashon Njoroge, later arrested for the crime, denied pulling the trigger, claiming he had long been a friend of Mboya. His statement to the police was short but memorable: 'Why don't you go after the big man?' It was assumed he meant the President, but as with Pio, I found it hard to believe Kenyatta would condone such an act. I knew Tom visited the pharmacy regularly and knew the family who ran it. He would also park his car in the same place each time, by the nearby Ismaili Hotel. His assassins had also known this. I called in to the pharmacy and spoke to the family. One young woman was still in shock. She had been greeting Tom, who was very popular and had friends everywhere, when, as she embraced him, she heard someone shout, 'Tom Mboya is here!' Seconds later a bullet had passed by, touching her hair. The next one had hit Tom.

Mboya's funeral was to be a big affair, and this time, unlike for Pio, who had been a nobody in the eyes of the public, Kenyatta would be attending. The feeling among Luos, Tom's tribe, was that Kikuyus should stay away. With emotions running high, scores of police and soldiers had been drafted in, lining the roads as the mourners, led by Pamela and the children, arrived at All Saints Cathedral. Kenyatta was flanked by a tight group of security men. There was quite a crowd, with Kenyans of all faiths coming to pay their respects. Among them was Jeremiah Nyagah, a great friend of Tom's. He was, however, also considered a Kikuyu, and when some Luos spotted him driving in they lost control. Surrounding his car, they began banging on the windows, shouting abuse and threatening to kill him. I rushed up and urged them to be calm, and that if they wanted to punish anyone it should be whoever killed Tom. It was fortunate I was not a Kikuyu, and eventually the protestors dispersed. After the moving service, as the congregation filed out, trouble flared again. Suddenly, people were running everywhere, some crying, not from grief now, but tear gas fired by the security forces, lashing out with batons to disperse the crowd. Around the world, newsreels showed Tom Mboya's funeral ending in scenes of chaos, anger and violence.

Like a lot of people I was utterly shocked by Tom's murder. What had happened to Pio had left me very shaky, but the level of anxiety and disbelief now seemed even worse, and I had to resort to Valium. Bruce McKenzie was also noticeably affected; one of those men who are brilliant in their own way, and can be totally ruthless with it, McKenzie was nonetheless quite shaken, not only because he liked Tom, but because I believe he now thought that if this could happen to a man like Tom Mboya it could happen to anyone; he might even have feared being next on the list. This might have been why, along with his second wife wanting to settle in England, he retreated from the centre of politics, citing ill health as the reason. Some said he was pushed, that he had outlived his usefulness to the Government. Before long though he would appear to be prospering again, and go on to buy a house next door to mine, adding a tennis court and swimming pool, all the trappings of luxury. One could only speculate about where he was getting the money, but dramatic events would in time reveal a lot more about Bruce's activities.

On the 25th of October 1969, just a few weeks after Tom's death, Kenyatta arrived in Kisumu to officially open the new Russian Hospital, a project that Odinga had set up. It was believed he wanted to signal his authority in this

Luo-dominated area of the country. Teachers and children were waiting to sing songs and read poems for the President. Also waiting were a contingent of angry Luos with placards that read: 'Where is Tom Mboya.' As Kenyatta and Odinga began a heated exchange of words, the mood quickly turned hostile, violence broke out, and Government troops opened fire into the crowd. When the shooting stopped, 11 people were dead, with hundreds more injured. Odinga was arrested and placed in detention.

On the 8th of November, before the sun had risen, and with no public announcement, Njoroge was hanged for the murder of Tom Mboya. In the aftermath of the Kisumu Massacre, the Kenya People's Union had been officially banned. Kenya was now a one-party state.

Bruce Mackenzie and me in Nairobi

Myself with Bruce Mackenzie, Pranlal Sheth and Oginga Odinga

Chapter Fifteen

The Asian Exodus From East Africa Accelerates

The Early 1970s

Tom Mboya's chief claim to fame in Kenya's history is that he kept the freedom flag flying through all the years that Kenyatta was in prison. He had worked hard in the Kenyan trade union movement and when it was banned, and J.D. Kali, Makhan Singh and others imprisoned, had helped to keep its spirit alive. These achievements, along with the educational airlift programme, would make him a lasting inspiration to Africans, and to all those who continued to struggle for justice the world over. Having known Tom for many years and seen how he educated himself and how hard he worked, I can testify to his talents and dedication. Though making enemies in high places, he had remained the darling of the Africans. They used to call him 'Mr Tom' or just 'Tom', even when he became a Minister. He knew how to 'bembeleza' – the Swahili word for charm – any community at any time.

He had weaknesses too, and he certainly knew how to enjoy life. I remember on a delegation when we would be taken out for parties from around 10pm and not get back to the hotel until the early hours, but then over breakfast, while we talked, he would be busily writing several pages to the Government about the previous day's events. 'Here Fitz,' he would say, 'you're the lawyer, read this through please and tell me how I can improve it.' The wording was precise, comprehensive and with hardly a comma out of place, and as we discussed the content Tom wrote still more. I thought, what a fantastic man! Who else could do this? A piece that would probably have taken me three days, he had written in half an hour. I thought: he is more brilliant than I am, and I'm supposed to be a PhD.

The English and Europeans who, reassured by Kenyatta, had stayed on after independence and seen Tom Mboya as a safe Westernised leader, had also been disturbed at his assassination. They did, however, have Charles Njonjo, whom they regarded as their protector, and felt that as long as he was around they were quite safe. I remember once at the British High Commissioner's House on National Day for the Queen's Birthday, he made a speech as 'guest of honour' in which he paid glowing tribute to Britain, then sang 'Rule Britannia' with such gusto one would think he really was an English 'Sir' or Officer. Just like the MP Colonel Cole, who whenever he heard the National Anthem would stand absolutely rigid, not moving a muscle, and I used to think good God how does he do it? The British sense of patriotism was so strong that they believed the Queen was the embodiment of the greatness of their country and Empire. Many perhaps still do. My father used to tell me a story about his commanding officer Colonel Fitzpatrick, whose wife was rumoured, whenever they fell out, to wait until he was in the bath then play 'God Save The King' loudly on the gramophone over and over again, obliging the poor man to jump to attention and salute.

Another of Tom Mboya's legacies was his design for the Africanisation Programme. He had told me: 'Fitz, you cannot have a country here where the civil service is European or Indian.' He was not racist, but practical. Traditionally, the junior civil service posts had been almost exclusively filled by young Asian boys, and since India had become independent, there was a fear that these people were no longer as subservient as in the past. 'They don't have loyalty to this country... they will sabotage things, or they will sleep on things... we Africans will take part... it doesn't matter what people say, what we are doing to the constitution, we will have to have Africanisation.' Tom saw the civil service as the central pillar that supported the Kenyan Government and society, but realised that you couldn't just put new people into these jobs and expect them to be capable and committed. There was a need to train and educate them, and this had been the idea behind the airlifts; to send Africans to America and turn them into civil servants. Many went on to postgraduate study and gained doctorates.

The move to Africanisation extended beyond the state bureaucracy to a whole range of businesses that had traditionally been carried on by Asians or Europeans. After independence the estimated 180,000 Asians and 60,000 Europeans living in Kenya had either been granted Kenyan citizenship, or had been given the option of applying for it up until 1965. It was expected that most of the Asians would try to move to Britain, but in fact only around 50,000 would do so, many more delaying taking Kenyan citizenship. I remember when we discussed this at Lancaster House I had said, 'Look Asians being Asians, they will want to keep their legs in two boats. Those that want to settle here in Kenya should be made citizens immediately without needing to apply, and those that don't want to should leave.'

When the British objected to the idea of automatic citizenship, a compromise for which I was partly responsible was agreed upon: that those born in Kenya, and one or more of whose parents were also born there, could have immediate Kenyan citizenship, while those that had lived in the country legally for five years or more could apply within the next two years. One thing that had made so many of the Asians hesitate was the violent upheaval in the Belgian Congo; when the Belgians had started fleeing through Kenya, their cars piled high with furniture, carpets, crockery and cutlery, selling everything for a song, abandoning their cars if they had to, just to get back to Belgium, the Asians thought oh God, it could be us next if things go wrong in Kenya, and we'll want to escape, so we had better keep our options open. Then within three or four months of the deadline for Kenyan citizenship, thousands of Asians rushed to apply. Their failure to do so earlier was seen by many Africans as disloyal. Kenyatta was very angry about it, as was Odinga, who was Home Affairs Minister at the time, and they both dug their heels in and held up the applications, by a year, two years, even up to four years in some cases. Some of my friends waited so long for their applications to be processed that they gave up in the end.

Effectively denying citizenship to Asians in this way assisted the Africanisation Programme; there had for some time been elements in the Government that wanted not only to push all Indians out of the labour force, but also out of the country. For some unscrupulous officials, Asian traders had been a lucrative source of income. A typical trick was for a police officer to go to a bazaar, usually on a Friday, enter one of the textile shops and demand to see the import licence for a particular piece of cloth. With hundreds of rolls of fabric, it was very hard for the trader to find the relevant documentation straight away, and before he had the chance he would be whisked off to prison. Denied bail, food or visitors, he would then be seen by a particular lawyer and asked to pay a sum of money for his release, the cash being split between those running the racket. It was not only Africans doing this. The inspector carrying out most of these arrests was a Sikh.

Traders would come to me in despair at the frequency this was happening to them, but there was little I could do. Judges were a party to it, and certain magistrates were known quite openly to be very corrupt, and quickly becoming rich on the proceeds. They received quite large sums of money for each case, but whether it was all distributed to the people concerned I don't know. I do know that when the political cases came in, again they were told to go to the same lawyer, who would get the same magistrate made a judge, before whom they would always win. Eventually the judges would have a price for every case, and I would even see physical fights between them in the courtroom, each wanting to give judgment and be the one to pocket the bribe. I was amazed that the practice was so deep-rooted, and even some of my good friends in the judiciary, whom I thought were very honest people, I'm told became very corrupt and made money this way.

As it became increasingly harder for Asians to obtain work or run businesses, they had begun to sell up and leave. For 500 Kenya shillings you could get a one-way ticket for England. Some went in the winter wearing only T-shirts. As more and more arrived in the UK, concerns over the influx grew, and in March 1968, a few weeks even before Enoch Powell's infamous 'Rivers of Blood' speech, the Commonwealth Immigration Act was passed, restricting entry to Britain to those having a parent or grandparent born in the country. I was one of a trio that visited the House of Commons to lobby MPs about the dangers of Enoch Powell's views. When India also put up barriers, we had what became known as the 'Kenyan Asian Crisis'. Those arriving in Britain faced difficulties such as finding accommodation, but fortunately Indians help one another, especially among families, and I think Africans are the same. When my servant's brother or cousins used to visit him from Eldoret for example, he would ask me if they could stay in the house, and I would reply, sure, carry on. This was the custom, you cannot say no, with us it would be very bad manners, you've got to put people up.

As the displaced Asian community began to settle in Britain, Kenya continued to become more African. Africanisation in the judiciary had begun as early as 1964, when Kenyatta invited Cecil Miller to come to Nairobi and become the first black judge. Born in British Guyana in 1916, Miller had been in the RAF in World War Two, and was frankly a show-off, talking mostly about what a good fighter pilot he had been. Kitili Mwendwa's appointment as Chief Justice in 1968, replacing Farrel, had been a part of the same process, though Miller, who had been Called to the Bar in 1952, was I thought a slightly better judge. Mwendwa on the other hand, who had never practised law, was a better businessman, and even after becoming Chief Justice he was more interested in running his bus service from Nairobi to Uganda in partnership with Milton Obote's wife. In court you always knew when one of his buses had broken down, as he would get a message and suddenly adjourn in the middle of a case. Once I visited his chambers where he showed me a big board with pins and arrows on it showing the positions of all his buses. I thought this was very odd, and that surely he should have enough work to do as Chief Justice.

One day I received a letter from the company that insured Mwendwa's buses. Apparently there were outstanding premiums, and they were going to cancel the policy if he did not pay up, and wanted me to take legal action against him. When I spoke to him about it, he called the people from the insurance company to his chambers and threatened to put them in prison. I don't think people had a great deal of respect for him as Chief Justice. A few individuals were loyal to him, but those practising regularly were well aware that he knew nothing about the law and wasn't interested in a job he had been pushed into.

A lot of the Africanisation Programme seemed token and impractical. Many of those who had been handed businesses did little of the day-to-day running. Often, land that had been taken and given to Ministers was either left empty and unproductive, or the new owner would visit maybe once a week or once a month, or simply ring up to find out what had been done. They were referred to as 'telephone farmers'. I know this is what happened with all the sugarcane plantations that Moi had taken from the Mehtas and given to the locals, who did nothing at all, expecting the Mehtas to still clear and plough the land, plant the seed, weed, and cut the cane. What was the point?

One European parliamentarian who had so far held on to his post was the Speaker, Sir Humphrey Slade. Why had the African leaders settled on him? I think because those who had met him early on found him a very nice and very impartial man who, unlike many of the judges, only supported the Government up to a point and strove instead to uphold the freedoms of Parliament and be fair to the opposition, especially if he felt it to be under-represented. Whenever minority groups or individuals were taking part in a discussion, he would tend to give them a more than proportionate chance to express their views. I thought this was right, and as Deputy Speaker had done the same for Odinga's KPU, allowing them more time to speak than Tom Mboya and others, which had made the latter very angry with me. Though the Africans had been willing to keep Sir Humphrey on, he had felt no great desire to wait until his retirement date in 1970, and we had become such good friends that for some time he had been asking me if I would like to step into his shoes before then. When I politely declined, he said why, did I not feel that the position of Speaker was a good one? I assured him it was, but that I hadn't the patience to sit for four hours at a time listening to a lot of speeches!

Also, as Deputy Speaker I liked to take part in the debates, which the Speaker cannot. Sir Humphrey was a good speaker in every sense, and having heard many well-known speakers in Britain and India, I think he was better than all of them. Visiting the Indian Parliament once as guest of the Speaker proved a surprising experience. I was given the VIP seat, and as proceedings got under way, 20 to 30 people stood up at once to have their say. 'Sit down,' called the Speaker. 'No!' retorted the members. So it went on, with the Speaker and the members all shouting at one another and people constantly jumping up and down. No one tried to throw anyone out or call for a serjeant-at-arms to arrest them, and the chamber was more like a chaotic marketplace than a Parliament.

1971 brought further drama. A placard appeared with a handful of names and words to the effect that Kitili Mwendwa must go. Then Njonjo stood up in Parliament and said he must be removed. It was believed he had been plotting a coup d'état, along with General Joseph Ndolo and Gideon Mutiso, the MP for Yatta. Mutiso and others had been arrested and charged with conspiracy. Ndolo, implicated in Mutiso's confession was shortly after replaced. Kitili Mwendwa was also implicated in other confessions, and seeing the writing on the wall he resigned. I would not be surprised if it were true. Kitili was a tremendous conspirator and loved intrigue and conjecture about people. He had been only three years in his post, making him the shortest serving as well as the youngest ever Chief Justice. It played into Njonjo's hands, as he was very keen to get rid of competition. Hilary Ngweno has written about these events in detail in his book.

Earlier in the year meanwhile, over the border in Uganda someone really had overthrown the Government. Idi Amin, a former soldier in the King's African Rifles, had seized the opportunity of Milton Obote's absence at a Commonwealth meeting in Singapore to stage a military coup. The Asians in Uganda thought this was great and were dancing in the streets. Obote had visited China, and they thought he had become a socialist, was nationalising everything and might soon do so with the Asian businesses, mills and cotton works. Amin on the other hand they felt would be a benign, tolerant person. He made some good speeches to the Asian Federation, a clever fellow, with no education but a 'gut' politician, he knew what to say at the right time, and I think appealed to their needs.

Eighteen months later things were looking very different. Amin had decided to take over the "economic revolution" and was calling the Asians 'bloodsuckers' that were milking the economy, and at the beginning of August 1972 ordered them en-masse, an estimated 80,000 people, to leave the country. Two days later this was amended and only those who were not Ugandan citizens had to go, but this still put the figure at around 60,000 having to leave Uganda within a deadline of just 90 days. Many of the 50,000 or so who held UK passports headed for Britain, others to India. When the forced expulsion started hundreds of families came through Kenya by rail, often with little more than the clothes on their back. Fellow Asians, myself included, went to the station to see if there was anyone we could help by giving them a little money for food or a cup of tea. Moi and others had insisted that there should be no stopping and they should continue on out of Kenya. I pleaded that these people, many of whom had relatives in Kenya, should be allowed a few days rest at least to recover from the shock. 'No, no,' insisted Moi, 'they will swallow this place,' and the authorities refused even to let them off the trains. Arriving in England, the families would often discover that their luggage had been stolen or ransacked at the point of departure.

The impact on Asians in Kenya was one of shock, thinking the same could happen to them at any time. Even I thought we might have a coup tomorrow, led by someone following Amin's example. I was later told that a similar move to expel Asians from Kenya had been discussed by the cabinet. Amin's behaviour was not so much a revolution as a straightforward seizure of power. But to maintain power you have to use what I would call respite, and so he gave farms to people, gave the Mehta's tea factories to the football club, and the sugar factories to some Egyptians. Mahendra Mehta and I had become friends, and I remember us talking one day about the attitude towards the Wahindi Asians in East Africa and other places now. We lamented the fact that conflict and discrimination were so often the product of temperament not reason, and that the way things were going there was the danger the next war might be against Indians.

Jomo Kenyatta was now 80 years old and showing no sign of retiring. His health though was not perfect, and after he had suffered a heart attack in 1966 those around him continued to be concerned. When the South African surgeon Christiaan Barnard performed the world's first heart transplant in 1967, we approached him for advice. Barnard came to Nairobi for a meeting: he made it clear that in view of the President's age, such a procedure should not be attempted. People naturally began to talk about what would happen when Kenyatta was no longer around, and who might move up the ladder. As Attorney General, Charles Njonjo's far-reaching powers were already well known, but it was also quite widely believed in political circles that he was ambitious to rise still higher. This was brought home to me at a party I attended one evening at the Indian High Commission. A group of us, including Njonjo and the Indian High Commissioner, was discussing politics, when a dentist, Dr Devani, asked me, in the event of Kenyatta's death, which person I thought should succeed Moi as Vice-President, who, according to the constitution would become President. I said I thought the Finance Minister Mwai Kibaki should be the next Vice-President.

Before I describe the reaction, let me describe the man. Very humble, straightforward and friendly, Kibaki had as far as I knew never been involved in corruption or bribes, and never demanded a house, cars or motorcycle escorts and other such trappings of office. He also disapproved of girls coming out to dance and shake their bottoms at the President during official visits to schools, calling him 'Mutukufu Rais' – treating him as a god. I had first known Kibaki at the LSE, where I was a year above him. Most people there said he was bound to be President of Kenya one day. I felt sure of it myself. He was certainly one of the most brilliant students in England, and studying Banking and Finance, the hardest of subjects in Economics. My area, Politics and Government I thought much easier. Back then in London we were poor students, Kibaki a little poorer, and when he returned to Kenya he was kind enough to tell friends how when he was hungry I used to buy him a sandwich and a cup of tea. Although not openly supporting or joining any political group or individual, he was originally very pro-Odinga, and a very sincere socialist, who basically would not harm anybody.

Mwai Kibaki was therefore my preference for the next Vice-President. But after I said this at the party, everyone looked very worried. When Njonjo had moved away I was urged to go and apologise to him, and warned by the High Commissioner that I could be harassed for the rest of my life – telling me that Charles will do this to you, and that. 'Why?' I said. 'Oh, he does it to everybody,' he told me, 'you should never cross his path.' This was the Indian High Commissioner telling me this. 'Why should I apologise?' I said, 'what have I done? Someone asked my opinion and I gave it. I never said Njonjo was no good.'

We all knew that one of the reasons Charles Njonjo wanted to get into Parliament was to become Vice-President when Kenyatta's time came, and Moi took his place. Some speculated that there would then be a fatal motor accident for Moi, and Njonjo would be the top man. I was once asked if people obeyed Njonjo out of fear or because they wanted favours. I believe it was both. Among Indians this was very important; if you know a person has influence, you help them more, give them money and so forth, because you expect that when the time comes they will do the same for you. Everywhere Njonjo went, Indians in particular would do anything for him. A lot of Africans though felt antagonistic. He clearly supported Europeans far more, even saying publicly on one occasion that he would never fly in a plane with an African pilot, and being rumoured to use only European doctors, though I doubt this was strictly true. Despite this he had great status among Africans in the law enforcement services. Passing International House, next to the Nairobi Hilton one day, and seeing a lot of armed police and soldiers, I asked an officer what was going on. He told me that Njonjo, the most important man in Kenya, was about to arrive.

For most Africans though, certainly the Kikuyu, Kenyatta was still their god. As the 1970s progressed he would preside over a growing population, and, through trade and cooperation with American and European companies, a burgeoning capitalist economy. Yet though the fruits of this success were benefiting a number of people, the vast majority were seeing little improvement in their material circumstances. Perhaps this would take a lot longer than many had envisioned. Kenya had its independence, which owed much to those who had supported Uhuru from the early days and through the dark times of the Mau Mau and the Emergency, but political progress seemed to be at a sticking point.

Increasingly aware of the entrenched nature of tribalism and the virtually one-party system, I felt no longer useful. It was though chiefly a question of survival; first Pio had tried to change things, and then in his own way so had Tom, and both had paid the price. I thought, this is dangerous, the fellows that got them, they can get anyone. Not wishing to be next on the list I decided to bow out of Parliament. Most importantly, Romola and I had been blessed with children, and having little money I felt I should now try to make some in order to give them a good education. The first priority was my family.

Mwai Kibaki

Chapter Sixteen

Milestones

Romola and I arranged to spend three months in England, and also tour around Europe. I wanted the children to see and understand different people and cultures. We were also considering having them educated in England. Not long after my father's death, my mother had gone to live in Goa to look after her elderly mother and the family property. I had been visiting her there about once or twice a year, and I hoped that she would return to Kenya eventually. We also had other relatives and friends remaining in the country, as well as business interests, so we would not be cutting our ties and intended to keep our house on.

    My brother Rix and sister Iva were my closest relatives living in Nairobi. To backtrack a few years; after leaving school, Rix had been sent away to India, where he had stayed with my maternal aunt, whose first husband, a shop owner from Karachi, had died and left her a lot of money. She had used it to build 14 flats and was a millionaire, and some of her income had helped pay for Rix's further education. Initially he had studied medicine, but after a couple of years he gave it up. We don't know what happened. He then took a place at the Commercial and Industrial College, where I believe he worked very hard. Returning to Kenya though, he did nothing. My father forced him to interviews, at which he would tell the employers he had a degree, but when they asked him to produce the certificate he would come back and say he didn't want the job. This happened half a dozen times. My father got a bit worried, and asked me, 'Has he got a degree?' I said, 'I have never read it, never seen it, but I presume he wouldn't tell people so if he hasn't.'

Rix was a very good-hearted person. He had always looked after me, and walked ahead of me physically to safeguard me when we were children. But in life he did not think ahead. Eventually my father took him to see someone he knew, who spoke to another man who found Rix a job as a prison officer, first in Mombasa then Nairobi. Leaving there he worked for S.T. Shah in a gramophone shop in Nakuru, and soon after was unemployed again. Much of the time he spent smoking and reading Wild West novels, sometimes three or four a week. My father and I would give him money when he asked, but we did try to stop him from smoking. 'No-one has ever died from smoking,' he would reply. Our father had given up cigarettes by that time, but it was still not widely known or accepted that tobacco could damage your health. Meanwhile, Rix must have got through hundreds of Wild West books. These were harmless, but I used to say to him, 'Rix how can you; surely they are all the same?' 'Yes, I know,' he said with a smile, 'I can always tell you how the story ends.' Sometimes he would ask me what he should do, and in the end I would have to say, 'I don't know.'

Meanwhile, my father had been having a house built in Nairobi, incorporating a grocery shop, bar and restaurant. We subsequently left our house in Parklands and all lived together in the upper residential part of the new property. Then when I was due to go off on a tour of India, Rix asked if he could run the downstairs of the new place as a business, and agreed to pay a monthly rental back to the family. He could have made I think around 5,000 Kenya shillings a month net, quite a lot of money, so he was happy, and I went off to India. I toured all over, and saw and learned a lot about the country. By the time I was ready to take the ship back to Kenya I had almost run out of money, so I bought a deck ticket for 150 shillings, which was very cheap, and fine if you didn't mind sleeping in the open air.

The night before we sailed, a drunken sailor came wandering along the deck, chatting to everyone and telling me I could get food from the First Class compartments if I wished, and it would be all right. I told him no thank you, and that I just wanted to sleep. When I woke, someone said that because the sailor had continued being a nuisance to the passengers all night, he had been locked in a cabin, only to climb out of the porthole and fall overboard. Eventually, realising his cries for help were genuine, someone threw him a lifebelt, but sadly, unable to reach it, he had drowned. I said, 'Oh I am so sorry.' One of the ship's officers had then asked me, as a lawyer, if I would sign a memorandum about what had happened. I said, 'What are the facts?' They explained that because the sailor had been drunk and making a nuisance of himself, the crew had no choice but to lock him up, and had acted in good faith. I testified in writing to what I had seen of the sailor's behaviour, and no more. They seemed grateful, and gave me accommodation near the Captain, while the body of the unfortunate sailor was left for the port authorities.

I had been away in India for three months. Back in Nairobi there was no sign of any rent from Rix for the business he had been left to run. On going to see the new property I found it full of women, about 20 or more. They were drinking in the bar and then taking men upstairs. Rix told me he was so embarrassed; the woman he had let it to had moved all these other women in and not paid him a shilling in rent, so he had been unable to pay me. I told the woman concerned that she and her friends were trespassers, and that even if they paid the rent I didn't want them running a brothel there. When I asked them to leave however, they refused. By this time I was already quite senior in politics, so I went back with some police and had them thrown out.

Time went by, and our father passed away. My brother was by that time in his mid-forties, and I suggested that perhaps he should think about getting married and settling down. He said he could not afford to marry, so I gave him some money and off he went to India. Then, in 1970 my mother had received a telegram from him to say that he had met someone; a girl he was very keen on, from a very good family, and that her father was a dentist. We thought this sounded good and were pleased for him. The next we heard was that he was coming back to Kenya, and would be bringing the girl with him. I thought this was very strange, and wrote to ask Rix why she was coming. He replied that she had insisted on it. When they arrived I took Rix aside and asked what was going on; was he intending to marry her, had he had sex with her, what? I said, 'Look, tell me the truth, knowing Indians they would not let their unmarried daughter travel, and certainly not move to another continent like this, unless there was something secure; tell me, did you already marry her civilly?' He replied, 'I suppose.' I said, 'What do you mean, you suppose?' Anything that was not an arranged marriage was considered by most people to be immoral. Anyway, I gave Rix and his wife a flat and took him on as accountant for my building firm that was putting up houses.

Throughout this story I have so far said almost nothing about my sister Iva, except that when we first came to Zanzibar she stayed on in Goa with my aunt, and later, when I was studying in London and my father fell sick, she sent me money to travel back to Kenya. It was known quite early on that Iva had health problems, and one day when on holiday with Rix, she collapsed. At first the doctors thought it was epilepsy, then discovered she had a hole in the heart. Despite this she had always worked for her living, mostly for Gailey & Roberts, part of East African Industries, involved in railway construction. Their office was in Hardinge Street, now Mackenzie Street, and she would come to the pharmacy and talk to our father every day. When she met a good man and they wanted to marry, she already knew that her condition made it far too risky to have children. Her fiancé loved children, but he loved her too, and said this did not matter to him, and that he would pay for her to have an operation in England. I offered to pay half, but he would not hear of it.

In 1973, I accompanied the two of them to England and met Alan Yates, the Queen's surgeon. He told Iva there was only a 16 percent chance of her surviving the operation. She asked him how long he thought she would live without it. He told her a maximum of six months. Ok she said, but I want to go ahead. He then advised her against it, but she repeated that she wanted to proceed. Iva was very brave. While she lay unconscious in the theatre, her husband and I walked round and round the hospital. It was six hours later when Alan Yates came to tell us that Iva was all right, and the operation appeared to have been a success. Several years later when a team of heart surgeons and consultants came to Nairobi, among them was Alan Yates. By pure chance I bumped into him. I invited him to my house, and without telling Iva, asked her to come too. I said, 'You'll never guess who is coming to dinner tonight.' As soon as they saw one another, Alan rushed up and embraced her. He said, 'You know you are the bravest woman I have ever met, I was so afraid that day, I was almost shaking with fear that I was going to kill you. I am so happy, you have tremendous determination.' A steel heart, he said. I kept in touch with Alan, and later visited him in England. Iva and her husband lived very happily together, both living into their 90s.

Being so close to my father, I had always been curious about the other woman in his early life and wanted to meet her and see if she might be willing to talk about those days. After he had died, I thought I would try to find her. Not wishing to upset my mother, or the woman concerned or any family she might now have, I had to do so discreetly. It turned out she did have a family, but when I managed to locate them, they gave me the sad news that she had only recently died after falling ill at a dance. I offered my condolences and explained about my father having known her many years ago, before her marriage. They were very welcoming and invited me in and showed me photographs, telling me all about her children and that she had led a good and happy life. I said I was grateful for their friendliness and hospitality, and that I wished we could have met under happier circumstances.

Romola and I had remained good friends with many of the campaigners for Kenyan independence, including Sarjit Heyer and his wife, the economist Judith Cripps. It was in the early 1970s, however, that Sarjit became unwell, and was diagnosed with polyarteritis nodosa, a very rare condition. I spoke to someone and we managed to get a second medical opinion, and the advice that there might be more chance of a cure in England. However, once he got there Sarjit succumbed and sadly died. Sarjit's tireless commitment to equality, and his important contributions behind the scenes with research, devising strategy and writing speeches and briefings, working always towards the goal of freedom for the Kenyan people were a vital part of the nation's development.

In 1974 my mother was still living in Goa, and Rix seemed settled in Kenya and was starting a family of his own. Meanwhile, I had my legal practice in Kenya, as well as business interests, including the firm for which Rix was the accountant. There was also Maralal Safari Lodge and Thomson's Falls Lodge which I had bought for a relatively low price at the time, and which we ran on a shoestring. One day my friend Josiah Mwangi (J.M.) Kariuki informed me that he had gone to stay there and found the place in darkness, the electricity having failed. He then told me he had gone back and installed a generator. 'Thank you, how much do I owe you?' I said. When he refused to take any money I felt rather uncomfortable. A year or so earlier, while still Deputy Speaker, I had been asked to check one of Kariuki's parliamentary expenses claims. It stated he had driven to his Nyandarua constituency and back, then to Mombasa and back, all on the same day. I said, 'Look J.M. you're my friend but be reasonable and reduce it, we all have allowances but this is overdoing it.' He said, 'I drive very fast.' I laughed, 'You would have to have arrived in

Mombasa at midnight, waited two minutes and driven straight back.' I wondered now if he had somehow managed to get the claim paid after all, and, thinking it was me that had turned a blind eye, was belatedly thanking me.

But Kariuki was a very affectionate and charming person. I had first met him when he was a typist in Kenyatta's office, tapping away with one finger, and very friendly. He looked like a boy in those days. Like so many, he had been in detention during the Emergency, and over the years had developed into an intelligent politician, always saying the right thing at the right time. On the subject of corruption, including the unequal distribution of land, he was an outspoken critic. He was very popular with the people, but not the Government, who had tried to stop him campaigning in the 1974 elections. I really don't know what happened to the generator, but one always remained aware of what might be seen as bribery. In the area of work I was moving into, corporate law, companies making takeover bids, for example, were often willing to pay a lot of money or bend the rules to get their way, but I would always tell them to go to arbitration. The problem was that in many institutions in Kenya, corruption had become a way of life and those who opposed it ran risks. In the spring of 1975, J.M. Kariuki's charred remains were found on an anthill just south of Nairobi. He had last been seen alive at the Hilton Hotel, accompanied by Kenyatta's bodyguard. I was very sad when I heard, and I still don't know why they decided to do this. Probably it was personal, as sometimes happens. Someone hates your guts and worries you will worm your way into his boss's good books, thereby threatening his own interests. I don't think J.M. was a danger to the Government, but perhaps someone thought so and I could be wrong.

Meanwhile, a bitter conflict from another part of the world was about to be played out in East Africa and bring the enigmatic Bruce McKenzie once more into the picture. In mid-1976, just a few months after Bruce was said to have helped capture a group suspected of planning to attack an El

Al aeroplane out of Nairobi, a passenger plane from Tel Aviv was hijacked by two Palestinians and landed at Entebbe airport in Uganda. They threatened that unless 53 Palestinian prisoners in Israel and other countries were released, they would kill the passengers, many of whom were Jewish. Any rescue attempt would be made much more difficult by the fact that Idi Amin had declared his support for the hijackers. It is believed that Bruce stepped in again, flying Mossad reconnaissance agents over Entebbe and helping to persuade Kenyatta to let Israel's planes refuel in Nairobi and cross Kenyan airspace. On the night of the 3rd of July 1976, Israeli jets destroyed several Ugandan Air Force planes on the ground, while commandos killed around 36 Ugandan soldiers and brought the majority of the hostages out unharmed. Amin, furious, issued an immediate death sentence on hundreds of Kenyans living in Uganda.

Whether Amin knew of Bruce McKenzie's role at the time of Operation Entebbe is unclear to me, but two years later Bruce flew in his light aircraft to Uganda, apparently at the dictator's invitation. According to reports, on landing in Uganda he would always instruct his co-pilot not to leave the plane unattended for a second, or allow anyone to tinker with it. On this occasion, shortly after his meeting was due to finish, a phone call was received in Kenya asking if Mr McKenzie had returned.

Then came news of a plane coming down over the Ngong Hills. When I went to survey the site of the crash I got a terrible shock, seeing by an amazing chance among the wreckage what I felt sure were the metal plates of Bruce's jaw, rebuilt after his wartime injuries, the facial scars hidden by bushy whiskers. If his plane had been sabotaged, how had Amin managed it? The story that emerged was that just as Bruce had been about to take off, an official ran out to the plane with a last-minute gift from the President of a carved antelope's head. Inside the antelope was a bomb, timed to go off in mid-air over Lake Victoria, where the evidence would sink without trace, but the mechanism had apparently lagged. Bruce left behind him a wife and children from his two marriages, a reputation as a good farmer, and, as details of his long-standing relationship with both the American and Israeli intelligence services came to light, an intriguing life story.

Kenyatta had always been very conscious of the fact that, once a person was in power, everyone would run to him. As far back as Lancaster House he told me that he could change everything with the will and support of the people that were at the time opposing him, because as the head of their Government, they would need to come to him for lots of small favours. One could later see the effects of this, how he had stopped projects or developments in areas where he thought the people opposed him. If they wanted the development, they had to go and support him.

But Kenyatta never forgot his friends, and when independence came he had offered me not only farms, but ministerial posts, and jobs in Government and industry. He even apologised at one point for not making me Attorney General. It often seemed like he was the only one in the Government who was really nice to me. I was amazed that even now he would ring up now and again: 'Look you're the only person who has never asked me for a favour, you've never asked me for a job, for money, do you want a job, what can I do for you, would you like to come back into politics...?' If he saw me on the road he would slow down his car and wave, 'How are you?' I thought it was good of him to remember. Most people in politics forget you completely.

In 1978, there was renewed concern about the President's health. It had been revealed he had been suffering from intermittent comas, some lasting a few hours, others days. In the summer he held a large family reunion in Mombasa for which his son flew over from England. I was in England myself at the time. On the 22nd of August, switching on the radio I heard the sad news that Mzee Jomo Kenyatta, the founding father of the Kenyan nation, had died peacefully in his sleep.

Chapter Seventeen

After Mzee

There were varying reports as to Kenyatta's age, some newspapers saying he had been 86, others 89. Kenyatta, having no record of his birth, had never been certain himself. Attending the funeral were Nehru, numerous African leaders including Julius Nyerere, and representing Britain, Prince Charles.

What would happen in Kenya now? Earlier attempts to change the constitution and allow another Kikuyu to take Kenyatta's place had not succeeded. Daniel Arap Moi was therefore automatically instated, and in time duly elected President, while I was pleased to see Mwai Kibaki made Vice-President.

I had never really been close to Moi, though we had met on and off over the years. He had always seemed to me a very simple person; either that or a good actor. I recalled now the day I had been standing next to him by the docket stairs in Parliament. A car had drawn up outside and Charles Njonjo had put his head out and called, 'Moi, come here.' Moi raced down the steps and Njonjo said, 'I've heard a new story today,' to which Moi replied eagerly, 'Tell me, tell me Charles, what is it?' Njonjo then recited something to the effect of: 'Oh God, help me from my friends, because my enemies I know, but my friends I don't.' Moi laughed heartily. 'Oh Charles, you are such a very clever man, you always say these very clever things,' and he carried on laughing until Njonjo had driven off again. I thought, is Moi really so simple? – we've all heard this saying many times. I then realised he was just playing up to him. Njonjo was a very powerful man, and for Moi to become President, he needed his support. At the same time Njonjo probably thought he was using Moi for the same end. Neither were fools, and it was just a question of who was going to get rid of whom first. I remember on one occasion being furious about some legislation Njonjo was trying to put through. 'Charles,' I told him, 'you failed your Bar finals so many times, and you have the nerve to try to tell me what is the law.' Njonjo ceased to be Attorney General in 1980 and moved to being an MP and Minister of Constitutional Affairs. Three years later he resigned, as I understand it amid allegations of abusing his public office, and there were rumours he was trying to take over the Presidency. If so, he would fail in the attempt, but he was luckier than some less ambitious people.

In 1983, I had just arrived in Nairobi from England when I heard that my former parliamentary colleague Sir Humphrey Slade, who was now 78 years of age, had been attacked at his home. I immediately rang him then drove over. 'Fitz you won't believe it,' he said, 'these men came to the house and began banging on the door. I fired some shots in the air and they ran away. Then a few days later a chauffeur-driven Mercedes turned up and four people got out, all very smartly dressed. As I opened my door, however, they began beating me and saying, "Give us your gun, give us your gun!" I told them I had no gun. "You're telling lies, we heard you firing it the other day," they said. They beat me again, and the pain was so great that I fetched the gun and gave it to them.' Returning a few days later to see how Sir Humphrey was, I was told that he had died. A kind, well-meaning man, who strove, often against the odds, to bring a sense of fair play into Parliament, and would wish no one any harm, I would remember him as a true friend. Sir Humphrey, poor fellow, had simply wanted a quiet life in his retirement, and one couldn't imagine him racing about like some people seemed to.

On the 27th of September 1985, I was in Kenya driving along the road when a car overtook me at high speed. I remember thinking: this man is in a hurry to get to heaven. It was the one-time Chief Justice Kitili Mwendwa, taking a suitcase of money to pay his farm workers their wages. A few kilometres further on the car was found overturned. Kitili was rushed to the Government hospital at Thika, where he was later pronounced dead. The family's questions about this accident have never been satisfactorily answered: in particular; where the suitcase of money went, and more importantly, why he was taken 25 kilometres to Thika, when the Aga Khan, a better-equipped hospital, was much closer. In a public statement, Njonjo referred to Kitili Mwendwa as an eccentric man with a passion for fast cars.

There had also been sad news in our family, with the sudden death from a heart attack of my brother Rix. A talented sportsman in his youth, he had always been an amiable happy-go-lucky person who had brightened the lives of his relatives and friends, and I would never forget his brotherly care for me when we were growing up. Rix's three children would all go on to do quite well. My mother, meanwhile, was still in Goa. Her own parents having both long ago passed away, I was hoping she might now agree to come back to live with us in Kenya, although I was in fact now dividing my time between Kenya and Britain, where since 1982 our children had been attending schools in London. Previously, our two girls had gone to Loreto Convent School, Msongari, and the two boys, nearby St. Mary's. A concern for standards, among them reports of pupils seen smoking, had hastened our decision to send them to the UK. Good contacts at the British High Commission had advised us to get them into new schools before, or at the 'O' Level stage, and ideally three years prior to the start of their 'A' levels. We were made aware though that they would first need to pick up almost completely new syllabi, with a British rather than Kenyan focus, on history and geography in particular.

When the UK school fees had turned out to be double the original quote, I had been obliged to take out a loan and undertake work in Kenya and Britain to pay for it. Romola, meanwhile, was staying in London with the children during term times and bringing them out to Nairobi so that we were all together in the holidays. The finances though were proving a strain. One day in Nairobi, as I was playing golf with my good friend and client Mahendra Mehta, he asked what was troubling me. 'What do you mean?' I said, 'I played all right didn't I?' Mahendra replied, 'Yes, you played fine, but I can see you are not your usual self. Is something bothering you – are you finding London more expensive than you expected?' When I admitted this was so, he offered to pay all the expenses for our family in London, right up until the time the children finished their education. I would not accept this, and nor, when I told her, would Romola. Mahendra then said he had been paying me too little for my services anyway, and insisted on giving me a raise. It was a great help, and I would end up working in part for Mahendra for almost 20 years.

Sunni and Mahendra Mehta

In Goa my mother was receiving what they called 'poscare', living with adopted servants and children from the churches or missions. The foundlings would get food and a home, and in return take care of those that had taken them in. Over the years I had sent tickets for my mother to bring her to Kenya, but been unable to coax her from Goa. Then suddenly one day when I was visiting her she said, all right, I would like to come. Ok I said, just give me your passport and I will arrange everything. She handed me a small box in which she kept all her important papers including the deeds to the property. When I looked inside the box I found that her passport had been eaten away by insects, leaving only the covers. It was unusable. Back in Kenya I rang the Indian High Commissioner, Placido D'Souza, who, though no relation, had known my father, and he arranged a new passport to be sent. Just after it arrived, I received a phone call to say that my mother had died. She was 92.

Eventually, Romola and I would both spend more time with our family in Britain and have the pleasure of seeing all four of our children go on to university and have successful careers and happy marriages. I would practise commercial law in Kenya until my retirement, and Romola would continue similarly in her profession of medicine. We had enjoyed very happy as well as dramatic times together in Kenya, and I recall vividly our regular gatherings for friends and colleagues at our home in Nairobi. These had always been lively and sociable occasions, with much political debate. Romola invariably organised the catering and everything else with great energy and efficiency, and although not officially involved in politics, she had in fact always been more resolute in her ideas than I was; a firm believer in ending the practice of sati in India for example, in abolishing the caste system, absolutely straight down the line when it came to honesty and anti-corruption, and a great source of moral strength to me. When she left her paid position at the Pumwani Maternity Hospital, she had later returned on a voluntary basis to help the African mothers and babies.

In addition to her professional and vocational achievements, anyone that knows Romola will have no hesitation in agreeing with me that her wisdom, good humour and hard work, along with her many talents, is the foundation of our family; as a loving and devoted mother, the health and happiness of all of our children has always been her absolute first priority.

Kenya continued to draw me back however. I had after all spent much of my adult life there and witnessed some remarkable events. Following Kenyatta, Moi would remain President for the next 24 years, surviving an attempted military coup and a supposed takeover plot by Charles Njonjo, who lost his shortly held parliamentary seat after findings that he had abused his office, though it seemed he continued to prosper in business. Mwai Kibaki would serve as Vice-President for 12 years, until being dropped by Moi, and in 2002 he would become Kenya's third President.

Jomo Kenyatta, whose statue has stood in Nairobi since Kenyan independence will always be known as the founding father of the nation. The other members of the Kapenguria Six with whom he was incarcerated must be remembered too. But what happened to them in the years following their release? The stories of their lives after independence are somewhat diverse, and as we have seen, in the early days they were not a unified group, but subject to intense rivalries, political, tribal and personal, and during their long ordeal of imprisonment, one or more of them was even alleged to have been involved in an attempt on Kenyatta's life.

Kung'u Karunga did not go into politics after independence but resumed his commercial career. In 1974, he went on a business trip to Idi Amin's Uganda and was never seen again. Fred Kubai had been welcomed back by the trade unions in 1961, served as an MP and was an assistant Minister of Labour and Social Services from 1969 to 1974. Sharing Kaggia's political principles up to a point, eventually Kubai gave up, decided to have a comfortable life, bought a farm, and ran expensive cars. He died in 1996.

Paul Ngei was the youngest of the six. A volatile character with an allegedly colourful love life, he was also an opportunist, and was suspended briefly from the Government in 1966 on charges of smuggling maize out of the country. Some Kenyans I believe referred to him as one of the 'Wabenzi' – the kind of powerful figures who drove big Mercedes. I have read that Ngei got his Mercedes in 1971, and asked the dealer to forward the bill to the Government. When the Government declined to pay, the dealers, knowing who Ngei was, let him have the car; the same apparently happened in restaurants. As I say, when I discovered that he was the son of a senior chief of the Akamba, his cavalier attitude to life made a kind of sense. After Kenyatta, Ngei tried initially to thwart Moi's succession, then worked his way back in, filling a series of ministerial posts. In 1991 he was declared bankrupt, his health failed and he died aged 81 in 2004.

Branded a communist for his criticisms of the way independent Kenya was being run, Bildad Kaggia had continued to follow a very simple life and to maintain his socialist views. The only trouble was, once Pinto was gone he had no one to work with, or at least no one who would sacrifice their life for the principles in which he believed, and this is the sad part. Released from jail after six months, in 1970 he more or less retired from politics and lived among the poor in Muranga. He ran a little maize mill in nearby Makutano where he would meet and talk to the people coming to get their grain milled, until his death in 2005.

Achieng Oneko, after winning the Nakuru Town seat in 1963 and being appointed as the Information, Broadcasting and Tourism Minister by Kenyatta, defected in 1966 to side with the socialist KPU and Odinga. Arrested in Kisumu in 1969 – the year Tom Mboya was killed – he was detained until 1975. After being released from prison

Oneko was blocked from getting a position and found it hard to gain any support. He returned to politics only when multi-party elections were allowed in 1992, as an MP in Odinga's FORD-Kenya party. He was the last surviving member of the Kapenguria Six when he died in 2007 aged 87.

With Fred Kubai, Dennis Pritt, Bildad Kaggia and Achhroo Kapila in our garden in Nairobi

Although not one of the Kapenguria Six, I must mention James Gichuru again. He was an affectionate and amiable man that everybody liked, but the one person he disliked was Odinga, whom he described as an imposter. I was surprised by this, perhaps it was personal, something to do with their schooling. At some point, Gichuru felt himself to have reached the top of his career and would go no further. He lost interest in proper politics and spent much of the time sitting in his bar. I was surprised that a man of his ability could do that. I remember him going to State House once and talking with Kenyatta for a long time, and afterwards I realised he must have been asking to keep his job as Finance Minister. Appointments could be decided on what seemed like a whim sometimes. Kenyatta once told me he was going to make me Minister of Lands, but the next day he said Jackson Angaine was feeling ignored because an Indian was getting a ministry and he was not, and had reminded him of the old days when Kenyatta used to stay with him. Did I mind therefore, Kenyatta asked me, if he made Angaine Minister of Lands instead of me? 'No, absolutely not,' I replied, 'you are the one to decide.'

James Gichuru

A very different kind of life was that of Makhan Singh. In 1961, an internal memo written by the British authorities discussing whether or not he should be released, described him as 'an able, shrewd and inveterate communist agitator'. (From the *Socialist Review* February 2016.) As Kenyan independence looked increasingly certain, there was probably little choice but to free him that year along with Kenyatta and the others. When the newly independent Government of Kenya was being put together, Singh was reportedly unwilling to have myself or others approach

Kenyatta for a place in KANU and a position in Parliament. Seen as a political radical alongside Odinga and Kaggia he found himself an outsider, his communist label making him especially incompatible with the country's new leadership, in which Tom Mboya, the seasoned trade union leader, was leaning strongly towards the West, America in particular. Given the sacrifices he had made, and his long commitment to independence, Singh would naturally feel a keen sense of rejection. The assumption that he was a communist though, was not unanimously shared. Achieng Oneko recalled that 'When he came out in 1961, he talked of betrayal. Some of us who had asked for positions were directed not to associate with Singh because he was a leftist. But he was not a communist, as purported by the British, but a law-abiding citizen with so much love for his country.'

When the long struggle for independence had been achieved, Makhan Singh was not only effectively barred from politics, but he found it hard to get a job. A position as secretary of the Historical Association of Kenya, and writing about the development of the Kenyan Trade Union movement, were marginal activities, unlikely one would think to have satisfied a man who had been used to intense political engagement. It was said that like many of us, he found Pio's assassination in 1965 devastating. More recently, the *Daily Nation* described Pio as Singh's 'comrade-in-ideology'. In the same article, Singh's son Hindapal said that his father '...almost became a recluse... he fundamentally lost his drive and died of frustration at 59, while my mother died at 83.'

It was said that on his passing in 1973, Makhan Singh had nothing to leave his family other than the 35 Kenya shillings in his savings account. His son Hindapal did not appear to be bitter, and attributed his father's demise to the political direction taken by post-independence Kenya: 'The ideology had shifted and we could not blame anybody... people like Kaggia, Kubai, Oneko, and Odinga suffered the same fate. This was a decision the leaders of that time made, and whether they were right or wrong, that is for history to judge.' Some made their judgement early on; Bildad Kaggia, who was said to have been disillusioned with the main nationalist movement, the Kenya African Union, said in his autobiography that when he heard Singh speak, he felt that 'He had the fire I admired, and was a real revolutionary.' Makhan Singh never rejected the label of communist; some say he chose it himself, and as I recall he wore it with pride.

There were many people – Africans, Asians, and Europeans – who stood up for human rights in Kenya, both in the run-up to independence, and years before, when such a thing must have seemed almost impossible. My friend Tom Mboya must be mentioned again in this context, as some time after independence Tom's widow Pamela invited me to a party at which in her after-dinner speech she remarked, 'Ladies and gentlemen, if not for Mr de Souza, we Africans would not be free.' It was a generous gesture on her part. Then one day Pamela told me, with tears in her eyes, that she had cancer of the uterus and there was only a slim chance of a cure. Not long afterwards one of her daughters rang to give me the sad news that she had died.

From the beginning of colonisation the African people of Kenya had been stripped of their rights and exploited by the European settlers through a series of policies, primarily the seizure of their land. There was also forced labour that, according to author Tiyambe Zelaza in his article 'The Colonial Labour System in Kenya', was 'widely used and became institutionalised during the first few decades of colonial rule in Kenya.' (Sourcewatch, Colonialism in Kenya website.) Confined to reserves with limited means of subsistence and subjected to poll and hut taxes, many Africans were obliged to move around and to graze their cattle and grow what they could as squatters on the Europeans' farms. To prevent competition with the settlers' produce however, Africans were forbidden to plant the more profitable cash crops of coffee, tea and sisal. Finding it hard to make an independent living from agriculture, the majority of squatters had little choice but to accept work on the settlers' farms.

By 1930, this source of cheap and plentiful labour was providing most of the manpower for Kenya's European masters, with an estimated 120,000 squatters occupying more than 20% of the settlers' farmland. In many cases it was land that the squatters or their forebears had originally inhabited. To further monitor and control the African population, the colonial authorities introduced the pass law which from 1920 stipulated that any African man leaving his reserve must have a pass, known as a kipande, bearing his name and fingerprint, together with his ethnic group, the name of his previous employers and the signature of his current employer. The Kikuyu kept their passes in a small metal container worn round their necks and called it a mbugi, meaning goat's bell, as the imposition of this law made them feel like livestock, owned by the white men. Any man found without his kipande would be fined heavily and often imprisoned.

With more and more indigenous Africans becoming excluded from their own land, they migrated to the cities in search of work, and it is estimated that between 1938 and 1952 the population of Nairobi doubled. In an earlier chapter I described how the authorities arrested and attempted to murder Peter Koinange during the Emergency. Peter's father was a Kikuyu chief, and both men may have been at one time office bearers for the old Kikuyu Central Association (KCA), which had campaigned for the return of tribal land from the British. Formed in the mid-1920s after the vocal Young Kikuyu Association of Harry Thuku was banned, the KCA's first president was Jomo Kenyatta. When, in 1940, the KCA was also banned, the vacuum was filled by the Mau Mau, many of whose members, whether violently or peacefully inclined, still regarded themselves as the KCA. From the KCA would emerge the KAU, then KANU.

Peter had studied at American universities and then gone to Cambridge, England as a Rhodes Scholar, but neither education nor social status could guarantee his safety. Any African could be locked up without good reason, especially if they were believed to have had past or present connection with the Mau Mau or its forerunner the KCA. If arrested, such people never appeared in court. Often they were never heard of again. I met George K. Ndegwa, the last secretary general of the KCA. He said to me, 'I am one of the leaders of the Mau Mau, I started it, and I want it to go on. You must tell them.' He was a huge man; over six foot four with big square shoulders, and wore a large overcoat, like an army greatcoat. He told me that he and others had been fighting in the war against the British and that they had to kill them, throw them all out. I didn't argue with him then. I didn't tell him violence was wrong. I just kept quiet and listened to him. I was impressed by his authority, and by his personality. He was a strong man and would have been a very strong political leader, but the fact was he had already burned his boats as far as moderation was concerned, and for this reason I don't think the British would ever have accepted him as part of any negotiating process. I don't know what happened to him. It was like a lot of other people; one just lost touch with them as events moved on.

Many of us who first met in Nairobi or London in the late 1940s and 1950s, as students or political activists, have drifted in and out of each other's lives at various times, and we have not all travelled in the same direction. My earliest association with Charles Njonjo was at the East African Students Association in London, and not so long ago when Romola and I were living in London he telephoned and left a message asking to see us. I had not seen him for some years, but he did not leave a number and we were unable to call him back.

And what of Joe Murumbi? We hear very little of the legacy of what might be called the African-Asians of whom he was one, being of Goan and Maasai parentage. In 1990, he was ill in hospital and asked to see me. When I arrived I was sad to learn that he had passed away. I was grateful though that he had remembered me, and I and countless others would always remember him, and his huge contribution to the independence movement, his integrity, and all he had done since; his important collections and promotion of African art and culture, and his positive influence on the country.

One person I never lost touch with was Fenner Brockway. A few months into the Emergency, in 1953 he had urged the House of Commons to form a commission of enquiry on the 'shoot to kill' order against Kenyans allegedly trying to escape or resist arrest. Imprisoned for his pacifist beliefs during 1914-18, he took a different view of fighting in the Spanish Civil War and against the Nazis, accepting that fascism must be resisted. Chairmanship of the Movement for Colonial Freedom followed, along with continued campaigning for world peace, a peerage, and authorship of more than 20 books on politics. Fenner remained a lifelong friend and I was honoured to have joined him in celebrating his 99th birthday.

Along with the strength of tribal loyalty in Kenya, one thing that has struck me about the world in general is the sweetness of power and money, how people whom you have known so well for years, thinking them sincere, honest and incorruptible, when they are offered high rank, take it. It reminds me of the famous joke about the film star who asks an attractive woman, 'Darling, will you come away with me to the Bahamas for a hundred thousand pounds?' She replies, 'Of course.' Then he says, 'Would you come for ten pounds?' 'Certainly not!' she retorts, 'what do you think I am, a prostitute?' 'No, no, you misunderstand,' replies the film star, 'I've already established you are a prostitute, I'm just looking for your price.' In some ways, this reflects a fact of life. George Bernard Shaw said that we are all prostitutes; for money we will sell our souls; the worst may be certain politicians, lawyers, etc., but in one way or another we all sell ourselves.

When people go to extremes for money or power of course, it becomes much worse. I used to say about Moi, it doesn't matter about all the things that have happened at least he has never killed anyone. Then in February 1990, Robert Ouko was murdered. A very nice, modest, friendly person, I liked Robert a great deal. I had talked with him just a few days earlier on Parliament Road. He asked me to stop my car, and we both parked and walked down towards the Parliament building together. As Minister for Foreign Affairs he had recently been to Washington with Moi as part of a delegation. I hadn't seen much of him in the previous two or three years. I had been to his house for dinner, and I remember one day bumping into him at the Hilton Hotel, where he was attending a reception given by the German Embassy. I was there for some other reason. He came up and embraced me and asked how I was doing, at which point I noticed the German Ambassador waiting nearby to receive him. I said, 'Your host is waiting, you had better say hello.' Robert replied, 'No, no, you and I haven't had a chat for a long time, don't worry about the host.'

As we walked down to Parliament that day, Robert explained that he was getting the molasses factory restarted and wanted to do it properly and get rid of the corruption. He himself told me there was a lot of corruption there and he was threatening to stop production to stamp out the bribery. Whether he went too far in this, stepping on the toes of people who were planning to make money from the plant I don't know. His murder, as far as I am aware, has never been convincingly solved, though many people thought it was after what happened in Washington, when the Americans were backing him to replace Moi. Robert was a warm, affectionate person. I really liked him so much.

If asked what I thought of Kenya after Moi when Kibaki was in power, I would say we had a government and a judiciary that was basically ok. The country had become very corrupt, and it was certainly not perfect even after Moi's time, the crime wave being one thing that worried me; I wondered why people were being attacked, houses ruined, and why the police seemed so weak – were they demoralised? Was the Government not being firm enough?

I thought that as Environment Minister John Michuki was firm certainly, and did his job as far as the matatus were concerned, whereas transport minister Ali Makwere let things slide back into chaos again. After Moi it seemed we had basic human rights in Kenya, we were not having people tortured, and I would have felt much happier living there under Kibaki. A brilliant student when I first met him in London, he was also a very modest, humble man, and continued to keep in touch with me over the years. He had been very pro-Odinga originally, one of our group in England, a left-winger. When he returned to Kenya he didn't join any group, and neither did I, but Kibaki was a very sincere Fabian socialist, who didn't believe in torture and wouldn't harm anybody. After he came to power I saw him only on rare occasions, but he was always very warm and friendly and we didn't discuss politics at all, except once mentioning a referendum that he thought he would win by a big majority. I must have looked a bit startled because he then assured me that his intelligence officers had told him he would win. I remember thinking to myself: this is what happens to people in power, the so-called intelligence officers give you the information you want to hear, they let you down.

It has been said that when Kibaki was President there was a failure to control corruption, but how much realistically could one man have done, and would things have been any different under another government? I don't know. I still think Kibaki was the best President we could have had, and at that time I couldn't really see anybody who could compete with him in the next elections, and envisaged Kibaki against either Raila Odinga or Kalonzo Musyoka. Did I feel then that any of the opposition parties could have done better? I knew them all very well; they were all my friends. I remember a few years ago meeting Raila Odinga on the road one day. He had just got into politics and he said, 'You are my father's lawyer, can you advise me what I should do?' I thought it was a very modest thing to say considering he was a leader and I was a nobody.

Can anyone be sure that they, or someone they support or advise, if they become a president or any kind of leader, that they will not become corrupt? It's a very big question! So what do we do? I have long retired from politics now, and am very happy to say I don't have to take these decisions.

We should remember that the history of modern Kenya is not just one of political infighting, bloodshed, alleged political assassination, corruption and tribalism, though all these have featured. There is infinitely more that is good about Kenya. Its beautiful landscapes and majestic wildlife draw thousands of tourists each year from all over the world. The country is independent and it has modernised in many areas, but there is still much to be done to improve healthcare provision, basic living conditions and access to education. Suffering and hardship exists, but so does the capacity to alleviate it, to achieve real progress for all, social and economic. Despite so many Kenyans being very poor, I believe they are largely honest, kind and hard-working people who love their families, and seek above all to live in peace and harmony with their neighbours. Ultimately, Kenya is my home.

My home in Nairobi

Romola and me with our children and grandchildren in 2005. (We have four more grandchildren now.)

Our grandchildren on holiday in Goa, January 2017

Printed in Poland
by Amazon Fulfillment
Poland Sp. z o.o., Wrocław